Hollywoodhell

An unusual history of Hollywood, the movie industry, and those movie industry employees that died early as a result of being part of the Hollywood culture

By Willie Ward

Table of Contents

The history of Hollywood is darkened by the stories of actors who were attracted to the splendor of movie and television careers, only to learn too late that the glitter was gold, but the lifestyle was deadly.

Hindsight tells us this: extreme psychological damage often results from failure to realize the dream of achieving a successful career in the film or television industry. It is a soul-wrenching experience to achieve fame and all of its many accoutrements, and then lose it; to rise to stardom, and then fall back to commonality. There is danger associated with being in the public's eye, being the public's idol, for worship often leads to envy, and for some twisted minds, sometimes murder, and, of course, because Hollywood offers easy access to, and to some extent popularizes the use of drugs and alcohol, the weak fall victim.

Chapter One: the beginning

Motion Pictures could be said to have their origin in 1872, when Edward Muybridge setup twelve cameras on a race track where they took pictures of a running horse in sequence. The first movie film was invented by George Eastman and William Walker in 1885. Perhaps the most famous of the earliest movies is *The Great Train Robbery*, which was created in 1903 by Edwin Porter.

The Santa Monica Mountains divide the Los Angeles area into a coastal plain to the south, and a valley in the north. In the early 1880s, the drainage basin formed by the Ballona Creek that lay between the Baldwin Hills and the Santa Monica Mountains was referred to as the Cahuenga Valley. **Cahuenga** (also, Cabeugna and Cabuenga) or "place of the hill" is a former Tongva and Tataviam (Fernandeño - Gabrieleño) Native American settlement in the San Fernando Valley. Its precise location is unknown. Linking the valley to the coastal plain is Cahuenga Pass, and standing above the valley is Cahuenga Peak.

The name Cahuenga Valley came into use when farmers disovered a frost-free strip of land that followed the base of the Santa Monica Mountains. Soon, this amazing farmland became renowned, for here bananas, oranges, and lemons thrived, and vegetables could be harvested early in the wintertime for transport to eastern markets.

In 1836, Yaanga, the Indian village, was moved to what later became the corner of Commercial and Alameda Streets. It was again moved in 1845 to the area that became Boyle Heights.

Americans brought disease, and this took many Indian lives. The population of Los Angeles, between 1848 and 1880, f ell from 75,050 to 12,500.

.On April 4, 1850, Los Angeles was incorporated as an American city, and. Five months later California was admitted into the Union.

Remarkably, the Gabrielino Indians survived. In 2006, the *Los Angeles Times* reported that there were 2,000 of them still living in Southern California.

Hollywood. Showing Orchard Street and Orange Drive, circa 1905. Courtesy of the USC Libraries – California Historical Society Collection.

Orchard street and Orange drive today

Harvey Wilcox, a man from Kansas, bought 160 acres of land west of Los Angeles in 1900. He intended to establish a conservative community there. The community was incorporated under the name Hollywood in 1903.

In 1910, Hollywood became a part of the city of Los Angeles in order to share the city's water and sewage systems.

David Horsley purchased the Blondeau Tavern on Sunset Boulevard in 1911 and renamed it the Nestor Film Company. This was Hollywood's first movie studio.

Francis Boggs was born in Santa Rosa, California. While still in his teens, Boggs began an acting career in San Francisco. He later moved to Chicago where he continued to work in theatre. It was in Chicago that he first met William Selig who caused him to move to Los Angeles in 1902.

In 1907, Boggs went to work for Selig at Selig's Chicago based Polyscope studios. Among his earliest films was *The Count of Monte Cristo*, and he also worked on *The Fairylogue and Radio-Plays* which involved L. Frank Baum presenting a slide show and films of his Wizard of Oz stories.

In 1909, he went back to the west coast and filmed *In the Sultan's Power*, one of the first films shot entirely in Los Angeles.

In October, Boggs rented a house in the Edendale district, where he gave Roscoe "Fatty" Arbuckle his first role in *Ben's Kid* (1909).

Selig came to Hollywood in 1911 to see the new studio, and on October 27th, as Selig and Boggs talked together, Frank Minnematsu, the studio janitor shot Boggs, crying "Mr. Boggs was my best friend, He was always very nice to me. But a man told me he was evil and had to die." Convicted of murder the Japanese janitor lived his final twenty-six years in San Quentin prison.

A one reel movie ran five to 8 minutes. Most of these were made in New York City by Biograph, Lubin, Selig, Essenay, Pathe Brothers, Vitagraph, and Edison. Of the nearly 200 one-reel films Boggs wrote and directed, only three survive. He was a man of immense talent, but today he is primarily remembered because he was the victim of the first movie-land murder.

The first feature-length film, *The Squaw Man*, was released in 1914. Its creators – Samuel Goldwyn, Cecil B. DeMille, and Jesse Lasky, made the movie in a barn that was a block away from what is now the corner of Hollywood and Vine.

The Charlie Chaplin Studios were built just south of Sunset in 1917.

Chapter Two: the Silent Years

Movies of more than one reel in length were first shown in the United States when Adolph Zukor distributed Pathé's three-reel *Passion Play* in 1908. The Motion Picture Patents Company (MPPC) was founded that year as a result of conflicts between the various production companies. The MPPC ended the domination of foreign films in the U.S., standardized the way films were distributed and exhibited in America, and in the process, improved the quality of U.S. motion pictures. When Vitagraph produced the five-reel film *The Life of Moses* in 1909, the MPPC forced it to be shown as a serial.

It is said that the first movie made in Hollywood was *The Squaw Man*, which was directed by Cecil B. DeMille in 1914, but the fact is that DW Griffith shot *In Old California* in 1910.

Feature films made motion pictures attractive to the middle class American by providing a format that was like legitimate theatre. These movies were used to produce popular middle-class novels and plays. The middle class audience had more spending power. This allowed movie producers to increase their budgets, thus offering higher quality and theater comfort.

By 1916 there were more than 21,000 movie theatres in the United States. This fact allowed the rise of the Hollywood studio system, which ruled movie exhibition from the 1920s to the '50s. Before the new studio-based monopoly could begin, however, the power of the MPPC had to end.

The basic principle of the newly founded 'movie trust' was own all patents, and sell licenses. The Trust's inability to overpower the independent movie companies and end their resistance to its policies cost a fortune in patent-infringements. Something else the MPPC over-looked was the power of the 'star system'. This system involved the management of publicity for major performers, known as 'stars'.

The end of the MPPC came in August, 1912, when the U.S. Justice Department brought suit for "restraint of trade", acts that violated the Sherman Antitrust Act. This resulted in the movie industry moving to southern California.

Because of the popularity of the nickelodeon, exhibitors, who were now showing three separate programs over a seven-day period, required as many as 20 new films every week. Most movies were being shot outdoors, and were therefore dependent upon available light. There just wasn't enough light on the east coast, and so, beginning in about 1907, production companies, such as Selig Polyscope, started sending units to south and west. It was apparant that a new movie industry capitol was needed.

These companies tried shooting in San Antonio, Texas, Santa Fe, N. M., Jacksonville, Florida, and even Cuba, but none of these could match Hollywood for the needed movie making qualities

By 1915, the motion-picture companies in Hollywood were working approximately 15,000 people.

Owen Carter, a camera man, drowned while filming *Across the Border* (1914).

William Elmer Booth was born on December 9th, 1882 in Los Angeles. While still a teen, Booth toured with stock companies before becoming involved in the young movie industry. Between 1911 and 1915, he appeared in forty movie shorts. He is best known for his performance as The Snapper Kid in *The Musketeers of Pig Alley*, directed by D. W. Griffith and released in 1912.

Booth was killed in an auto accident on June 16, 1915 in Los Angeles. It is said that Todd Browning was responsible for Booth's death.

Billie Ritchie (William Moro) was born in Glasgow, Scotland on September 14th, 1874. He began to work in the theater in 1887, performing in vaudeville, acting, and doing pantomime

Billie's parents were variety artists before him. Billie was trained while working in the Theater Royal at Plymouth, England's oldest theater. He soon started his "drunk" career by playing "father" in *Ten Nights in a Bar-room.*

Billie later joined the Karno Fun Factory and Comedy Troupe, a traveling show that featured stars such as Stan Laurel and Charlie Chaplin at various times.

Billie went to work for Henry "Pathe" Lehman in 1914. Lehman's nickname came from the method used by Lehman to get a job with D. W. Griffith. He liked, representing himself to be an employee of the French film company, Pathe.

While working in a comedy film for Fox, Billie was attacked by three wild ostriches. He suffered severe injuries, and was forced to stop working.

After two years, mostly spent in bed at his Hollywood home at 1200 North McCadden Place, Billie died at age forty-two. He is buried in Forest Lawn Memorial Park, Glendale. Los Angeles County, California, Plot: Section C, Lot 27.

The most successful companies in the new Hollywood were independents. Among these were the Famous Players, Lasky Corporation which became **Paramount Pictures** in 1927, **Universal Pictures, Goldwyn Picture Corporation**, Metro Picture Corporation, and Louis B. Mayer Pictures

Chief among the Directors/Producers at his time was D.W. Griffith, who was known as "the father of film technique," "the man who invented Hollywood," and "the Shakespeare of the screen." Griffith was the first filmmaker to realize that motion-pictures could create great persuasive power over an audience, or even a nation.

Griffith began his film career in late 1907. He played the lead in *Rescued From An Eagles Nest* which was released in 1907. In June, 1908, the Biograph Company used him to replace director, George McCutcheon, on the film, *The Adventures of Dollie.* Griffith released a fresh and exciting film, and the movie resulted in a full-time director's contract with Biograph.

As part of his new contract, Griffith made two independent features per year, the first being *The Clansman*, which was title of the book by Thomas Dixon, which the film adapted. Shooting on the film began in 1914. When the film opened in 1915, it was renamed *The Birth of a Nation*, and was a great success. There were controversial aspects to the film, such as appeals to racism, that provoked fear and disgust, and as the film's popularity swept the nation, denunciations followed. Many, who had praised it, changed their minds. After the film had caused riots in several cities, it was banned in eight Northern and Midwestern states.
First Amendment protection was not given to movies in the U. S. until 1952.

Taking the lead in protesting against The Birth of a Nation was the NAACP, which had been founded six years before the film's release.

At the height of his fame, Griffith decided to produce a film that protested against what he saw as a flaw in human character that had endangered civilization throughout history. This film was the epic *Intolerance*, which was released in 1916.

The temple of Babylon sequence from *Intolerance*.

Charlie Chaplin was earning $130 a week in 1913. A year later, he was paid $10,000 a week. This is an indication of the rapid popularity of motion pictures as a major form of public entertainment.

By the 1920s, the major studios had adopted the 'Star system'. Theda Bara, for example, was a 'created' star. She was born, Theodosia Goodman, a daughter of a tailor, she became Theda Bara, a mysterious European, the child of a French artist and his lover, an Arab woman.

Florence La Badie (IMDb says that her real name was Florence Russ) was born on April 27th, 1888 in New York City (some reports have her born in Austin, Texas). Little is known of her early life. It is thought that she was adopted by a Canadian attorney and his wife.

Florence went to New York City to become a fashion model, but in 1908 she accepted a role in the theatre. Later, she toured with a road company across the eastern U. S. She became friends with Mary Pickford during this stage of her career.

Mary introduced Florence to the film industry, and Biograph offered Florence a small role in one of their films. This led to roles working for D. W. Griffith. Her first credited role was in *The Politician's Love Story*.

In 1911, Thanhouser Films signed her to a contract, and made her their major star. Among the films she worked in for Thanhouser were, *The Tempest*, released in 1911, *Dr. Jekyll and Mr. Hyde*, released in 1912, and *The Million Dollar Mystery*, a serial that was released in 1914 and 1915.

Florence appeared in 185 movies between 1909 and 1917. On August 28th, 1917, Florence and her fiancé were driving in New York State when her car's brakes failed. The car rolled over, and Florence was seriously injured. She died on October 13 from an infection and was interred in an unmarked grave in the Green-Wood cemetery in Brooklyn, New York.

During the 1920s in the U.S., movie stars salaries went sky high. The studio system became standard, much like Thomas Ince had designed between 1914 and 1918 at Inceville. His studio was in the Santa Ynez Canyon near Hollywood. With some modification, it prevailed as the dominant mode of Hollywood production for the next 40 years.

Camera man **Alvin Knechtel** and stunt pilot **William Hauber** were killed when their plane crashed during filming of *The Aviator* in 1920.

Olive Thomas was born October 20, 1894 in the Pittsburgh-area. Her father died in 1906, and she was forced to leave school at age fifteen to help support her mother and two younger brothers

In 1914, after answering a newspaper ad, she won "The Most Beautiful Girl in New York City", a contest run by commercial artist Howard Chandler Christy. She then modelled for artist Harrison Fisher and appeared on the cover of Saturday Evening Post.

Fisher wrote to Flo Ziegfeld about Thomas, and she was given a part in Ziegfeld's follies. She later danced in the risqué *Midnight Frolic*, an after-hours show and became the center-of-attention for the in-crowd. Thomas soon found herself pursued by a number of wealthy men who showered her with expensive gifts. It was said that the German Ambassador gave her a $10,000 string of pearls.

Thomas posed nude for Peruvian artist Alberto Vargas. She later signed a contract with the International Film Company, becoming the leading lady in Harry Fox movies. Thomas appeared in more than twenty films over the next four years. She moved to Triangle Pictures in 1916, where she worked with Thomas Ince.

In December 1918, Thomas went to Selznick Pictures Company. In 1920, she played a teenager in *The Flapper*, and became the first actress to be described by that term.

On September 5, 1920, while vacationing in Paris with her husband, Jack Pickford, the younger brother of Mary Pickford, Thomas died after accidentally ingesting a mercury bichloride solution, which had been prescribed for her husband's chronic syphilis. He brought her body back to the United States, and she was interred in a crypt at the Woodlawn Cemetery in the Bronx

Ormer Leslie "Lock" Locklear, born on October 28, 1891, in Greenville, Texas. Fascinated with flying, he joined the U.S. Army Air Service. He trained in Austin, Texas and was a 2nd Lieutenant when World War One ended.

After leaving the service in 1919, he became a member of a group of stunt pilots; this led to work in films in Hollywood.

Locklear died during the filming of *The Skywayman* in 1920. He was attempting to dive his plane toward some oil derricks and making it seem to crash. The film crew failed to follow instructions and Lock was blinded him with their powerful lights, He hit the derricks.

Lock is buried in Fort Worth.

Virginia Rappe was born to the unwed mother, Mabel Rapp (a chorus girl, said to have been a prostitute) in New York City. Her mother died when Virginia was eleven years old, and Virginia was sent to Chicago to live with her grandmother.

At age fourteen, she began working as an art model in Chicago. By the time she was fifteen she had undergone at least two abortions.

In 1916, she relocated to Los Angeles where she became nationally known when she was named the cover girl for the sheet music to the popular song *Let Me Call You Sweetheart.* In 1917, she won a role in *Paradise Garden* and then co-starred with Rudolph Valentino in *Over the Rhine.*

While working for Mack Sennett, Rappe had numerous sexual encounters with both cast and crew members. An epidemic of pubic lice (for which she was blamed) caused Sennett to have the studio closed and fumigated.

During a party held on September 5, 1921, in Arbuckle's suite at the St. Francis Hotel in San Francisco, Rappe was injured; she died four days later of a ruptured bladder and peritonitis.

The exact events of that party are unknown. Witnesses told various versions of what happened, one being that Arbuckle had savagely raped her, causing her death. Arbuckle went through three manslaughter trials, but was finally acquitted.

She is buried in the Hollywood Memorial Cemetery in Los Angeles, California.

William Desmond Taylor was born William Cunningham Deane-Tanner in Ireland in 1872. He immigrated to America in 1890 and married Ethel Hamilton on December 7, 1901. She was a member of the Florodora Sextette, and the daughter of a wealthy Wall Street broker who loaned Tanner the money to start an antiques business. Tanner suddenly vanished in 1908, leaving his wife and daughter behind.

He moved to Hollywood where he found work as an actor and took the name William Desmond Taylor. In 1914, he directed his first film, *The Awakening*. All in all, he directed more than fifty films.

In 1919, close to the end of World War I, Taylor enlisted in the British Army. After leaving the military, he returned to Los Angeles.

In 1922, Taylor was shot to death. His bi-sexual valet, Peavey, discovered the body. Peavey had a criminal record that included charges of vagrancy and indecent exposure. He accused Mabel Normand of the murder.

It was said at the time that Mabel Normand and Taylor may have had a romantic relationship. Normand's popularity was falling, and she had already been involved in three previous scandals. During the same time, Taylor was actively engaged in developing Mary Miles Minter, a successful teenage actress's career. Letters were found in Taylor's home that revealed a sexual relationship between Taylor, aged forty-nine, and nineteen-year-old Minter. According to the letters, they had been engaging in sex since Minter was seventeen. Charlotte Shelby, Minter's mother owned a .38 caliber pistol that used unusual bullets similar to the type which killed Taylor.

In 1964, Margaret Gibson, an actress who had worked with Taylor, suffered a heart attack. As she was dying, she confessed to shooting and killing Taylor.

404-B South Alvarado (the northeast corner of Alvarado & Maryland), Los Angeles as it looked when Taylor lived and died there.

404-B South Alvarado (the northeast corner of Alvarado & Maryland), Los Angeles, as it looks today.

Taylor was interred in a mausoleum at Hollywood Forever Cemetery on Santa Monica Boulevard in Hollywood. The inscription on his crypt reads:

<u>In Memory of William C. Deane-Tanner,</u>
<u>Beloved Father of Ethel Deane-Tanner.</u>
<u>Died 1 February 1922</u>

Wallace Reid was born on April 15, 1891 in St. Louis, Missouri. His parents were both actors and his father worked in a variety of theatrical jobs.

Reid's father pushed him toward a career in the movie industry, and changed his own career from the theatre to acting, writing, and directing films. Wallace made his first film, *The Phoenix* in 1910. He was later in both *Birth of a Nation* in 1915 and *Intolerance* in 1916.

Wallace married actress Dorothy Davenport in 1913. He was twenty-two at the time and Dorothy was seventeen.

Reid was put under contract by producer Jesse Lasky after being involved with more than 100 shorts. He then starred in more than sixty films while working for Lasky's Famous Players film company, which later became Paramount Pictures.

Wallace was badly injured in a scene that involved a train crash while working in *The Valley of the Giants*, released in 1919. His injuries should have stopped him from completing the movie, but the studio dispatched their doctor to the location with a stock of morphine, thus allowing Wallace to continue working without being hindered by pain. He was scheduled to start another film immediately upon completion of *The Valley of the Giants*, and the studio saw to it that he had an ample supply of the drug so that would be possible. Wallace was already an alcoholic, and the use of drugs ruined his health. By 1922, he was spending large periods of time in sanitariums. He made his last picture, *Thirty Days* in 1922, and upon its completion he could hardly stand erect. Wallace died on January 18, 1923. He was just thirty-one years old.

Evelyn Nelson was born on November 13th, 1899, in Chloride, Arizona.

She moved to Hollywood at age twenty with her mother, where she landed a role in the comedy short, *Springtime* (1920). Between then and 1923, she had parts in fifteen movies, the last being *Desert Rider*, a western released in 1923.

Evelyn and her mother lived at 6281 De Longpre Avenue, Los Angeles, and it was here her mother discovered her body on June 16, 1923. Evelyn had committed suicide by filling the house with natural gas, resulting in asphyxiation.

She left two notes, one simply saying she was tired. The second note was more revealing, as it read:

I am just about gone and will soon be with my friend Wally.

Wallace Reid, also an actor, committed suicide on January 18, 1923. He was thirty-one years old.

Martha Mansfield was born on July 14, 1899 in New York City. In 1912, her father deserted the family. When she was eighteen, she began a stage career, working in the Ziegfeld Follies.

She first appeared in films in *Civilian Clothe'*, released in 1920. She became a star when she played in *Dr. Jekyll and Mr. Hyde* opposite John Barrymore. Her last role was in *The Leavenworth Case*, made in 1923.

She was working on location in San Antonio, Texas later that year on *The Warrens of Virginia*, when a discarded match set her costume afire. She died soon after arriving at the Physicians and Surgeons Hospital in San Antonio.

Thomas Ince was born in Newport, Rhode Island, the son of actors. He first performed on the stage at age six, and worked on Broadway when he was fifteen. Ince was hired by Biograph in New York where he worked exclusively in films at the rate of five dollars per day.

In 1910, a chance encounter led Ince to go to work at the Independent Motion Pictures Co, and that same year he was given a chance to direct. He was offered work by IMP's owner Carl Laemmle, and Laemmle sent him to Cuba to make films. Ince's output there was small.

In 1911, Ince applied to Charles Baumann at the New York Motion Picture Company. Baumann was trying to establish a West Coast studio at the time. Ince accepted an offer of $100 a week and left for California. In November 1911, he arrived at NYMP's studios where he began to revolutionize the filmmaking process. He established a method of pre-planning his films on paper which introduced the use of a "shooting script".

Ince left Edendale and found a suitable film making location in the Santa Monica hills.

In 1912, he purchased a 460-acre ranch and put a lease on 18,000 additional acres in the Palisades Highlands. There, Ince built a studio that was the first of its kind, offering offices, labs, and all film making necessities. While the site was being built Ince hired *The Miller Brothers 101 Ranch Wildwest Show*, including cowboys, horses, cattle and a Sioux Indian tribe, who set up their tepees on the property. When construction was completed, the streets were lined with a variety of structures, from small houses to magnificent mansions built in the architectural designs of various countries.

By 1913, Ince had ceased directing to concentrate on producing, giving the directing responsibility to brothers Francis and John Ford. John had come to Hollywood following his brother Francis, who was working as an actor. In John's film *The Quiet Man* (1952), Francis was seen for the last time in a film as an old man on his death bed, who suddenly sprang to life to rush out and witness a fist fight between John Wayne and Victor McLaglen.

In his last years, Ince made *Anna Christie* (1923), and *Human Wreckage* (1923), an early anti-drug movie.

Cecil B. DeMille acquired Ince Studios in 1925, renaming it the DeMille Studios. Pathé, RKO, producer Howard Hughes, and Desilu Productions also filmed on the lot at various times. In 1991, Sony Pictures Entertainment purchased the property and renamed it Culver Studios.

On Saturday, November 15, 1924, William Randolph Hearst, his mistress, Marion Davies, Charlie Chaplin, and newspaper columnist Louella Parsons went aboard Hearst's 280-foot yacht, the Oneida. They were celebrating Ince's forty-second birthday, but he arrived late and the yacht left without him.

Ince took a train to San Diego, and he joined the group there the next morning. After dinner that night, Ince complained of acute indigestion. He was taken ashore in San Diego, in the company of a doctor and put on a train to Los Angeles. He left the train at Del Mar and went to a hotel. Later, he left the hotel and was driven to his Hollywood home where he died the following day.

The front page of the Wednesday morning edition of the Los Angeles Times told another version; *Movie Producer Shot on Hearst Yacht*! The story mysteriously vanished in the evening edition, and Ince's body was cremated.

Los Angeles rumors began to circulate saying Hearst shot Ince in the head by mistake.

It was said that Hearst believed Davies and Chaplin were having an affair, and it was for this reason that he had invited them on board the yacht.

According to the story, he came upon the pair in a compromising position and pulled a pistol from his pocket. Davies began to scream, and Ince rushed to the scene. A fight began, there was a gunshot, and Ince was hit by the bullet meant for Chaplin.

According to Chaplin's secretary, Chaplin saw Ince's head "bleeding from a bullet wound". Whatever the cause of Ince's death, it was commonly believed that Hearst used his power to cover up the incident.

Chaplin denied that he was even there. Davies also denied the incident. She did not acknowledge that Chaplin or Parsons were aboard the yacht that weekend, claiming that Ince's wife called her that Monday afternoon to inform her of Ince's death.

After the Ince affair, Hearst gave Parsons a lifetime contract. He also gave Ince's wife a large trust fund, and she refused to allow an autopsy, ordering her husband's immediate cremation.

D.W. Griffith said of the incident, "All you have to do to make Hearst turn white as a ghost is mention Ince's name. There's plenty wrong there, but Hearst is too big."

Thomas Ince' home at 1051 Benedict Canyon Drive, Beverly Hills, California. This building was demolished in the early 1940s.

Most of the major film genres were established in the 1920s. Back then, the most popular was slapstick comedy. It could be said that Mack Sennett, at his Keystone Studios, was most prolific, employing the talents of such stars as Charlie Chaplin, Harry Langdon, Roscoe ("Fatty") Arbuckle, Mabel Normand, and Harold Lloyd. After having achieved fame, most of these quit Keystone and started their own production companies, a practice that wasn't possible later.

Roscoe "Fatty" Arbuckle was born on March 24, 1887 in Smith Center, Kansas. He is said to have weighed sixteen pounds at birth.

His first professional appearance was in 1904. He was paid $17.50 a week to sing illustrated songs for Sid Grauman at the Unique Theater in San Jose, California. He later worked in the Morosco Burbank stock company and traveled through China and Japan with Ferris Hartman. His last appearance on the stage was with Hartman in Yokahama, Japan, in 1913, where he played the Mikado.

When he was a teenager, Arbuckle traveled the West Coast on the vaudeville circuit. There, he got his start in films at the Selig Polyscope Company, and later went to work for Keystone Studios. Fatty started as a Keystone Cop, but his weight, between 250 and 300 pounds (he stood five feet-ten inches high), coupled with his graceful moves, soon made him Hollywood's most popular comedic star.

By 1917 Fatty had formed a partnership with Joseph M. Schenck, who was the husband of Norma Talmadge. The company they formed was called Comique and their movie shorts were released through Famous Players.

Fatty hired a young man he met in New York by the name of Buster Keaton. Keaton's first film was *The Butcher Boy*, released in 1917.

In 1919, Paramount Studios asked Fatty to start making full-length features for them. The first feature was released in 1920. It was titled, *The Round-Up. The Round Up* was followed by *Brewster's Millions* (1921) and *Gasoline Gus* (1921).

Fatty Arbuckle and Charles Chaplin

In 1921, Arbuckle decided to throw a grand Labor Day party. He chose the St. Francis hotel in San Francisco for the site and invited dozens of Hollywood's celebrities. Among them was Virginia Rappe who had a reputation for being a loose woman. The party was on the twelfth floor in a suite that contained rooms 1219 through 1221. Fatty greeted his guests in his pajamas, and even though prohibition was in effect, large quantities of liquor were available.

Around 3 o'clock, Arbuckle retired from the party in order to get dressed to go sight-seeing with a friend. What happened in the following ten minutes is disputed.

Maude Delmont, known as "Bambina", stated that Fatty took Virginia into his bedroom, saying, "I've waited for this a long time." A few minutes later, according to Delmont, party-goers could hear Rappe screaming. When Fatty finally opened the door, Delmont said Rappe was seen to be naked and bleeding.

In his own defense, Fatty said that when he went to his room to change clothes, he discovered Virginia in his bathroom. He said she had vomited, and he helped her clean up before taking her to a nearby bed to rest. He then left her, and returned to his party. Later he left to join a sight-seeing tour and then drove back to Los Angeles.

Virginia was not taken to the hospital for three days as most of the people who visited her considered her condition to be the result of drinking.

On the fourth day, Virginia was driven to the Wakefield Sanatorium, a maternity hospital. Virginia died the following day from peritonitis, caused by a ruptured bladder. Fatty was arrested and charged with Manslaughter.

When Arbuckle went on trial the newspapers had a field day. For the next three weeks, the headlines were about nothing but Arbuckle's trial.

As a result of the accusations made against him, movie theaters across the nation refused to book Fatty's films. He was tried three times, finally winning an acquittal of any wrong doing by a jury, and even received a written apology from the court.

Fatty appeared in 163 films between 1909 and 1933, eleven were uncredited roles made after the trials. His wife said that he became an alcoholic as a result of the bad publicity and the loss of income.

On June 29, 1933, Arbuckle died of a fatal heart attack in his sleep. Alcoholism is said to have been the cause. He was living at 649 W. Adams Blvd., Los Angeles when this occurred.

He was cremated at his wife's request.

Other sensational deaths involving Hollywood personalities, through murder or suicide or drug overdose, fueled the public furor.

To stop increasing efforts by state and local governments to censor the movies, the Hollywood studios formed a new and much stronger trade association, the Motion Picture Producers and Distributors of America, which was later renamed the Motion Picture Association of America. They hired Will H. Hays, to serve as it's head.

The MPAA advocated self-regulation as an alternative to government control. Hays ordered the industry to follow a series of rules that regulated various forms of immoral behavior shown in the movies. For example, stories of lawbreaking social transgression always have good and morality triumph in the end.

Max Linder (Gabriel Leuvielle) was born on December 16th, 1883 in Saint-Loubès, Gironde, France. His parents were winegrowers. He spent most of his working life in France, starting as a stage actor, and then appearing in his first film role in 1905. Linder can be said to be as important to the history of film as Charles Chaplin or Harold Lloyd because he originated the classic style of silent slapstick comedy years before they first appeared on-screen (the "mirror routine," which the Marx Brothers' used in *Duck Soup* in 1933) was first performed by Linder, in *Seven Years Bad Luck* in1921.

After making his first film appearance, he quickly became famous and successful as a slapstick comedian in both France and the U. S. By 1912, he was the highest-paid film star in the world, with a salary of one million francs a year.

Linder starred in more than four hundred short comedies between 1905 and 1925. He not only acted, but directed as well.

Linder was drafted when World War One began and was gassed. His health suffered for the remainder of his life.

Linder traveled to the USA in 1916 where he was to produce eight movies. But only three were finished before he was forced to return to Europe by poor health. He returned to the U. S. to make several films for United Artists in the early 1920s, but as a result of his failing health, these short comedies failed to exhibit the spirit seen in his earlier work.

He married and after the birth of his daughter, the emotional problems he struggled with became apparent when he and his wife attempted suicide in Vienna in 1925. They were found and revived from an overdose of barbiturates.

Then on November 1, 1925, the couple succeeded by injecting morphine and slitting their wrists.

Max is buried in the Catholique cimetière de Saint-Loubès.
The Hollywood sign, which originally reads "Hollywoodland," was erected in 1923. It was an advertisement for a Hollywood Hills housing development. After the advertisement was over, the sign remained and was neglected.

Barbara LaMarr was born Reatha Dale Watson on July 28, 1896 in Yakama, Washington. While still a child, she appeared on stage in several plays produced in nearby Tacoma. Her mother took her to Hollywood in 1909 where she danced professionally in Los Angeles theaters. LaMarr looked older than thirteen and had a well-developed body. Her mother took advantage of this and put her to work in a burlesque house, which resulted in Barbara's arrest. The judge returned her to her parents' care.

At sixteen, LaMarr ran off to Yuma, Arizona where she married a cowboy. The new husband died of pneumonia several months after their marriage, and she returned to Hollywood. Within a few months after arriving in Hollywood, LaMarr married attorney Lawrence Converse. Converse did not tell her he already had a wife and three children. Lawrence was charged with bigamy and jailed. He beat his head on the cell bars and died three days later from blood clots on the brain. Witnesses say Converse was screaming LaMarr's name while he bashed his head.

At age twenty, LaMarr married again. She divorced the man after he was sent to San Quentin for forgery. She, then, had affairs with several men, including Ernest Hemingway. In 1920, she began playing minor roles in the movies. Douglas Fairbanks cast her in *The Nut*, and again in the 1921 hit, *The 3 Musketeers*. This led to a contract with MGM.

While working on the film, *Souls for Sale*, LaMarr was involved in an accident. The studio doctors gave her morphine for pain thus allowing her to finish the film. She soon became addicted to drugs and alcohol.

She continued to be successful, starring in *The Prisoner of Zenda* in 1922, and *Thy Name is Woman* in 1924. Critics called her "the greatest actress of her time". Her lifestyle led to a nervous breakdown in 1925, and she was diagnosed with tuberculosis. Paul Bern gave her a house in Alta Dena (Bern had been begging her to marry him for years), and she began a life of isolation. Bern cared for her until she died in 1926, just 29.

Officially she died of anorexia, but her friends said she died of a drug overdose. Sound came to film in 1927-1928. As a result, Loews, 20th Century Fox,

Warner Brothers, Paramount, Columbia, and Universal pretty much took over the industry. While they didn't control all distribution of movies in the U.S., they had 25 to 35% of it.

The first Academy Awards ceremony and banquet took place in the Blossom Room of the Hollywood Roosevelt Hotel on May 16, 1929..

Ray Raymond divorced his wife in 1921 and married Dorothy Mackaye. They both acted in vaudeville and on Broadway. In the late 1920's, they headed to Los Angeles.

Mackaye was a comedic actress, "the toast of the theatrical world" as one newspaper put it, while Raymond was a song-and-dance man who traveled around the nation working such jobs as he found whether on Broadway, in motion pictures, or vaudeville houses. The Raymonds socialized with a heavy-drinking crowd that included actor Paul Kelly. Soon Kelly and Dorothy began sneaking off together, often staying out all night long. Raymond gave Kelly a stern warning to stay away from his wife, but Kelly continued his pursuit and finally openly declared his love for Dorothy.

On April 16, 1927, Kelly confronted Raymond in front of the Raymonds' maid and daughter. According to the maid, they were both drunk. Kelly bashed Raymond's head against a wall and knocked him out. The following morning, Dorothy called a doctor, who sat with Raymond while Mackaye visited Kelly. Ray Raymond died two days later of a brain hemorrhage.

Dorothy tried to convince the police her husband had died of natural causes. The maid told them what she had seen and Kelly was charged with first-degree murder. Dorothy was indicted for felony cover-up.

Dorothy denied having an affair with Kelly, but the actor's houseboy testified otherwise. Then the police found a stack of Kelly's love letters tucked under her mattress.

Kelly finally admitted his love for Dorothy and argued that the fight with Raymond was a duel, not a murder. The jury handed down a manslaughter conviction. Paul Kelly got one to ten years. Dorothy MacKaye received one to three years.

Julia Bruns was born in 1895 in St. Louis; unfortunately not much is known about her early life. On October 12, 1913, when she was eighteen, she flew with pilot Tony Jannus in his Baldwin Red Devil to an altitude of 4000 feet, remaining airborne for twenty minutes. This was just ten years after the Wright Brothers made their first flight.

She became a renowned model, appearing on magazine covers and in nationwide news reports. Her first theatrical role was in *The American Maid*. She appeared in three movies in Hollywood: *No Place for Father* in 1913, *At First Sight* in 1917, and *Quand on aime* in 1919.

Bruns was introduced to drugs by fellow thespians and soon became an addict. In 1925, in an effort to get money for purchasing drugs, she stole jewellery in Chicago worth more than $1000 and, as a result, was jailed.

Bruns died of alcohol poisoning in a cheap furnished room in New York City in 1927.

Grauman's Chinese Theatre had its Grand Opening in Hollywood on May 18, 1927. The film shown that evening was Cecil B. DeMille's *The King of Kings*. A riot breaks out as onlookers try to see the stars entering the theater for the premiere.

Ralph Yearsley was born in London, England on October 6, 1896. Although he had gone to medical school, the lure of Hollywood, and the film industry was too much, so he pulled up stakes and moved to the United States to pursue a career as an actor.

Yearsley made his motion picture debut in the 1921 silent film comedy in *Pardon My French*. That same year, he appeared in *Tol'able David*, directed by Henry King and the film won Photoplay Magazine's Medal of Honor. Ralph appeared in twenty films between 1921 and 1928, but is probably best known for his part in Harold Lloyd's 1927 film, *The Kid Brother*.

He was married to Grace Yearsley with whom he had a daughter, Diana Satterwhite.

In 1928, for reasons unknown, Yearsley committed suicide and is buried in the Forest Lawn Memorial Park Cemetery in the Hollywood Hills.

During the filming of *Hell's Angels* in 1929, three stunt pilots were killed.

Arthemus (Art) Ward Acord was born on April 17th, 1890, in Stillwater, Oklahoma Territory. As a boy, he worked on a ranch, and this experience led him to take up rodeo competition. In 1912, he became the world rodeo champion.

Art worked for William 'Wild Bill' Cody in 1911. His rodeoing resulted in his meeting some of the top cowboy movie stars of that era, such as Hoot Gibson, Tom Mix, and Broncho Billy Anderson. Because of their influence, Art went to Hollywood where he found work as a stunt man and supporting actor with Bison Film Company. His first movie role was in *The Two Brothers,* released in 1910. Between 1910 and 1930, he appeared in 112 films.

When World War One broke out, Art enlisted in the Army. It is said that he was awarded the Croix de Guerre for bravery by the French Government.

After the war, Art made a series of short films for Universal Pictures, but failed to make the cross-over to talkies because of his voice. As a result, Art became an alcoholic and a belligerent tough guy. He broke Victor Fleming's nose when the director (who would later direct *Gone With the Wind*) suggested that Art was not really part American-Indian as he claimed. Art spent time in jail for bootlegging, and his acting career came to an end.

Art married Edythe Sterling in 1913, and they divorced three years later. Edythe first appeared on film in 1913, and earned seventy-four film credits over a period of ten years. She died in Hollywood in 1962.

Art's next marriage was to Edna Nores, dates unknown. This marriage also ended in divorce, and he then married Louise Lorraine who, though only five feet one inch tall, was known for her work in cliff-hanger serials. She also played the role of Jane in several Tarzan movies. Between 1920 and 1932, Louise appeared in sixty-nine movies. Her marriage to Art ended in divorce in 1928. She died in New York City in 1981.

Art attempted to earn a living working in road shows, and failing at this, he moved to Mexico where he went back to rodeo work, worked in a mine, and in foolhardy stunt designed to bring him publicity, faked his own kidnapping. The plot failed.

On January, 4th, 1931, Art was rushed to a hospital, where he died. The official ruling was death by suicide. According to Chihuahua police, Art told the doctor treating him that he had purposely swallowed cyanide poison. There are some of Art's friends who believed that he was, in fact, murdered by an official who learned that Art was involved with the man's wife, and that the Mexican police and authorities engaged in a conspiracy to cover up the fact.

Art's body was shipped to Los Angeles, and he was buried in Forest Lawn Memorial Park Cemetery, in Glendale, California.

Art Acord threatens sleazy saloon owner Dick Nores to stay away from Vivian May in "The White Outlaw".

The White Outlaw, released in 1929 by J. Charles Davis Productions, was silent and filmed in black and white.

When dynamite exploded on a ship in 1931, **Varick Frissell**, co-director, and **Alexander Penrod, a** cameraman, were killed while working on the film, *The Viking*. Twenty-five of the ship's crew were also killed.

Tom Forman was born February 22, 1893 in Mitchell County, Texas. Little is known about his early life, but in 1914, he was working for the Jesse Lasky production Company, where he directed and acted in *The Doom of Duty* and *Within the Noose*, both released in 1914. He served in World War One, later acted in *Lights and Shadows*, starring Lon Chaney, as well as the 1923 version of *The Virginian*.

Forman was contracted to direct *The Wreck* for Columbia Pictures, starting on November 8th, 1926, but on the evening of the day before, in Venice, California, for unknown reasons, he committed suicide by gun shot.

During the filming of *Noah's Ark* (1928), three people died while shooting the great flood.

The Chateau Marmont opened its doors in February, 1929. The 63 room French-style castle is sited into the edge of the Hollywood Hills, and has been there since the Sunset Strip was unpaved and West Hollywood was a newly established town on the Western edge of Los Angeles. The hotel has appeared in Oliver Stone's biopic *The Doors*, and Sofia Coppola's 2010 *Somewhere*. But the hotel is most notable because the mysterious, and often scandalous, haunt of Hollywood's famous.Lindsay Lohan was evicted from Suite 33 in 2012 for running up a $46,350 bill. Kate Moss and Johnny Depp were regulars in 1994, and John Belushi died in Bungalow 3 in 1982.

Jean Harlow is said to have had an affair with Clark Gable there in 1933 while she was on her honeymoon with her third husband.

James Dean won his role in *Rebel Without a Cause*, by jumping through the roof of Bungalow 2.

Led Zeppelin's drummer road his motorcycle through the lobby, and Jim Morrison either jumped from a fourth floor window or simply fell while shimmying down a drainpipe.

Columbia Pictures former head, Harry Cohn, told his stars, "If you are going to get into trouble, do it at the Chateau Marmont."

You can stay at the hotel for about $415 per night.

Jeanne Eagels, born on June 26, 1890 in Kansas City, Missouri, was educated at Morris Public School, but because of her father's death and her mother's resulting poverty, she quit school before graduating in order to take a job in a department store.

Jeanne left Kansas City in 1905 after joining the Dubinsky Brothers' travelling theatre show. She began as a dancer, and in time worked her way up to leading lady parts in comedies and dramas produced by the Dubinskys.

In about 1911, she moved to New York City and took a job in a chorus line which led to her becoming a Ziegfeld Girl. A year later she was getting roles in the Broadway theatre. She starred with George Arliss in three plays in 1916 and 1917.

In 1922, Jeanne appeared as the female lead in *Rain*. She toured in *Rain* for a total of three seasons, giving a final performance on Broadway in 1926.

In 1927, she went to Hollywood to work with John Gilbert in *Man, Woman and Sin*. The following year she appeared in two "talkies" for Paramount Pictures.

On October 3, 1929, Eagels died suddenly at a private hospital in New York City. The exact cause of death was not reported, but evidence pointed to alcohol and heroin.

Chapter Three: the Thirties

On Valentine's Day, 1931, Universal Pictures released *Dracula*. The film was the highest earning movie of the year, bringing the studio out of a downward spiral.

Alma Rubens, born in 1897 in San Francisco, began performing at a young age.

In 1917, she was given her first professional stage opportunity when she replaced a chorus girl who had become ill. The stock company she was with traveled to Los Angeles where Franklyn Farnum, a friend, talked her into joining him in films.

In 1916, Alma was given a part in the movie *Reggie Mixes In* and worked in six more films in that same year. She appeared with Douglas Fairbanks in *The Half Breed* in 1917. In 1924 she was given the female leads in *The Price She Paid* and *Cytherea.*

Rubens played the part of Julie in the 1929 version of *Show Boat*, her next-to-last film. She found it hard to get parts after that because of an addiction to cocaine. As cocaine took charge, she experienced a series of trips to insane asylums, drug rehabs, and even jails. When she became destitute, the publishing millionaire, William Randolph Hearst, contributed to her support at the request of her friend, Marion Davies.

Alma's final stage appearance was in early 1930 when she was given a small part in a play at the Writer's Club in Hollywood. She was arrested later that year on a drug charge by Federal officers in San Diego.

Rubens died of typhoid asthenic pneumonia in 1931, brought on by excessive drug use. She is buried in Ararat Cemetery in Fresno, California.

Paul Bern, film director, screenwriter, and producer for MGM, was born Paul Levy, on December 3, 1889 in Wansbeck, Germany. His parents were Jewish. In 1898, due to the rising tide of anti-Semitism and high unemployment in their country, his father moved the family to New York City hoping for a better life. Pursuing a career as an actor, Paul studied at the American Academy of Dramatic Arts.

While living in New York, Paul met Dorothy Millette, who became his common-law wife. Millette suffered from various mental and emotional problems and spent time in a sanatorium, but Paul always supported her financially.

When he realized acting really wasn't his calling, Bern moved to Hollywood to work in the film industry. There, he worked as a film editor, screenwriter, and director before becoming a producer for MGM.

In 1930, he met the actress Jean Harlow and while helping her further her career, the two fell in love and married July 2, 1932.

Two months after the wedding, Paul was found dead in their Beverly Hills home. He had been shot in the head, and the coroner ruled his death a suicide.

There was a note by the body that read:
> "Dearest Dear,
> Unfortunatly [sic] this is the only way to make good the frightful wrong I have done you and to wipe out my abject humiliation, I Love [sic] you. Paul You understand that last night was only a comedy".

Bern's butler discovered the body and called the head of MGM Studios, Louis B. Mayer, who made it to the scene before the police. Mayer took the suicide note and only gave it to the police after a great deal of pressure was applied. It seems that Bern's "wrong" might have been that he had to use a phallus in order to have intercourse with his bride.

An interesting note to this sad story is Bern's abandoned common-law wife travelled to Los Angeles and is thought to have visited him on the night of his death. Two days later, Dorothy Millette's body was found in the Sacramento River. It appears she committed suicide by throwing herself off a steamboat. There was much speculation that she killed Paul, and the studio covered it up to protect Jean's movie reputation as a blond bombshell.

Paul Bern's last project was production assistant to Irving Thalberg on the great film *Grand Hotel*, which was released after Paul's death. The film went on to win the Academy Award for best picture for 1931–32, but the award was presented to Thalberg. Paul was not mentioned.

Paul's ashes were interred in the Inglewood Park Cemetery.

Actress **Martha Mansfield** died on November 30, 1933 while filming *The Warrens of Virginia*. She was sitting in an automobile, resting between takes when someone walked by and threw a match into the car after lighting a cigarette. The match ignited her costume, and she died in the hospital the following day from severe burns. She was twenty-four.

Karl Dane was born Rasmus Karl Therkelsen Gottlieb on Oct 12, 1886, in Copenhagen, Denmark. His father built a toy theatre where Karl and his brother would perform for the crowds. Although Karl later said this experience inspired him to pursue acting, in 1900 he became an apprentice machinist, a job he would perform on and off throughout his life.

Even though he was married and had two children, on January 25, 1916, Dane left them behind and sailed alone for the United States, intending to send for his family later. Speaking no English, he boarded a ship with twenty-five dollars in his pocket. Upon arrival and clearance through Ellis Island, he moved in with a friend in Brooklyn.

In late 1917, Dane appeared in a Vitagraph Studios short film that was made in New Jersey. This led to a part in the Warner Brothers film, *My Four Years in Germany*. He followed that with *To Hell with the Kaiser*, and completed three more films in 1919 before moving to Hollywood. During this time, Karl found out his wife no longer wanted to join him in America, so they divorced.

In 1921, Dane married a Swedish immigrant, quit acting, and moved to Van Nuys, California, where he and his wife started a chicken farm. His wife died two years later while giving birth. The child also died.

Devastated by his loss, Dane married again in March of 1924, but the marriage ended after only a few months. Karl, then returned to Hollywood.

In December 1924, he won a role in *The Big Parade* starring John Gilbert. The movie became the second highest grossing silent film in history. He also appeared with the Latin heartthrob, Rudolph Valentino, in *Son of the Sheik*. He then appeared as the comic relief in several films, including *La Bohème*, and *Alias Jimmy Valentine*.

In June of 1928, a month before Karl became an American citizen and legally changed his name to Karl Dane, he met and fell in love with a Russian dancer. Although Dane and the dancer claimed to be married and lived together in Dane's home, in November of 1928, she moved out and filed a breach of promise suit against him which she eventually dropped.

Because his thick Danish accent made it difficult find to find work after sound films became popular, Dane's last film, *The Whispering Shadow* made in 1932, starred Bela Lugosi.

By the summer of 1933, Dane had given up looking for movie roles and tried his hand at mining. He spent three months driving up and down the West Coast trying to find a good mining deal. The venture never took off, and he ended up losing $1,100. Dane then took on several jobs, including mechanic, waiter, and carpenter. He even purchased a hot dog stand outside MGM Studios in 1933, but the business soon failed. He then tried to get work as an extra or a carpenter, but had no luck.

On April 13, 1934, a pickpocket stole the last of Karl's money, a total of eighteen dollars. He had plans the next day to see a movie with a young woman named Frances. When he didn't show, she became worried and went to his apartment, where she found Karl slumped in his chair with a revolver at his feet. He had shot himself in the head.

On the table, next to his scrapbook filled with photos and memorabilia chronicling his acting career, she found his suicide note.

"To Frances and all my friends-goodbye."

When no one claimed the body, MGM agreed to pay for the funeral. Fifty people attended the service. Karl Dane is buried in the Hollywood Forever Cemetery.

George William Hill was born on April 25, 1895. He began his career in the movie industry when he was thirteen years old working with D. W. Griffith as a stagehand. He later became a cinematographer during the silent film era. Eventually, he was hired by the rapidly growing movie studios as a director. Hill's reputation as a director grew, and he was soon making films that utilized the talents of such stars as Marion Davies and Jackie Coogan. He directed Lon Chaney's money-maker, *Tell It to the Marines*, released in 1926, and four years later directed *The Big House*, starring Wallace Berry.

In 1930, he married Frances Marion, a screenwriter he worked with.

In 1931, he directed Wallace Beery and Marie Dressler, pairing them in *Min and Bill*, a script his wife wrote. Playing two alcoholic tugboat owners in this wildly popular film, *Min and Bill* thrust Beery and Dressler into stardom. Frances and George divorced in 1933.

Just as his career was taking off, Hill was badly injured in an automobile accident. It is thought that pain from his injuries was the reason he shot himself in 1934.

Born on January 14th 1908 in Camden, New Jersey, **Russ Columbo** was born Ruggiero Eugenio di Rodolfo Colombo and was the son of Italian immigrants. He studied the violin while still a child and performed professionally at the age of thirteen.

Russ quit high school when he turned seventeen and joined a band. For the next few years he traveled with bands, playing the violin, and singing.

When Russ was twenty, he appeared in a Vitaphone short while a member of the Gus Arnheim orchestra. He managed The Club Pyramid in Camden for a while, but quit when he was told he had the potential to become a singing star.

After signing with a manager, he moved to New York City where he landed a job with NBC. A recording contract with RCA Victor followed, and he became a singing sensation adored by his female fans.

He composed <u>Prisoner of Love, Too Beautiful for Words, When You're in Love</u>, and several other songs that became hits.

His music has been used in nineteen television and film productions, and between 1929 and 1934, he appeared in movies.

Russ was romantically involved with Carole Lombard in 1934, and he was being considered by Universal Pictures to play the role of Gaylord Ravenal in *Show Boat*, when he was killed in a shooting accident.

Russ went to visit his friend, Lansing Brown, a photographer, on September 2nd, 1934. Brown had a firearm collection, and the two were looking at the guns when a fowling piece, held by Brown, fired accidently. The ball glanced off a table and struck Russ above the left eye. Surgeons at Good Samaritan Hospital in Los Angeles attempted to remove the ball from Russ' brain, but he died during the operation.

Russ is buried in Forest Lawn Memorial Park in Glendale, California. His funeral mass was attended by many of the Hollywood elite, including Bing Crosby and Carole Lombard.

Lou Tellegen, christened Isidor Bernard Von Dammeler, **was born in Holland in** November 26, 1881, the illegitimate son of an army lieutenant. He first appeared on stage when he was five years old, thanks to the fame of his mother, a dancer.

Tellegen ran away when he was sixteen, traveled through much of Europe, was sentenced to prison in Russia for theft, and upon release returned home, only to discover that his father had disinherited him.

He worked his way to Paris, where August Rodin, generally considered the progenitor of modern sculpture, hired him as a model. Tellegen posed for *Eternal Springtime*, which is now in the Metropolitan Museum. In 1903, he married a countess and they had a daughter, but the marriage failed.

Following trips to Egypt, Africa, and South America, he returned to Paris and joined Sarah Bernhardt's show. In 1910, he accompanied Bernhardt to the United States.

He first appeared on the New York stage as the leading man in *Maria Rosa* and became an immediate star. Offered his first film role, he spent the next fifteen years traveling between New York and Hollywood and was considered one of the most handsome screen stars of that time.

In 1916, he married a well-known opera singer, Geraldine Farrar. They divorced in 1923. He, then married Nina Romano, an actress. They were divorced, and in 1930, he married for a fourth time, a silent film star named Eve Casanova. That marriage lasted two years.

His career ended when his face was badly damaged in a fire. He was heavily in debt at the time and had just been told he had cancer.

On October 29, 1934, just forty-three years old, Tellegen committed suicide in a friend's bathroom. Standing in front of a full-length mirror, he stabbed himself seven times with a pair of sewing scissors. None of his four ex-wives attended his funeral.

He was cremated and his ashes scattered

Pepi Lederer, born on March 18, 1910. She earned the nickname "Pepi" for her high-spirited personality. Later she formally adopted the name. Her mother was a stage actress and the sister of Marion Davies.

After her Aunt Marion became involved with William Randolph Hearst, Hearst took responsibility for Pepi and her several siblings, who included Charlie Lederer, later a well-known screenwriter. Pepi spent much of her childhood at Hearst Castle.

The Hearsts arranged for Pepi to get a few small parts in movies such as *Her Cardboard Lover*. Hearst also gave her a token job on his magazine, *The Connoisseur*.

Pepi was known to be a lesbian. She associated with Tallulah Bankhead and Louise Brooks, and while living in Europe for five years, she took up with Monica Morris. Monica, once involved with Tallulah Bankhead, had earned the nickname of "the Stage-Door Ferret" because of her predatory ways. Morris moved in with her and apparently introduced Pepi to drugs.

When Pepi returned to Los Angeles with Monica, they stayed at the Hearst Lexington Avenue house. Marion and Hearst were living in his San Simeon mansion at the time. Having learned of Pepi's drug use, Marion and Hearst decided to have her committed to the psychiatric section of Good Samaritan Hospital for a cure.

On June 11, 1935, Pepi was in bed in her sixth floor room at the Good Samaritan when she asked her nurse for something to eat. The nurse, about to leave, heard a noise and turned to see Pepi kill herself by leaping through a window. She died of a broken neck.

Pepi is interred in a crypt in Marion Hearst's private mausoleum at Hollywood Cemetery.

Aleta Freel was born in Jersey City, New Jersey, on June 14, 1907. Her father was a medical doctor. She was educated at the Bergen School for Girls in Jersey City and graduated from Smith College. She then joined a stock company, and in 1933 was given a part in the New York City Ritz Theater production of *Double Door*. She married Hollywood actor, Ross Alexander following a backstage romance.

Freel shot herself in the temple with a rifle on December 6, 1935 and died the following morning at Emergency Hospital in Los Angeles. Ross told police that he and Miss Freel had a "small spat" during the prior evening and that she had been disappointed about unsuccessful screen tests. There was an investigation of her death but no evidence of foul play was developed. Ross soon remarried. One year after Freel's death, he committed suicide. It is said, he used the same gun that she had used to kill herself. Freel died in the house located at 7357 Woodrow Wilson, Los Angeles. She is buried in the Bayview Cemetery in New York.

Thelma Todd was born on July 29, 1906 in the state of Massachusetts.

While still a teenager, she started competing in beauty contests. In 1925, she was crowned Miss Massachusetts, and as a result, received an offer from a Hollywood talent scout. Thus began her career in film.

In 1927, Todd was given the female lead in, *Fascinating Youth*; this led to more offers, and she became a star. Thelma was highly regarded as a comedian, and she played opposite other popular comic actors. She appeared in the 1931 film *The Maltese Falcon*, and in a total of 119 movies, but was probably best known for her roles in *Monkey Business*, and *Horse Feathers*, playing opposite the Marx Brothers. Todd continued her work in short-subject films through 1935. Her last film was *The Bohemian Girl*.

Todd had a long lasting affair with director Roland West (fourteen films between 1913 and 1936). West was married, and it is said that their relationship was often rocky. West suggested that Todd open a restaurant, and she accepted his advice. She found a location Pacific Palisades near Santa Monica Beach and named the place *Thelma Todd's Sidewalk Cafe*. It became a popular eating spot well-known movie celebrities as well as mobsters.

On the morning of Monday, December 16, 1935, Todd was found lying in the front seat of her car wearing an evening gown, diamonds, and a mink coat. Her death was caused by carbon monoxide poisoning, and a Grand Jury ruled it to be a suicide. Some believed that Lucky Luciano had her killed when she refused to allow him to operate illegal gambling in her popular restaurant.

It is said that in 1952, shortly before he died, West confessed to murdering Todd, saying the murder resulted when they argued about Todd, already drunk, attempting to go out again. No charges were filled, and the case is still open.

17531 Posetano Road in Pacific Palisades, where Thelma Todd's café was located.

Thelma's body was cremated, and after her mother's death in 1969, Thelma's ashes were placed in her mother's casket and buried in Bellevue Cemetery in her hometown of Lawrence, Massachusetts.

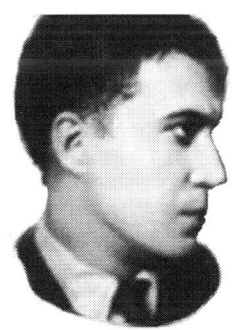

Arthur Edmund Carewe was born Hovsep Hovsepian **in** Trabzon, Ottoman Empire, on December 30, 1884. His family fled the Empire after his father, an influential banker, died due to the Hamidian massacres. In 1896, Arthur immigrated to the United States where he joined his two brothers. Having decided on a stage career, he attended the American Academy of Dramatic Arts in New York City. By 1910, he had taken the stage name Arthur Carewe, and then pulled a publicity stunt by faking a suicide attempt over a dancer.

For some reason, he gave up his plans to be an actor and moved to Chicago in 1914, where he started a furniture store. On February 17, 1915, Arthur married Canadian soprano Irene Pavlowska. (They divorced in 1921.)

On June 28, 1918, Arthur Carewe became an American citizen. When his furniture store failed, he moved to Hollywood, and landed a role in *Romance and Arabella*.

Within a few years, Carewe had become a well-known character actor, and was given parts in *The Phantom of the Opera* (1925), *Uncle Tom's Cabin* (1927), and *The Cat and the Canary* (1927). Altogether, Carewe appeared in fifty films, most of them made during the silent film era.

He had a stroke in 1936 after finishing *Charlie Chan's Secret*. No longer able to act because of facial paralysis, he took his life on April 22, 1937, with a gunshot to the head.

He was cremated and his ashes scattered.

A stunt man was killed during the filming of *The Charge of the Light Brigade* in 1936. The man fell from his horse and hit a broken sword lying on the ground. Thirty-six horses had their legs broken during the making of this film due to the use of trip wires. As a result, the U. S. Congress passed laws that protect animals during the production of movies.

John Gilbert was born July 10, 1897 in Logan, Utah. His parents, both actors, were abusive, causing him to run away to Hollywood while still a teenager. He soon found work with the Thomas Ince Studios, first as an extra, and then as a writer.

Gilbert quickly established an acting reputation, appearing in films such as *Heart o' the Hills*. Fox Film gave him a three year contract and featured him in *The Monte Cristo* and *The Wolf Man*.

Gilbert quit Fox in 1924 and signed a contract with MGM. In 1925, he played the lead role in *The Big Parade*, which became the second highest silent film money maker ever released.

In 1922, Gilbert married Leatrice Joy. They had one daughter, and then divorced in 1924.

He co-starred with Greta Garbo in *Flesh and the Devil*, and they became romantically involved. Gilbert wanted to marry, but Garbo did not.

Gilbert's first appearance in a sound film, *The Hollywood Revue of 1929*, was well received by audiences, and praised by a few critics. His next talking endeavor, *His Glorious Night*, also released in 1929, was a disaster. (See the "I love you, I love you, I love you" parody in *Singing in the Rain*.)

Severe depression caused by second-rate films and not enough offers, coupled with a marriage to that ended in as quick divorce, led to extreme alcoholism, and by 1934 his health had deteriorated considerably.

Gilbert died on January 9, 1936 of a heart attack brought on by his excessive drinking.

He was buried in Forest Lawn Memorial Park in Glendale, California.

Paul Johnston McCullough was born on March 27th, 1883 in Springfield, Ohio. While still a young child, Paul met Bobby Clark at the YMCA. They remained friends, and when adults developed a vaudeville act that they performed in vaudeville reviews and circuses.

In 1922, the men landed work in the Irving Berlin Music Box Revue, and in 1928, they moved to Hollywood. Over the following seven years they starred in thirty-five movie shorts.

Paul had a serious problem with mental depression and in 1936, he placed himself in a sanitarium in Medford, Massachusetts. He was released a few months later, and on his way home stopped at a barber shop, where he requested a shave. While the barber was shaving Paul, Paul suddenly grabbed the straight edge razor from his hands and slashed his own wrists and neck. He was rushed to a hospital but died two days later.

Bobby Clark continued a career as a solo act until his death in 1960.

The comedy team of Clark & McCullough has generally been forgotten despite their great popularity in the 1930s. One reason for this is that their short films were not packaged and sold to television in the 1950s, as were *The Three Stooges* and *Laurel & Hardy*. The Clark and McCullough films were considered risqué and were written for adults, thus the television audiences of the 1950s would have found them vulgar.

Adele Blood was born on April 23, 1886 in San Francisco, California. She first appeared in a production of the California Theatre in San Francisco. She appeared in many stage plays after that, usually as the leading lady. She became known as "the most beautiful blonde on the American stage".

Adele had roles in two motion pictures, *The Devil's Toy,* released in 1916, and *The Riddle: Woman,* released in 1920.

She committed suicide on September 13, 1936, by shooting herself in the head. Her daughter, Dawn, seventeen at the time, reported that Adele was having money problems.

Three years later, Dawn killed herself.

Silent film star **John Bowers** (John Bowersox)**,** was born on December 25, 1885, in Garrett, Indiana. After college, he moved east and began working on the New York City stage. He landed his first film role in 1916 and appeared in ninety-four movies between 1916 and 1936, becoming one of Hollywood's most popular leading men. He frequently co-starred with Marguerite De La Motte. They married in 1924, but divorced in 1936.

Like many silent film stars, when movies became "talkies," John's voice did not make the transition. After renting a sailboat and sailing to Catalina Island, where he failed to land a roll in a Gary Cooper movie being filmed there, he apparently committed suicide on November 17, 1936 by drowning himself. His body was found on the Santa Monica beach the next day. He was cremated and the location of his ashes is unknown.

Marie Walcamp was born in Dennison, Ohio in 1894. After finishing her formal education, she went to the East Coast in search of work on the stage.

She appeared in 105 films between 1913 and 1927, mostly shorts. Her final film was *In A Moment Of Temptation* released in 1927.

She married actor Harlan Tucker in 1927. Failing to find work after that she became depressed over the prospects of her career and on November 17, 1936, committed suicide by overdosing on prescription drugs.

She was cremated and her ashes given to someone in her family or a friend.

Marie Prevost was born Marie Bickford Dunn on November 8, 1898 in Sarnia, Ontario. At age three, her family moved to Los Angeles where she grew up.

She worked as a secretary for a while after graduating high school. Soon bored with her job, she decided to try and find work in the movies. Her first application was with Mack Sennett.

Sennett, who grew up in a town near Montreal, took his fellow Canadian under his wing. He nicknamed her "French girl", added her to his lineup of beautiful bathing beauties, and changed her name to the more exotic sounding Marie Prevost.

In 1919, Prevost agreed to marry wealthy Los Angeles socialite Sonny Gerke. The wedding was kept secret, and six months later Gerke left her. He did not attempt to divorce her because he was afraid of his mother. The lady had strictly forbidden him to have any association with Prevost or any other actress. Prevost was afraid the publicity from divorce proceedings would damage her movie career and so the pair remained secretly married for four years.

Prevost's first successful role was in *Love, Honor, and Behave* which was made in 1920.

Prevost completed three films for Sennett and then moved to Universal in 1921. When Marie's mother was killed in an automobile accident in 1926, she was devastated and started drinking

Howard Hughes saw Prevost in *The Beautiful and Damned* and decided to give her the lead part in his upcoming film *Racket*, completed in 1928.

Hughes and Prevost became romantically involved during the making of the film, but Hughes ended their relationship abruptly for an unknown reason, leaving Prevost disillusioned and severely depressed. She became a serious alcoholic and developed a reputation for not being dependable. That and a significant weight gain destroyed her future in the movie industry for good.

By 1934, she was broke, and on January 21, 1937, at the age of thirty-eight, she died from heart failure brought on by acute alcoholism and malnutrition. Marie's body wasn't found until two days later, when her neighbors complained about her dog barking.

Her funeral, which was at the Hollywood Memorial Cemetery was paid for by her friend, Joan Crawford. Other notable stars who attended were Douglas Fairbanks Jr., Clark Gable, Wallace Beery, Mack Sennett, and Barbara Stanwyck. Her remains were cremated and mixed with her mother's.

Ross Alexander (Alexander Ross Smith) was born in Brooklyn on July 27, 1907. He grew up in Rochester, New York, and took parts in little theater productions while still in high school. After graduating he won a part on Broadway in the long-running comedy *Enter Madame*. He then appeared in *Let Us Be Gay* in 1929, and as a result, was introduced to producer John Golden. This led to Paramount offering him a part in *The Wiser Sex*, which was released in 1932. He returned to Broadway that same year to take a role in *The Stork Is Dead*. He continued in stock and, while working at the Winchester Playhouse in Mount Kisco, New York, he met and became friends with Henry Fonda, and Fonda's first wife, Margaret Sullavan. It was here that he met Aleta Friele. In February 1934, Alexander married Friele with Fonda serving as best man. Shortly thereafter,

Hollywood once again called; this time the studio was Warner Bros. He and his new bride moved to Hollywood where they bought a home in Laurel Canyon.

Alexander's youthful appearance and happy-go-lucky attitude won him lead roles in *Flirtation Walk* (1934), *A Midsummer Night's Dream* (1935), and *Captain Blood* (1935).

Between 1932 and 1937, Alexander appeared in seventeen movies.

Warner's began featuring him in roles castoff by Dick Powell, and in other B-grade movies. Their purpose was to limit his exposure after deciding it was too much trouble to try and conceal his homosexuality.

Alexander's marriage with Aleta Freel ended with her suicide on December 6th, 1935.

Alexander was known to have become obsessed with Bette Davis in the spring of 1936 as he openly worked hard at being given a co-starring role with the queen of Warner Brothers. He was reported as saying that she would respond to their love scenes "like a wildcat" and they would become real-life lovers as well as co-stars.

A friend of Davis commented, "It was really pathetic... I knew Bette well enough to know that Ross wasn't her type. He was a handsome enough kid, with a good body and a wry, offhand, cynical charm that made him great in certain roles, but she could always spot a bisexual component in a man, and that she needed like a hole in her head at that stage."

Ross then tried another marriage of convenience, this time with Anne Nagel. They had met on the sets of *China Clipper* in 1936, and *Here Comes Carter* made that same year.

Alexander and Nagel

Alexander became involved in a sex scandal shortly thereafter, and Warner Brothers gave up on him. Aware that he would get no more film parts, Alexander shot and killed himself on January 2, 1937, thirteen months after Aleta's suicide. Some reports say he used the same rifle to shoot himself as Aleta did. Others say he used a pistol.

He is buried in Forest Lawn Memorial Park in Glendale, California.

Alexander's suicide evidently caused Nagel to become seriously depressed, and as a result, Universal began giving her roles in second-rate serials and B westerns. Fed up, she left Universal, but was only able to find work with second-tier studios such as Republic, Monogram, and PRC, the lowest rung on the ladder. Nagel's appearance in *Armored Car Robbery*, released in 1950, is now considered a classic, and was the best movie she had appeared in for many years. Nagel married an Army Air Corps officer in 1941, but the marriage was unsuccessful and they divorced in 1951. She had parts in five more television and film productions, and quit acting in 1957. She was said to have become an alcoholic, and she spent the last years of her life in poverty, dying of cancer on July 6th, 1966, at fifty years of age.

Marvel Rea was born on November 9, 1901 in Nebraska. In 1910, her family moved to California, and at the age of seventeen, she joined the Keystone Film Company, becoming a Mack Sennett Bathing Beauty.

Rea worked in films for five years, from 1917 through 1921. She earned twenty-five screen credits during that time. Among them were *A Clever Dummy*, made in 1917, *The Summer Girls*, released the following year, and *For Land's Sake*, which was completed in 1920.

On September 2, 1936, while out walking, Rea was approached by three young men who offered to drive her to her home; she refused. The men then threw her into a truck and drove her to a grove of trees in South Los Angeles where they assaulted her. She was left on the ground in a semiconscious state. The men were later captured and booked on suspicion of kidnapping.

In January 1937, the men were sentenced to prison terms of from one to fifty years, but in 1939, they were freed on technicalities regarding their trials.

On June 17, 1937, depressed by the experience, Rea killed herself by eating ant poison. She is buried at the Pacific Crest Cemetery in Redondo Beach, California with her family.

Rosamond Pinchot was born in New York City on October 26, 1904. Her father was a wealthy attorney. She was discovered by Max Reinhardt at age nineteen while on an ocean cruise, and he gave her a role in the Broadway production of *The Miracle*. Pinchot made just one appearance in a movie; the 1935 adaptation of *The 3 Musketeers*.

In 1927, when she was twenty-three, Pinchot was named "The Loveliest Woman in America" by The New York Times. She married William "Big Bill" Gaston the following year, and later had an affair with Jed Harris, the notoriously belligerent director of numerous Broadway and Hollywood productions.

On January 24, 1938, Rosamond Pinchot committed suicide by sitting in the family auto in a closed garage while the engine was running and inhaling carbon monoxide gas. She left two suicide notes, but what they contained was never revealed. She is buried in the Pinchot family plot in Milford Cemetery in Milford, Pennsylvania.

Dorothy Hale was born Dorothy Donovan in Pittsburgh, Pennsylvania on January 11, 1905. Fourteen years later after attending a convent and a drama school, she ran away from home. Her family hired detectives to find her, but she finally came home when her money ran out. At age seventeen, she landed a job in the chorus of the Broadway production of *Lady, Be Good*, and in 1927 at age twenty-two, she married Gardner Hale, a society portrait artist.

Hale spent several seasons working in stock companies and had a few jobs as a dancer and Ziegfeld girl. She was left penniless in December, 1931 after her husband was killed when his car went over a Santa Maria cliff. No longer able to maintain her wealthy lifestyle, Hale began to accept gifts of money from rich lovers and generous friends, one of whom was Clare Booth Luce.

In 1932, a friend who knew Samuel Goldwyn helped Hale land a role in *Cynara*, which was followed by a role in *Catherine the Great*, released in 1934.

After many scandalous affairs, in 1937, Hale became romantically involved with Harry Hopkins, the administrator of the WPA and policy advisor to Franklin D. Roosevelt. Hale moved into Hampshire House, an expensive apartment building in Central Park South, and began buying a trousseau in preparation of marrying Hopkins, but Hopkins broke off the affair without an explanation. The gossip columnists who had been reporting the fairy-tale romance with rumors of a White House wedding, much to Dorothy's embarrassment, also played up the stories of her "cruel jilting." Later, it was said the White House was disturbed about the Hopkins/Hale engagement.

On October 20, 1938, Hale invited friends over, explaining that she was leaving on a long trip. After the party, she and her friends went to the theater. Evidently despondent over the failed engagement and her financial situation, Dorothy Hale committed suicide at 1:15am the next morning, throwing herself out of the window of her sixteenth floor apartment wearing the same evening dress she'd worn to her party.

It is unknown where she is buried, but Dorothy will not be forgotten. Her friend, the Mexican artist Frida Kahlo, commemorated the event of hers death in the famous painting, *The Suicide of Dorothy Hale*, depicting Hale's plunge from her apartment to the pavement below.

Florence Lawrence was born Florence Annie Bridgwood in Hamilton, Ontario, January 2, 1886. After her father's death, Florence, her mother and two older brothers moved to Buffalo, New York. She graduated high school there, and joined her mother's dramatic company. The company disbanded in 1906, and Lawrence and her mother moved to New York City.

That same year, at age twenty, she appeared in her first motion picture. The following year, she appeared in thirty-eight movies while working for the

Vitagraph Company. In 1906, she played Daniel Boone's daughter in *Daniel Boone*, an Edison Manufacturing Company film.

She went back to work for Vitagraph in 1908, and played the lead role in *The Dispatch Bearer*. Because she was an excellent horseback rider, she worked in eleven movies over the next five months. She also met and married Harry Solter, a fellow actor, in 1929.

Lawrence joined the Independent Moving Pictures Company of America in 1909 and made fifty films for them over the next eleven months. After that, she joined a film company headed by Siegmund Lubin and was teamed up with Arthur Johnson. They cranked out forty-eight films together.

In 1912, Lawrence and Carl Laemmle formed their own company, the Victor Film Company. They set up a film studio in Fort Lee, New Jersey where they made many films starring Lawrence. In 1913, they sold out to Universal Pictures.

Although she had declared herself retired, in 1914 Lawrence agreed to make a film for Universal. While shooting *Pawns of Destiny*, a fire broke out and Lawrence was badly burned and suffered a serious fall. She spent months recuperating. She returned to work for Universal in 1916, and completed *Elusive Isabel*, but suffered a relapse and was paralyzed for four months. She divorced her husband in 1920, because she blamed him for making her do the stunt that caused her so much pain and misery. In 1921, she married again, and divorced in 1931.

When the Great Depression struck in 1929, Lawrence was no longer popular with movie goers and the stock market crash took most of her fortune. She also lost her mother in 1929, and spent a large amount of money for a commemorative bust to place on her gravesite.

Florence married again in 1933, but divorced him five months later citing severe abuse.

Broke, discouraged, and dealing with a bone marrow disease that caused her a great deal of pain, Florence was found in her West Hollywood apartment on December 27, 1938. She was rushed to the hospital where she died. She had killed herself by eating ant poison.

Although the site is now marked thanks to The National Film Preservation Board and actor Roddy McDowell, she was buried near her mother's grave in an unmarked plot in the Hollywood Forever Cemetery in Hollywood, California.

Chapter Four: The World War Two Years

George Periolat was born in Chicago, Illinois, on February 5, 1874. He worked for a while as a Broadway actor, and then made his first film for the Essanay Studios in Chicago. In 1911, he moved to Hollywood and began a career that included over 170 films.

Sound brought an end to Periolat's career, as it did many silent film stars. His last appearance was in the 1932 film, *What Price Hollywood?*

He killed himself on February 20, 1940, by ingesting arsenic. There is no record of where he is buried.

In 1941, during the filming of *They Died With Their Boots On*, three of the horsemen died during the final cavalry charge. One of these, **Jack Budlong**, threw his sword away when his horse tripped and fell. The sword hit the ground hilt first, and Budlong was impaled on the blade.

Helen Morgan (Helen Riggins) was born on August 2nd, in Danville, Illinois. Her father was a farmer. Helen quit school after the eighth grade. She worked at various jobs; including film extra in local films, took voice lessons, and became a popular singer in Chicago speakeasies. It is said that the venue put her on the road to alcoholism.

While dancing in the chorus of *Sally* in 1923, she was brought to the attention of Florenz Ziegfeld. This led to a job in the *Ziegfeld Follies* in 1931. In 1927, shortly after *Show Boat* opened, she was arrested and charged with violation of liquor laws. This led to an indictment, and she was found innocent in 1929.

Following her appearance in the 1929 film version of *Show Boat*, she returned to Broadway to star in Kern and Hammerstein's musical *Sweet Adeline*.

Her last role in a movie came in 1936, when she played the tragic part of the mulatto, Julie Laverne in *Show Boat*.

Helen married three times. She had a child in 1926, and gave it up for adoption. In 1940, Helen was hospitalized in after playing Julie La Verne for the last time in a Los Angeles stage revival of *Show Boat*. She fell onstage during a performance of *George White's Scandals of 1942,* and died at age 41, in Chicago, of cirrhosis of the liver, resulting from acute alcoholism, on October 9, 1941. She is buried in the Holy Sepulcher Cemetery, Alsip, Cook County, Illinois.

Helen was a famous stage and film star in the 1920s and 1930s, but she is pretty much forgotten today, except by film and theater musical fans. Her recordings are hard to find stores, and unfortunately her best film performance, the 1936 version of *Show Boat* was dropped by most TV and film producers when Paul Robeson, a main character in the film, was blacklisted by HUAC n 1950. Today, the 1936 version, considered by many to be the best of them all, is shown by Turner Classic Films

Stars that worked with the USO overseas during World War Two were dressed in military style uniforms and given officer's rank just in case they were captured by the enemy. The precaution protected them from being accused of being a spy, and hopefully guaranteed them better treatment. Thirty-six performers were killed during the war and more injured, usually as the result of plane crashes.

Following are the stars that served in World War Two

➢ **Don Adams**: enlisted in 1941 in the Marine Corps. He took part in the invasion of Guadalcanal and was the only man in his platoon to survive. He later served as a Marine drill instructor.

➢ **John Agar:** Sergeant, Army Air Corps.

➢ **Robert Altman:** joined the Army Air Forces in 1943. He flew as a crewman on a B-24 bomber, making more than 50 bombing missions in Borneo and the Dutch East Indies

➢ **Eddie Albert:** before World War Two began, Albert worked in South America for U.S. Army intelligence. He joined the Navy in 1942, and was awarded the Bronze Star with Combat "V" (for valor), for rescuing forty-seven Marines while piloting a boat during the invasion of Tarawa.

➢ **Steve Allen:** U. S. Army

➢ **James Arness:** served as a rifleman with the 3rd Infantry Division. He was badly wounded during the invasion at Anzio, Italy.

➢ **Desi Arnaz:** Arnaz was a Cuban citizen when the war started. He attempted to join the U. S. Navy, but was declined as a non-citizen. Then, in May 1943, he was drafted. After messing up his knee playing softball he was forced to give up hopes of becoming a flyer, and entered the infantry where he taught illiterate soldiers to read and write. Next he was assigned to the psychological section of a hospital where his job was to make returning wounded soldiers feel better. Lucy assisted him in that work by bringing in young starlets. He remained there until the war ended.

Bea Arthur: U. S. Marine Corps, truck driver and typist, 1943 to the war's end in 1945.

Mel Brooks: enlisted in the Army in 1944. Combat Engineer specializing in deactivating mines.

Barry Brown: U. S. Navy. Gunners Mate on D-Day landing craft.

Sid Caesar: Coast Guard.

Lee J. Cobb: Air Force.

Chuck Connors: West Point graduate. He was a tank-warfare instructor, stationed at Camp Campbell, Kentucky.

➤ **Jackie Coogan:** enlisted in the Army when the war started and transferred to the Army Air Forces as a glider pilot. He became a flight officer and volunteered for the 1st Air Commando Group. He flew British troops to a raid 100 miles behind Japanese lines during the Burma campaign.

➤ **Jackie Cooper:** Cooper's guardian kept him out of the draft until the end of 1942 when Cooper joined the Navy's officer training program. A criminal charge of contributing to the delinquency of a minor (two girls ages fifteen and sixteen) caused him to be dropped from the program. He was tried, found not guilty and the navy sent him to Boot Camp. After graduating he became a drummer in a Navy band.

➤ **Nicholas Colasanto:** Navy.

➤ **Mike Connors**: Army Air Forces.

➤ **William Conrad:** Army Air Forces fighter pilot.

➤ **Elisha Cook Jr.:** Although he was only 5 feet 5 inches tall and weighed 123 pounds, he was accepted into the U. S. Army.

➤ **Jeff Corey:** Navy Combat Photographer aboard U. S. S Yorktown when it was hit by kamikaze planes.

➤ **Broderick Crawford**: Sergeant, Army Air Corps. Served as announcer for the Glen Miller Orchestra in Briton.

➤ **Richard Crenna:** served in the army infantry as a Radioman. He was in combat in the European theater in the Battle of the Bulge. Later he served in the Pacific theater decoding Japanese messages.

➤ **Richard Cromwell**: Coast Guard. Three years service in the Pacific.

➤ **Robert "Bob" Cummings:** Army Air Force Flight Instructor.

➤ **Tony Curtis:** after enlisting in the navy, Curtis served aboard a submarine tender until the end of the war. He witnessed the Japanese surrender ceremony in Tokyo Bay from his ship's signal bridge.

➤ **Dan Dailey**: Army officer, Signal Corps.

➤ **Bill Dana**: Army Infantry. Co A, 263rd INF, 66th Div, Battle of the Bulge.

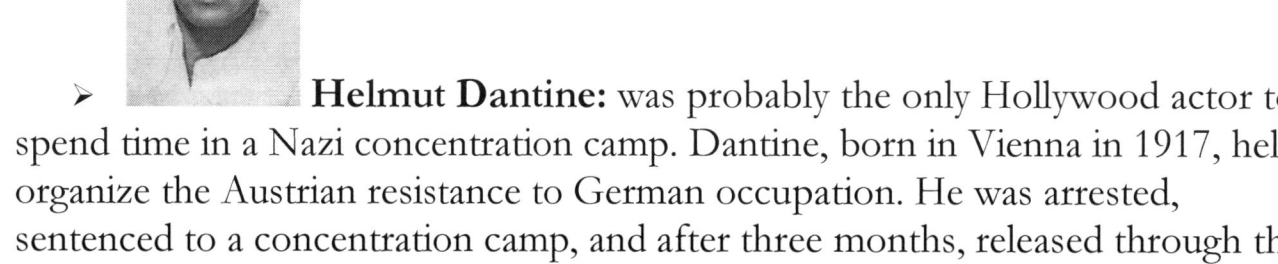

➤ **Helmut Dantine:** was probably the only Hollywood actor to spend time in a Nazi concentration camp. Dantine, born in Vienna in 1917, helped organize the Austrian resistance to German occupation. He was arrested, sentenced to a concentration camp, and after three months, released through the aid of his uncle, a Consolidated Aircraft VP (the US had not entered the war yet).

➤ **Sammy Davis Jr.:** Army entertainment Special Services unit.

➤ **Dennis Day**: Navy Lieutenant.

➤ **Gabreal Dell**: Merchant Marine.

➢ **Richard Denning**: Yeoman First Class on a submarine.

➢ **James Doohan:** Army; landed at Normandy on D-Day.

➢ **Kirk Douglas:** enlisted in the United States Navy in 1941, graduated Midshipman School, and was assigned to a Patrol Craft. His boat dropped charges on a Japanese submarine and Douglas was badly injured when a charge exploded prematurely. He was medically discharged for war injuries in 1944.

➢ **Melvyn Douglas:** became a Private in the Army at age forty. Later he was commissioned Captain and transferred to Burma where he worked in entertainment.

➢ **Charles Durning:** Drafted into the army at the start of the war, he served in Europe with the 3rd Army Support troops and the 386th Anti-aircraft Artillery Battalion. Durning was awarded the Silver Star for valor and 3 Purple Heart medals.

➢ **Buddy Ebsen:** Ebsen was commissioned Lieutenant, Junior Grade in the Coast Guard. He served as executive officer on a Coast Guard-manned Navy frigate.

➢ **Richard Egan:** served in the army as a judo instructor.

➢ **Douglas Fairbanks Jr.:** Joined the Navy in April, 1941 and was commissioned a Lieutenant. Saw combat aboard several ships and was then assigned to Lord Louis Mountbatten's Commando staff in the United Kingdom. He was given a Silver Star for action at Salerno.

➢ **Peter Falk:** Merchant Marine.

➢ **Norman Fell**: Air Force Tail Gunner, Pacific.

➢ **Henry Fonda:** in 1943, on the day after completing filming of *The Ox Bow Incident*, Fonda enlisted in the Navy. He initially served as a Quartermaster 3rd Class on a destroyer; and was later commissioned a Lieutenant Junior Grade in Air Combat Intelligence in the Pacific. Awarded the Navy Presidential Unit Citation and the Bronze Star.

➢ **Steve Forrest**: Army, wounded in Battle of the Bulge.

➢ **Glenn Ford:** assigned in 1943 to active duty at the Marine Corps Base in San Diego. He was sent to Marine Corps Schools Detachment (Photographic Section) in Quantico, Virginia.

➢ **John Ford:** Commander, in the Navy; head of the photographic unit for the Office of Strategic Services; made documentaries for the Navy Department.

➢ **John Forsythe:** Army Air Force.

➢ **Clark Gable:** at forty-one, Gable went through Army Air Force OCS. He eventually became a Major, flew five combat missions as an observer-gunner in B-17 Flying Fortresses, and because of his tendency to take too many risks, was awarded an Air Medal and sent back to the states.

➢ **Theodore Geisel** (Dr. Seuss): U. S. Army. Headed the Frank Capra Signal Corps Animation Department.

➢ **Alan Hale:** Coast Guard.

➢ **Sterling Hayden:** joined the British Commandos, broke his leg, and returned to America. He tried to join the Navy as an officer, but was refused because he only had a tenth grade education. He then enlisted in the Marines as a private, and while in Boot Camp at Parris Island he was recommended for Officer Candidate School, commissioned a second lieutenant and transferred to the OSS. His service included parachuting into fascist Croatia. He became a Captain, received the Silver Star, a Bronze Arrowhead device for parachuting behind enemy lines, and a commendation from Yugoslavia's Marshal Tito.

 ➤ **Van Heflin:** combat cameraman in the Ninth Air Force in Europe.

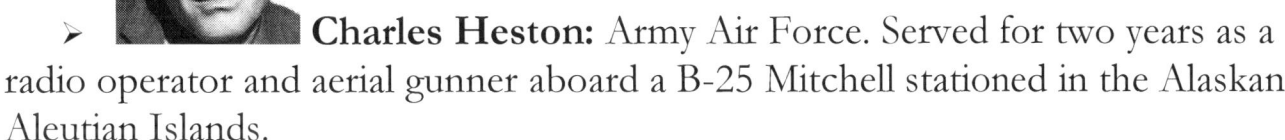 ➤ **Charles Heston:** Army Air Force. Served for two years as a radio operator and aerial gunner aboard a B-25 Mitchell stationed in the Alaskan Aleutian Islands.

➤ **Hal Holbrook:** U. S. Army.

➤ **William Holden:** enlisted in the Army Air Corps in April. 1942. After graduating OCS he became a 2nd Lieutenant and worked as public relations officer.

 ➤ **William Hopper**: Navy Frogman; underwater demolition.

 ➢ **Rock Hudson:** aircraft mechanic for the Navy in the Philippines.

➢ **Rick Jason:** Army Air Corps.

➢ **Russell Johnson:** joined the Army Air Force; commissioned second lieutenant; flew forty-four combat missions as a bombardier in B-25 bombers.

➢ **Brian Keith:** served as a Radio-Gunner in a Douglas SBD Dauntless dive-bomber in a Marine squadron.

➢ **Gene Kelly:** enlisted in the Naval Air Service in late 1944; commissioned lieutenant junior grade. He was involved in writing and directing documentaries.

➤ **George Kennedy:** Army officer; served under General Patton in Europe.

➤ **Jack Kerouac:** Joined the U. S. Naval Reserves in 1942, and was kicked out after just ten days. Said to have been drunk when he enlisted in the U. S. Army, the basic training instructors declared him "restless and apathetic" and transferred him to a psychiatric ward where he was diagnosed with several psychotic disorders including schizophrenia. He was then given a medical discharge.

➤ **Ted Knight:** Army Combat Engineer; earned five battle stars serving in the European Theatre.

➤ **Alexander Korda:** This British director, who came to America in 1926, was married to Merle Oberon. He worked for British Intelligence, making pro-British films, and assessing American attitudes toward Briton and the war with Germany.

➤ **Don Knotts:** Army Special Services (entertainment).

➤ **Alan Ladd**: joined the Army to much publicity and headlines, and was shortly thereafter discharged because of a double hernia.

➤ **Burt Lancaster:** Army Special Services (entertainment).

➤ **Jack Lemmon:** graduated the Harvard naval program and was informed by his commanding officer that he had made the lowest grades ever made by any officer commissioned by the ROTC.

➤ **Guy Madison:** Coast Guard

➤ **Carl Malden:** Army Air Force

➤ **Raymond Massey**: Massey was too old for service, but he attempted to join the Marines. They were going to make an Intelligence Officer out of him, but the Canadian Government (his home country), made a better offer. He was commissioned a Major, and wound up involved in entertainment.

➢ **Walter Matthau:** served in the Air Forces in England as a B-24 radioman-gunner.

➢ **Strother Martin:** served as a swimming instructor in the Navy.

➢ **Tony Martin**: managed to obtain a rank of Chief Specialist in the Navy, did some recruiting, and then became involved in a bribery trial after he gave a car to the man aided him in getting his rank. He was finally kicked out of the Navy and had to report to the draft board. He entered the Army as a Private and went into the Army Air Corps. Glenn Miller requested that Martin be assigned to his Army Band. All band members were officers, so Martin was sent to OCS where he graduated in the top third of his class. He was given Second Lieutenant's bars and orders to join Miller, and the next day an officer told him that he was no longer commissioned, was not joining Miller's band, and was sent to a unit composed of undesirables. The brother of a friend of Martin's, a General, intervened, and Martin joined Henry Mancini's band.

➢ **Lee Marvin:** Marine Corps; 4th Marine Division, wounded in action on Saipan. Awarded the Purple Heart.

➤ **Tim McCoy:** Colonel, Army Air Forces.

➤ **Ed McMahan:** He was a Marine Corps flight instructor.

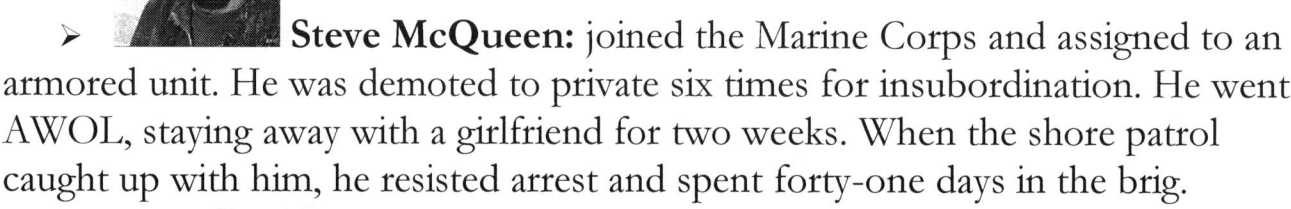

➤ **Steve McQueen:** joined the Marine Corps and assigned to an armored unit. He was demoted to private six times for insubordination. He went AWOL, staying away with a girlfriend for two weeks. When the shore patrol caught up with him, he resisted arrest and spent forty-one days in the brig.

➤ **Jan Merlin:** Torpedoman, in the Navy. Served on three successive ships in the North Atlantic and Pacific Fleets. Awarded ten battle stars. Entered Japan's Inland Sea with the first group of Occupation Forces.

➤ **Burgess Meredith**: enlisted in the Army as a Private. He graduated the Army Air Corps Intelligence School and was commissioned a Second Lieutenant. He worked on films and eventually became a Captain. In 1944 he was discharged so that he could play the part of Ernie Pyle in the film, *The Story of G. I. Joe.*

➤ **Ray Milland:** refused entrance into the Army Air Corps because of a bad hand, became a civilian flight instructor at an Arizona base.

➤ **Glenn Miller:** was too old to be drafted but joined the Army Air Corps anyway. Commissioned a Captain, he organized the Miller Air Force Band composed of the nation's finest musicians. He took his band to England in 1944. On December the fifteenth, 1944, Miller was a passenger in a small plane flying to Paris. The plane did not arrive, and the fate of the men in it was never determined. It is generally believed that the plane iced up and crashed in the English Channel.

➤ **Cameron Mitchell:** served as a bombardier with the Army Air Forces.

➤ **Robert Mitchum**: avoided the draft until March, 1945 when he was inducted into the Army.

➤ **George Montgomery:** Army Air Forces.

➢ **Robert Montgomery:** Commanded PT boats in the Panama Canal area and in the South Pacific. He saw action at Guadalcanal and the Marshall Islands, was commissioned Lieutenant Commander, contracted malaria, and in 1943 was assigned to a destroyer that took part in the Normandy invasion. He received a Bronze Star.

➢ **Glen Morris:** served in the Navy; commanded an amphibious-assault landing craft.

➢ **Wayne Morris:** in 1941, Morris enlisted in the Naval Air Service. He became a fighter pilot, served on the Carrier Essex, and took part in raids on Iwo Jima, Wake Island, and Okinawa. He fought in both Philippine Sea battles. All in all, Morris flew fifty-six missions, shot down six Japanese planes, sunk a Japanese gunboat, two destroyers, and had a part in sinking a submarine. Three of the planes he flew had to be junked because they had so many bullet holes in them. Morris was awarded four Distinguished Flying Crosses and two Air Medals.

➢ **Audie Murphy:** Army; most decorated soldier in World War Two.

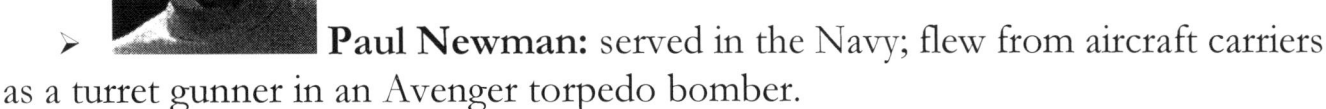

➤ **Paul Newman:** served in the Navy; flew from aircraft carriers as a turret gunner in an Avenger torpedo bomber.

➤ **George O'Brien:** enlisted in the Navy, serving on a Submarine chaser. O'Brien volunteered to be a Marine stretcher bearer and was decorated for bravery.

➤  **Carroll O'Connor:** Merchant Marine.

➤ **Jack Palance:** Army Air Forces.

➤ **Fess Parker:** Marine Corps Radio Operator.

➤ **Dick Peabody:** Navy.

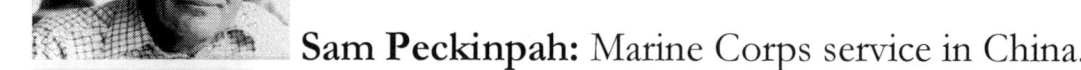

➢ **Sam Peckinpah:** Marine Corps service in China.

➢ **Tom Poston:** Army Air Forces pilot. Dropped paratroopers for the Normandy invasion; served in North Africa, Italy, France, and England.

➢ **Tyrone Power:** after completing filming of *The Black Swan* in 1942, Power enlisted in the Naval Reserve. Irritated by star treatment, in August, 1942, he joined the Marine Corps, was commissioned a Second Lieutenant, a pilot, and spent the next year doing very little. Finally, in August, 1944, he got his wish to see combat and was transferred to Saipan where he flew cargo and wounded Marines in and out of Iwo Jima and Okinawa.

➢ **Robert Preston:** Army Air Forces Intelligence officer.

➢ **Tony Randall:** enlisted in the Army in 1942 and served until the war ended.

➢ **Ronald Reagan**: joined the Army Calvary Reserves as a Lieutenant and was activated in April, 1942. He became a public relations officer in the Army Air Corps and later joined a film crew.

➢ **Steve Reeves:** Pacific service in the army.

➢ **Jason Robards Jr:** Navy Radioman. Served on a Heavy Cruiser in the Pacific. Ship was sunk by Japanese torpedoes. Robards was rescued by a destroyer.

➢ **Don Rickles:** Seaman First Class, Navy. Pacific sea duty.

➢ **Cesar Romaro:** Coast Guard Chief Boatswain's Mate. Served on an assault-transport at Saipan and Tinian.

➤ **Mickey Rooney**: MGM fought the draft tooth and nail to keep Rooney out of the military, and Rooney, married to Ava Gardiner was glad of it. He was afraid if he left town Gardiner would find someone else to party with. He finally appeared before the draft board and was classified 4-F because of high blood pressure (he blamed this on Gardner). In 1943, Rooney, now twenty-two, applied for a new examination and was classified 1-A (Ava had left him with a final remark, 'You know, Mick, I'm damned tired of living with a midget.') Rooney entered the Army where he had to fight several men over remarks about Ava and him. On leave, he attempted to visit Ava and found Howard Hughes there ahead of him. They got into a fist fight that ended in a draw with the two combatants shaking hands. Rooney then went to France as an entertainer.

➤ **John Russell:** Marine Second Lieutenant. Served on Guadalcanal in intelligence.

➤ **Robert Ryan:** became a naval gunnery instructor.

➤ **Rod Serling:** Army paratrooper. Served in combat on Leyte. Awarded Bronze Star and Purple Heart.

➢ **Red Skelton:** Army Special Services entertainer.

➢ **Robert Stack:** Navy gunnery instructor.

➢ **George Stevens:** Army Signal Corp film unit.

➢ **Jimmy Stewart:** Army Air Forces. Rose to Brigadier General in the reserves.

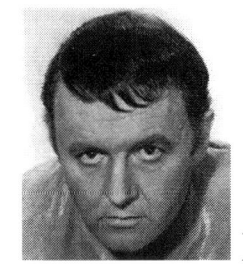

➢ **Rod Stieger:** Navy Seaman; served on a destroyer in the Pacific.

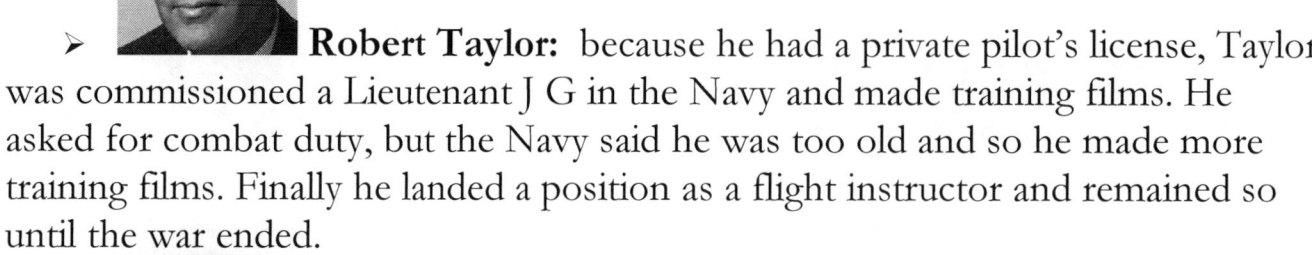

➤ **Robert Taylor:** because he had a private pilot's license, Taylor was commissioned a Lieutenant J G in the Navy and made training films. He asked for combat duty, but the Navy said he was too old and so he made more training films. Finally he landed a position as a flight instructor and remained so until the war ended.

➤ **Rudy Vallee**: was forty-two in 1942 entered the Coast Guard as a Chief Petty Officer. Later he was commissioned a Second Lieutenant. His service was all stateside.

➤ **Lee Van Cleef:** Served on a Navy minesweeper.

➤ **Dick Van Dyke:** Army Air Corps Special Forces entertainer.

➤ **Eli Wallach:** Army staff sergeant in a military hospital.

➤ **Jack Warden:** served as a paratrooper in the 101st Airborne Division.

➤ **James Whitmore:** Second Lieutenant, Marine Corps in the Panama Canal Zone.

➤ **Gig Young:** served as a pharmacist's mate in the US Coast Guard.

Some who did not serve in WW2 and why:

John Wayne avoided the draft by claiming exemption because he had three children.

Spencer Tracy was forty-one when the war started. He had served in the Navy in World War One. He and **Pat O'Brien** had joined together.

John Garfield had a heart murmur.

Humphrey Bogart was forty-three when the war began. He too had served in WWI. The scar on his lip, which caused his famous lisp, was the result of a military prisoner attacking him. Bogart shot the man.

Edward G. Robinson, forty-nine when the war started, also served in the Navy in WWI.

George Raft was forty-seven.

James Cagney was forty-three.

Errol Flynn did everything possible to avoid the draft. Finally giving in, he took his physical and to his sad surprise was informed that he had a heart murmur and tuberculosis. The doctor told him he probably only had a few years to live.

Frank Sinatra was World War Two's most hated star so-far as the men in the military were concerned. He was not in service, and he was constantly seen in the news surrounded by nubile young women. Sinatra was 4-F because of a punctured ear drum.

Gary Cooper was forty at the war's start. He was 4-F because of a crippled hip.

Cary Grant applied for Army Air Force OCS but evidently his studio shot that down by getting him classified 1-H (a person that Washington wanted held ready for service from time-to-time as needed). It is said that in actuality Grant was working for British Intelligence during the war.

Gregory Peck was 4-F because of a ruptured disk in his back.

Orson Welles was classified 4-F.

Dana Andrews was classified 4-F.

Ronald Colman was fifty and had served in WWI.

Ray Milland had a bad hand but did do some flight instructing for the Army Air Force. **Fred Astaire** had a low draft number and was not called. He was forty-three and had three children.

Phil Silvers was 4-F because of bad eyesight.

Jack Benny was forty-seven and ignored by the draft.

Peter Lawford had a bad arm.

Jess Barker a heart murmur.

Van Johnson suffered a skull fracture while filming and was recuperating during most of the war, but this did not stop him from making more films. **Marlon Brando** was 4-F because of near sightedness and a bad knee.

Sidney Poitier enlisted in the Army and then decided he did not like military service so he pretended to be insane. The army doctors threatened him with electric shock treatment and he admitted that he was faking. They discharged him anyway.

Stephen H Haggard was born on March 21, 1911, in Guatemala City, Guatemala. He was the son of Sir Godfrey Haggard, a British diplomat, and the great-nephew of H. Rider Haggard. After graduating university, he decided to become an actor and moved to New York City where he made his first stage appearance in 1934 in *Come of Age*. He then returned to London and garnered roles in plays such as *Flowers of the Forest*, and *The Seagull*.

In September of 1935, he married and fathered three children.

In 1938, Haggard once again travelled to New York where he appeared on Broadway in *Whiteoaks*. He then went to Hollywood for a part in *Whom the Gods Love*, which was released in 1936. In 1939, he appeared in Alfred Hitchcock's film, *Jamaica Inn*, and three years later in *The Young Mr Pitt*.

Haggard joined the British Army at the beginning of World War Two, serving as a captain in the Intelligence Corps. He was sent to the Middle East where he worked for the Department of Political Warfare. His wife and children moved to New York in 1940, where his father was serving as consul-general.

While serving in the Middle East in 1943, he met and fell in love with a married Egyptian woman. Overworked and believing with good cause that the war had destroyed his acting career, Haggard suffered a nervous breakdown when the woman decided to end their relationship.

He committed suicide by shooting himself in the head while on a train traveling between Cairo and Palestine on February 25, 1943.

He was buried in Heliopolis War Cemetery in Cairo, Egypt.

Carole Lombard was born Jane Alice Peters in Fort Wayne, Indiana, on October 6, 1908. When her parents separated in 1916, her mother moved the children to Los Angeles. Carole was playing a game of junior high school baseball when film director, Allan Dwan, saw her. This chance encounter led to her first movie role, a part in the 1921 film, *Perfect Crime*.

After that one part, she returned to public school for three years, and then quit to join a theater troupe. In 1925, she was given a screen test by Fox Films and signed to a contract. That year she played the female lead in *Hearts and Spurs*.

In 1926, an auto accident left her with a scar on the across the left side of her face, and Fox fired her. When Carole was seventeen, she was afraid the scar would ruin her career so she had plastic surgery to make it less visible. She then learned to hide the mark that was left using make-up and lighting. Mack Sennett gave her a few parts in 1928, and Fox gave her a part in *Me, Gangster* that year.

Carole had an appealing, sexy voice, and when sound became popular, she began to get more roles. Her first sound movie was *High Voltage*, released in 1929 by Pathe. She co-starred with William Powell in *Man of the World* in 1931. They later married, but the marriage only lasted two years.

No Man of Her Own, released in 1932, paired Carole with Clark Gable. Although they never worked together in another film, they reunited at a party four years later. Gable, who was still legally married to Rhea Langham, and Lombard soon became one of Hollywood's most popular couples, and were constantly asked when they would marry.

Their careers continued flourish, and Carole received a nomination for Best Actress for the film *My Man Godfrey* in 1936. She didn't win the award, but much beloved for her zany, spirited roles in the madcap comedies of the '30s, Carole became the highest-paid Hollywood movie star in the late 1930s.

Finally, in 1939, Rhea agreed to a large settlement and granted Gable a divorce. The happy couple married in 1939 and bought a ranch in Encino, California.

Carole made *Mr. & Mrs. Smith* in 1941. The film was directed by Alfred Hitchcock and co-starred Robert Montgomery. Her final film, which is said to be the happiest experience in her career, was *To Be or Not to Be* with Jack Benny and was made in 1942.

That same year, Carole went home to Indiana to take part in a World War II bond rally and raised over two million dollars. On January 16, 1942, anxious to get home, she boarded a commercial flight with her mother and Gable's close friend and press secretary, Otto Winkler. Flying back to California, the plane crashed near Mt. Potosi, thirty-two miles from Las Vegas, Nevada, and all aboard were killed. Carole was thirty-three years old.

Gable was devastated by her death, and shortly thereafter, joined the United States Army Air Forces. After officer training, he led a six-man picture unit and went to England to film aerial combat missions. In 1943, the United States commissioned the SS Carole Lombard. On the second anniversary of Carole's war bond drive, the ship was launched and used to rescue hundreds of survivors from ships sunk in the Pacific and taking them to safety.

Although Gable was married two times after Carole's death, he insisted on being buried beside Carole at Forest Lawn Memorial Park Cemetery in Glendale, California.

John Sydney Barrymore (Blythe) was born on February 15th, 1882, in Philadelphia, Pennsylvania. Because their parents, Maurice Barrymore (formerly known as Herbert Blythe) and Georgiana Drew Barrymore were both actors and required to travel, John and his siblings, Ethel and Lionel, were raised by their grandmother, Louisa Lane Drew in Philadelphia. John often spoke of the summer of 1896 when he and Lionel roughed it, acting like Robinson Crusoe with their black servant as their only companion.

John's grandmother and his mother both died when John was fifteen. His mother died of tuberculosis. His father was often committed to a mental institution. It is said that because of these childhood difficulties John was emotionally unstable and became an alcoholic.

Caught by the police in a whore house at the age of sixteen, John was kicked out of the exclusive Georgetown Preparatory School. Then, at age nineteen, John had an affair with the well-known showgirl, Evelyn Nesbit. Popular rumour had it that Evelyn was impregnated by young Barrymore and had an abortion.

Several years later, Nesbit was involved in a national scandal. Another one of her lovers, the well-known society architect, Stanford White, was murdered by Nesbit's husband, Harry K. Thaw, a Pittsburgh millionaire. John Barrymore was subpoenaed to testify at Thaw's trial as the defence hoped to reveal Barrymore's relationship with Nesbit, but they both swore under oath that there had not been a relationship or an abortion.

He graduated King's College in Wimbledon, Pennsylvania, and then moved to New York to attend the New York Art Student League. His first employment was an artist, doing sketches for the *New York Evening Journal*. His inclination was to act however, and in 1903, he appeared in the stage production of *Glad of It*. Because of his performances in *The Fortune Hunter,* he became quit famous. He became known as "his generation's most acclaimed Hamlet".

John's first film was a short produced by the Lubin Company, titled *The Dream of a Moving Picture Director*, released in 1912.

John Barrymore as Dr. Jekyll (1920)

John married Katherine Corri Harris in 1910. They divorced six years later, and he then married Blanche Marie Louise Oelrichs in 1920. The marriage produced one daughter, Diana. John and Louise divorced in 1925. In 1928, he married actress Dolores Costello. That marriage produced two children: Ethel Mae and John Drew Barrymore. John Drew Barrymore is the father of actress Drew Barrymore. His marriage to Costello ended in 1935. One year later he married Elaine Barrie. They divorced by 1940.

Between 1912 and 1941, John appeared in sixty-five film productions.

Alcoholism plagued John early on in his life and by 1936, when he was fifty-four, it began to interfere with his work. He had a difficulty remembering his lines, and was offered fewer film roles. In order to support his extravagant lifestyle, he started working in radio. John collapsed while rehearsing for *The Rudy Vallee* radio show on May 19th, 1942. He was taken to the Hollywood Presbyterian Hospital. The diagnoses was cirrhosis of the liver, pneumonia, atherosclerosis, and hemorrhaging ulcers. John died on May 29th, 1942 in Los Angeles, California. He was sixty years old.

John's final speech was:

"Die? I should say not, dear fellow. No Barrymore would allow such a conventional thing to happen to him".

He is buried in Calvary Cemetery in Los Angeles, California.

Jeanette Loff was born on October 9, 1906 in Orofino, Idaho. In 1907, when she was a year old, her family moved to Canada where her father found work as a violinist. They lived there until Jeanette was sixteen, when her family moved to Portland, Oregon, where she completed her musical education as a trained soprano.

Loff moved to Hollywood in 1924, where she landed an uncredited role in *Uncle Tom's Cabin*. After seeing her performance, Cecil B. DeMille gave her a contract and began casting her in small parts. She had a role in *The King of Jazz* in 1930, and then decided to quit acting for an unknown reason. Even though she was still under contract to Universal Pictures, she made no additional films and went to New York City where she performed in various musicals.

Loff returned to Hollywood in 1942 and played a role in *Mating Time*. That was her final movie appearance.

On August 4, 1942, age thirty-five, she died after swallowing ammonia. The coroner's report was inconclusive as to whether she ingested the ammonia accidentally or intentionally. She is buried in Forest Lawn Cemetery in Glendale, California.

Woodbridge Van Dyke, Jr. was born on March 21, 1889, in San Diego, California. Following the lead of his parents, he became a child actor on the vaudeville circuit.

Moving to Hollywood at age twenty-seven, he was given the position of assistant director on the D. W. Griffith's classic film *Intolerance*, which was released in 1916. He directed many well-known films after that, including, *Trader Horn* in 1931, and *Tarzan the Ape Man* in 1932. Known as one of Hollywood's most versatile directors, he soon earned the nickname of "One-Take Woody."

Van Dyke directed four of the *Thin Man* movies, with Myrna Loy and William Powell, and six of the eight Jeanette MacDonald-Nelson Eddy films. He is credited with saving MacDonald's life in 1939 when she tried to kill herself after hearing that Eddy had married someone else.

In 1936, he also directed San Francisco starring the earthquake scene credited to have some of the best special effects ever filmed.

Van Dyke enlisted in the US Marine Corps at the start of World War Two, and even set up a recruiting center at MGM. After learning that he had cancer in late 1942, he returned to Hollywood, directed his last film, *Journey for Margaret*, the movie that made five-year-old Margaret O'Brien a star. He then said his goodbyes to his wife and children, and rather than face a death by cancer, committed suicide on February 5, 1943. He is buried in Forest Lawn Memorial Cemetery in Glendale, California.

Lupe Velez was born María Guadalupe Villalobos Vélez on July 18, 1908 in San Luis Potosí, Mexico. Believing her to be undisciplined, Lupe's parents sent her to Texas to be educated in a Catholic convent school at the age of thirteen. After she returned home, she took dancing lessons, and in 1924, at the age of sixteen, she performed at the Teatro Principal in Mexico City. Shortly thereafter she left home and returned to Texas where she danced in vaudeville shows.

At the suggestion of fellow vaudevillians, she moved to Hollywood, where she worked for a while as a sales assistant and then met the comedienne Fanny Brice (*Funny Girl*), who promoted her to the studios as a dancer. That same year, in 1927, Hal Roach gave her a movie part in *The Gaucho*, which starred Douglas Fairbanks. Over the next few years, she performed in *The Wolf Song* (1929), *Lady of the Pavements* (1928); and Tod Browning's *Where East is East* (1931).

Velez then became known as a comedian, playing opposite other comedians such as Laurel and Hardy and Jimmy Durante.

She left Hollywood to perform on Broadway when she was thirty, appearing in *You Never Know*, and then returned to Hollywood to play the lead in *The Girl from Mexico* (1939) which became to be known as the first of a series of *Spitfire* films.

The *Spitfire* movies restarted her movie career. Over the next few years she once again was the star of musical and comedy films, working for RKO, Universal Pictures, and Columbia Pictures.

Velez was said to have been romantically involved with several men, including John Gilbert and Gary Cooper. She married Johnny Weissmuller in 1933. They divorced in 1938.

Lupe's Hollywood career faded after the ending of the *Spitfire* films, and she began to involve herself with more and more men, first other stars, then less known actors and stuntmen. In 1943, she was sexually involved with Harald Maresch and became pregnant. On December 14, 1944, faced with the rules of Catholic morality, which forbade abortion, she made a decision. Lupe was living in one of Hollywood's grand homes. The mortgage was overdue, but she still had credit. She filled the house with flowers, invited friends over for dinner, and served a large catered meal followed with expensive brandy. After announcing her intention to commit suicide, she went to her bedroom, filled the room with lighted candles, and then took her life with an overdose of Seconal. Her alleged suicide note read:

> To Harald: May God forgive you and forgive me, too; but I prefer to take my life away and our baby's, before I bring him with shame, or killing him. How could you, Harold, fake such a great love for me and our baby when all the time you did not want us? I see no other way out for me so goodbye and good luck to you.   Love, Lupe.

Unfortunately, fate destroyed Lupe's dream of a grand finale. The next morning, her maid discovered Lupe's body in the bathroom. The Seconal, mixed with the grand dinner and brandy caused her to throw up. Hollywood rumors allege that when she rushed to the bathroom she fell, struck her head on the corner of the commode, and drowned in the commode while unconscious.

Lupe is buried in the artist area of the Panteon de Delores Cemetery in Mexico City.

Russell Hopton was born on February 18, 1900 in New York City. All in all, he appeared in 105 films. His most noted part was in *Street Scene* which was made in 1931. He also appeared in *Min and Bill* in 1930, *Law and Order* in 1932, *I'm No Angel* in 1933, *G' Men* in 1935, *Made For Each Other* in 1939, and *Tall in the Saddle* in 1944. After that, his work was reduced to an occasional unaccredited minor role in "B" rated films and he became despondent.

He committed suicide on April 7, 1945 by overdosing on sleeping pills. He was buried in Holy Cross Cemetery in Culver City, California.

Rags Ragland (John Lee Morgan Beauregard "Rags" Ragland) was born August 23rd, 1905 in Louisville, Kentucky. As a teenager, he worked at various job before moving to Los Angeles at age 22. His early entertainment experience came in LA where he worked for the Minsky burlesque shows as a house comic, performing with Phil Silvers in partner routines.

Ragland signed a long-term contract with MGM in 1941. His first film was *Panama Hattie*, released in 1942. He made more than 20 films for MGM, the last being, The Hoodlum Saint, released in 1946.

Ragland, a serious alcoholic, died of uremic poisoning on August 20th, 1946, at age 40, in Los Angeles, California. Doctors were unable to help him, saying that his liver and kidneys were ruined by his drinking.

Panama Hattie (1942)
Ragland, Ben Blue, Red Skelton and Ann Sothern

Elizabeth Short (known as "The Black Dalia"), was born in Boston, Massachusetts, the third of five daughters of Cleo and Phoebe Sawyer. Troubled by asthma and bronchitis, at the age of sixteen, Elizabeth was sent to live in Miami, Florida. For the next three years, she stayed in, Florida during the winter and in Medford, Massachusetts during the summer.

When she was eighteen, Elizabeth learned that her father was living in Vallejo, California, and she moved there to be with him. They moved to Los Angeles in 1943, but then they had a fight, and she left. She worked for a while at the Post Exchange at Camp Cooke, California, and then moved to Santa Barbara.

Arrested for underage drinking, she was sent back to Medford by the juvenile authorities. Her next move was back to Florida where she met Air Force Major Matthew Michael Gordon Jr. Later, she told friends that Gordon had written her a letter from India proposing marriage. She said that she had accepted his proposal only to learn later that he had been killed in an airplane crash.

Elizabeth returned to Los Angeles in July 1946 to visit an old boyfriend she had met in Florida during the war.

Short's severely mutilated remains were found some months later on a Los Angeles vacant lot. She was nude, cut in half at the waist, and drained of blood.

Her killer was never identified.

She is buried in the Mountain View Cemetery in Oakland, California.

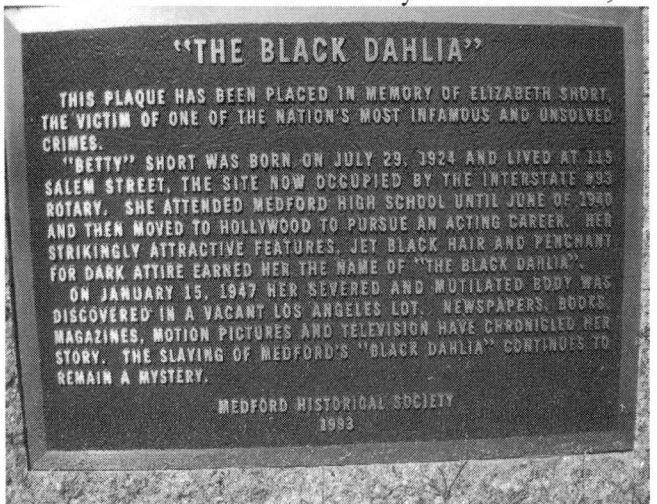

W. C. Fields was born William Claude Dukenfield on January 29, 1880 in Darby, Pennsylvania. After only four years of formal education, he was made to leave school so he could help his father sell vegetables from a horse drawn cart. Fields often fought with his father, who was an alcoholic, and he once struck his father on the head with a shovel. Finally, when he was eleven years old, he had enough and ran away from home.

For two years, he managed to stay alive by stealing food and an occasional piece of clothing. At one point, he lived in a hole behind some rundown buildings, but he survived.

By the time he was thirteen, he had become a skilled juggler and found employment using those skill performing in vaudeville. He later traveled in the U. S. and Europe under the title, The Eccentric Juggler. He married Harriet Hughes, in 1900 and in 1904, they had a son.

In 1906, Fields first performed on Broadway in *The Ham Tree*, a musical comedy, but his marriage failed, and he and Harriet separated in 1907.

He met Bessie Poole while they were performing at the Amsterdam Theater in New York City, and they had a son together, but never married. Bessie was killed in a barroom fight in 1919, and Fields supported his son until he graduated from high school.

Fields met Carlotta Monti in 1932, and they lived together until his death

Debilitated by his heavy drinking, Fields became extremely ill in 1936 and was forced to stop working. He starred in, *The Big Broadcast of 1938*, and that was his last film. He was extremely ill and having delirium tremens when he began to make radio appearances, working only occasionally, often with Edgar Bergen.

Fields died on December 25, 1946 from a stomach hemorrhage caused by his excessive use of alcohol.

The movie industry grew steadily after the introduction of sound, but, while ticket sales were high between 1945 and 1948, running an average of 90 million a week, by 1960 sales had fallen to 45 million. Television had a lot to do with this, but inflation did also. The biggest factor was the governments breaking the studio's hold on exhibition. It was ruled that for the studios to own the movies and the theaters was a monopoly.

In 1947, the House UnAmerican Activities Committee (HUAC) held nine days of hearings into the effect on the Hollywood motion picture industry that communist propaganda had had. As a result, more than 300 directors, radio commentators, actors and writers were boycotted by the movie studios. A few, such as Chaplin, Orson Welles, and Paul Robeson left the U.S. to find work elsewhere. Some writers used false names or gave the credit to friends. Later, as few as ten percent succeeded in regaining their careers.

Movie studio executives testified to the committee that some WW2 movies, such as *Mission to Moscow, The North Star,* and *Song of Russia,* could be thought of as pro-Soviet propaganda, but were valuable to the Allied war effort. Fearful of the House investigations, some studios released a few anti-communist propaganda films such *as Guilty of Treason (about the ordeal and trial of Cardinal József Mindszenty), The Red Menace, The Red Danube, The Woman on Pier 13,* and the *Red Planet Mars. I Was a Communist for the FBI,* was nominated for an Academy Award as the best documentary in 1951. It was also serialized for radio. International Pictures was the only major studio that did not produce such a film.

Herman Bing was born on March 30th, 1889 in Frankfort-am-Main, Germany. He moved to Hollywood in 1926, working for F. W. Murnau as Assistant Director.

Bing's first movie role was in Murnau's silent classic, *Sunrise,* released in 1927. He played the uncredited part of the streetcar conductor. Between 1921 and 1946 he appeared in 125 movies, acted on stage in burlesque, and did voice work in films like Disney's Dumbo where he was the Ringmaster.

Bing's thick German accent was unwelcome after the beginning of World War Two, and his career wasn't helped by rumors that he was a German sympathizer. Depressed by his inability to find work, Bing shot himself on January 9th, 1947. He is buried in Hollywood Forever Cemetery, Los Angeles, California.

Benny 'Bugsy' Siegel was born in Williamsburg, Brooklyn in 1906. In his teens, Siegel became a member of Meyer Lansky's mob, engaging in gambling and car theft. It is said that Siegel was the mob's hit man, and Lansky would hire him out to other crime families.

He later became a bootlegger, working with Albert "Mad Hatter" Anastasia. Siegel was one of the four gunmen who killed New York mob boss Joe Masseria on Luciano's orders.

In 1937, his bosses sent Siegel to California to help Los Angeles crime family boss, Jack Dragna. Once in LA, Siegel recruited Mickey Cohen as his lieutenant.

Siegel went to Southern Nevada in 1934, following Lansky's orders to explore other operations. They began providing illegal services to the crews working on the Hoover Dam. Lansky then turned the desert operation over to Siegel. Siegel turned the operation over to Moe Sedway and returned to Hollywood. Throughout the spring of 1946, Siegel was involved in black-marketing building materials, and other items then in postwar shortage.

Siegel then decided to take over control of the Las Vegas Flamingo Hotel, and at this time the Flamingo became syndicate-run.

He renovated the building and demanded the finest that money could buy. By October 1946, renovation costs were more than four million dollars.

In November 1946, the syndicate issued an ultimatum to Siegel: either provide better accounting of their money or their funding would end. After the syndicate ceased providing funds, Siegel began a private fund raising effort, selling nonexistent stock.

Under pressure to have the hotel show some income, he moved the opening date up. The hotel was not finished, but he expected to make enough money in the casino to finish the project and repay his debts.

Locals jammed the opening, but just a handful of celebrities drove in from Los Angeles; among these were June Haver, Vivian Blaine, George Raft, Sonny Tufts, Brian Donlevy and Charles Coburn. At the time, the hotel was noisy with construction, and the air conditioning quit working on a regular basis. Gambling tables were in use but the luxurious rooms and suites that would have lured customers were not ready.

The Flamingo's gambling tables had lost $275,000 after two weeks, and the operation was shut down. Lansky intervened and got an extension for Bugsy. Siegel did all that he could to turn the Flamingo around, but by the time profits began to appear the mob bosses were tired of waiting.

On the night of June 20, 1947, Siegel was sitting in Virginia Hill's Beverly Hills home when an unknown assailant fired at him through a window with a rifle, hitting him twice in the head. No charges were filed, and the crime remains officially unsolved. He is buried in the Hollywood Forever Cemetery in Los Angeles.

Carole Landis was born Frances Lillian Mary Ridste on January 1, 1919 in Fairchild, Wisconsin. Her childhood was marred by parental abuse, both physical and mental; a sad state compounded by extreme poverty.

Perhaps driven by an intense need to escape her situation at home, she married the nineteen-year-old boy next door in 1934 when she was fifteen. Her parents had the marriage annulled one month later. The obstinate pair ran away just five months afterwards and married again. The two separated and Carole took a bus to San Francisco.

Carole found work as a Hula dancer at the Royal Hawaiian Club and later sang with the Carl Ravazzia Orchestra. Her next move was to Los Angeles. Her mother and Carole's estranged husband, hearing of Carole's success, soon joined her.

Her first appearance in films was as an extra in *Gold Diggers of 1937*. She continued to find work in films through 1937, 1938, and 1939, always in unaccredited minor roles until 1940 when Hal Roach gave her the female lead in *One Million B.C.*, co-starring with Victor Mature. That part made her a star.

Landis next signed a contract with 20th Century Fox and established a sexual relationship with Darryl Zanuck. This move garnered her roles in top level movies such as *Moon Over Miami*, in which she shared billing with Betty Gable. She starred in *I Wake Up Screaming* that same year (1941). Then she made the mistake of breaking up with Zanuck and her career went down the tube.

She, Martha Raye, and Kay Francis did a USO tour through England and North Africa in 1942. In 1944, she traveled with Jack Benny to the South Pacific. Carole volunteered more time entertaining troops than any other actress in World War Two. She caught amoebic dysentery and malaria while in the Pacific and nearly died of the debilitating diseases.

After the war ended, Carole starred on Broadway in *A Lady Says Yes*. Jacqueline Susann, who also had a part in the play is said to have had an affair with Carole at the time. Susann said later that the character Jennifer North in her book *Valley of the Dolls* was based on Landis.

By 1948, Carole's acting career took a nose-dive. She became romantically involved with Rex Harrison, but he refused to divorce his wife, Lilli Palmer and marry her.

Despondent, Carole committed suicide on July 5, 1948, by taking an overdose of Seconal. Harrison fell into disfavor in Hollywood as a result of the scandal surrounding Carole's suicide and did not work there again for many years.

Carole Landis is buried in the Forest Lawn Memorial Park in Glendale, California.

1465 Capri Drive, Pacific Palisades, where Carole Landis died

The Hollywood Chamber of Commerce removed 'land' from the Hollywood sign in 1949.

Leona Hutton was born in 1892. Between 1913 and 1916, she appeared in forty-three films. She was seen the first time on film in *The Crimson Stain*, released in 1913, a three-reel drama short. Her final role was in *The Man Who Would Not Die*, made in 1916.

During World War One, Hutton worked in Europe with the American Red Cross.

Hutton fractured her leg in 1949 and was confined at home for ten weeks. Evidently depressed, she killed herself by taking an overdose of codeine.

She is buried somewhere in St. Joseph, Missouri.

Chapter Five: The Fifties

The Hollywood movie industry of 1950 was threatened on several fronts. Television was rapidly becoming the most popular entertainment source in the U. S., and anti-trust laws that required separate ownership for movie production companies and theater chains had gone into effect on January 1, 1950. The viewing public was moving to the suburbs, causing downtown first-run movie theatres to face the possibility of falling bankrupt. Finally, both the morality and the patriotism of Hollywood movies as well as their creators were falling fast.

The release of the Charlie Chaplin movie, *Limelight*, in 1952, was damaged by a pressure campaign started by the American Legion. Chaplin was accused of being immoral, and of having Communist sympathies.

There was a political uproar that began in the early 1950s with Senator Joseph McCarthy's fabricated brandishing lists of Communists in the U. S. Government, and with the HUAC investigations.

Director Elia Kazan said in 1952 that the studios were trying so hard not to offend that "Actors are afraid to act, writers are afraid to write, and producers are afraid to produce." Critic

Solutions to these problems began to be put into practice starting in the 1950s by younger producers such as Stanley Kramer, Harold Hecht, and Burt Lancaster, men who became powerful figures in the movie industry.

Maria Montez (her real name was Maria Africa Gracia Vidal de Santo Silas), daughter of a Spanish diplomat was born on June 6, 1912 in Barahona, Dominican Republic.

Maria was working as a model in New York City when Universal offered her a contract. She moved to Hollywood and in 1941 began appearing in small film roles. Because of her exotic accent, Universal began to use her in low-budget productions playing opposite stars like Sabu, Turhan Bey, and Jon Hall.

Her adventurous and sometimes sexy films soon became popular, but interest in the "flying carpet" genre dried up after World War Two ended.

Her inabilities to act, dance, or sing contributed to the demise of her career, and her propensity to gain weight closed it.

She left Hollywood and moved to Europe with her husband, Jean-Pierre Aumont, where she appeared in a few French and Italian films. On September 7, 1951, at age 34, her maid found her drowned in her bath tub. The cause is unknown and was deemed accidental.

Maria is interred in the Cimetiere de Montparnasse in Paris, France.

Mayo Methot was born in Portland, Oregon on March 3, 1904. When she only four, she began performing on stage and was known as "The Portland Rosebud." Barely five feet high, she worked in the Baker Stock Company until she was eighteen, and then moved to New York City where she met George M. Cohan. Through his connections, she began to find work on Broadway, and spent the next eight years performing in plays such as *All the King's Men, The Song and Dance Man, The Medicine Man and Great Day* where she introduced the popular classic song, <u>More Than You Know</u>, in 1929.

In 1932, Methot moved to Hollywood where she won a contract with Warner Brothers Studios. Warner Brothers usually had her playing tough second leads in crime films such as *Jimmy the Gent* and *Marked Woman*. It was here that she met Humphrey Bogart in 1938.

Bogart became her third husband, and the pair drank a lot. Methot had a reputation for being a nasty drunk, and resulted in several serious fights between the two. She once stabbed Bogart with a kitchen knife, cut her wrists in a botched suicide attempt, and even threatened to kill Bogart with a pistol.

During World War II, Methot and Bogart often travelled around Europe, entertaining the troops. The army placed a ban on using married couples as entertainers for the remainder of the war because of their habit of borrowing guns while intoxicated and "shooting up the place" for fun.

Methot's drunken rampages eventually destroyed her acting career, and in 1945, Bogart divorced her and married Lauren Bacall.

After Bogart left her, Methot moved back to Portland, sank into depression and alcoholism, and died of liver failure in a cheap motel room on June 9, 1951.

Mayo is buried in the Portland Memorial Mausoleum in Portland, Oregon.

Marion Aye was born April 5, 1903 in Chicago, Illinois and was discovered by Max Sennett, who always had an eye out for girls who looked good in swimsuits. She was very active in films between the years of 1919 to 1926, including eighteen westerns opposite the actor, Bob Reeves.

After she retired and was isolated from the film industry, Marion grew despondent. From 1935 until 1951, she tried to commit suicide several times. Each attempt seemingly coincided with a failure to revive her show business career. Then, on July 10, 1951, after what her father said was a failure to win a part in a television play, Marion was found semi-conscious in a motel room. She had swallowed poison.

Marion Aye died on July 21, 1951 and is buried in the Forest Lawn Cemetery in Glendale, California.

Robert Walker was born Robert Hudson Walker in Salt Lake City, Utah, on October 13, 1918. His father edited a newspaper. His parents separated when Robert was very young. As a result, he became depressed and angry. He was expelled several times from school because of his rebellious behavior. While attending the American Academy of Dramatic Arts in New York City, Walker met Phylis Isley, who later became the film star Jennifer Jones. They were married in Tulsa, Oklahoma on January 2, 1939, and then moved to Hollywood to find work in the film industry.

Unsuccessful in this first attempt, they returned to New York where Walker found work in radio while Phylis stayed at home and gave birth to two sons.

Phylis returned to auditioning, and she was discovered in 1941 by producer David O. Selznick. Now named Jennifer Jones, she began an affair with Selznick, and she was given the role of Bernadette in the 1943 Twentieth Century Fox production, *Song of Bernadette*, released in 1943.

Walker and Jones returned to Hollywood where Selznick helped Walker land a contract with MGM. Walker immediately started work on the war drama, *Bataan*. He appeared in the male lead in Selznick's *Since You Went Away* in 1944, co-starring with his wife; by that time the Selznick and Jones' affair had become public. Jones and Walker separated in November, 1943 and were divorced in 1945.

Walker co-starred in *The Clock* opposite Judy Garland in 1945. He continued to work steadily in Hollywood, but he was greatly depressed over the divorce from Jones, soon became an alcoholic, and then suffered a nervous breakdown.

Walker married Barbara Ford, director John Ford's daughter, in 1948 and she divorced him five months later because of his erratic behavior and arrests for DUI. By this time, Robert was so despondent and self-destructive that he was committed to an asylum and was not released until late 1949.

Alfred Hitchcock gave Walker a starring role in *Strangers on a Train* in 1951, and this has been considered to be his finest film.

His final movie appearance was in the title role in *My Son John*, made in 1952.

On the night of August 28, 1951, Walker became so agitated and out-of-control that his psychiatrist was called. The doctor gave him an injection of Sodium Amytal. It is believed that the amount of alcohol in his blood caused him to have an acute allergic reaction to the drug and he died at age thirty-two.

Robert was buried in Lindquists Washington Heights Memorial Park in Ogden Utah.

Paul Hurst was born Oct 15, 1888 in Traver, California. He had supporting roles in several hundred movies during the 20s, 30s and 40s. Hurst is best remembered for his role as the Yankee deserter who is shot by Scarlett in *Gone with the Wind*, released in 1939, of his characterization of the drunken and sadistic vigilante Smith in *The Ox Bow Incident* released in 1943 and the rancher who refuses water to a Quaker family in the movie *Angel and the Badman*. It was after this role that Republic Pictures signed him as the comic sidekick in Monte Hale's Western series. He made his last appearance in John Ford's *The Sun Shines Bright*.

In 1952, Hurst was told that he had cancer, and he committed suicide a few months later. He is buried in Reedley Cemetery in Reedley, California.

Duke York was born Charles Everest Sinsabaugh on October 17, 1908 in Danby, New York. Known as the second-string Lon Chaney, Jr. he is most remembered for his performances in the Three Stooges short film playing monsters and the like.

He also played King Kala in the serial, *Flash Gordon* and had parts in *Alias*

Boston Blackie (1942), *Destination Tokyo* (1943), *The Paleface* (1948), and *My Favorite Spy* (1951).

His first marriage ended in divorce, and then he dated Catherine Moench who lived in Beverly Hills. She ended the relationship saying Duke was too jealous and misunderstood her past.

On January 24th, 1952, Duke called Catherine and tried to mend the relationship. When she was resistant, he kept threatening to commit suicide. While still on the phone with her, he shot himself in the head.

He is buried in the Hollywood Forever Cemetery in Hollywood, California.

Hiram King "Hank" Williams, Sr. was born on September 17, 1923 in Mount Olive, Butler County, Alabama. Hank is considered one of the most influential musicians of all-time. He recorded thirty-five singles that reached the Top 10 of the Billboard Country & Western Best Sellers chart. Eleven ranked number one. Hank is credited for contributing music to 139 movie soundtracks between 1952 and 2012. He appeared in two television productions, *The Kate Smith Evening Hour*, and *Perry Como's Kraft Music Hall*.

Hank's career in music started in Montgomery, Alabama in 1937, where he participated in a talent show at the Empire Theater. Singing his first original song, WPA Blues, (lyrics he had composed to the tune of Riley Puckett's Dissatisfied) he won first prize...fifteen dollars.

Hank sang and played his Silvertone guitar on the sidewalk in front of the WSFA radio studios. Because of his recent win at the Empire Theater and his street performances, he caught the attention of the radio station producers and they invited him to perform on air. So many listeners contacted the radio station asking for more of "the singing kid" that the producers hired him to host his own fifteen-minute show twice a week for a weekly salary of fifteen dollars.

He signed with MGM Records in 1948 and released the song Move It on Over which was a hit. Even though Hank could not read or write music he was accepted by the Grand Ole Opera, and later wrote Your Cheatin' Heart, Hey, Good Lookin, and I'm So Lonesome I Could Cry, all major hits. In August of 1952, the Grand Ole Opry released Hank, citing unreliability and frequent drunkenness.

Because Hank was born with spina bifida occulta, a disorder of the spinal column, he experienced lifelong pain. It is thought, to find some relief, he turned to alcohol and prescription drugs, which severely deteriorated his health. By 1952, Hank had developed heart problems.

He was supposed to perform at the Municipal Auditorium in Charleston, West Virginia on Wednesday December 31, 1952. Because of a winter storm in the Nashville area it wasn't possible to fly, so he hired a college student, Charles Carr, to drive him. When they stopped at the Andrew Johnson Hotel in Knoxville, Tennessee, Carr requested a doctor for Hank. It seems Hank was feeling the combination of the chloral hydrate and alcohol he had drunk on the way from Montgomery to Knoxville. Dr. P.H. Cardwell injected Williams with two shots of vitamin B12 that also contained a quarter-grain of morphine. When they left the hotel, the bellboys said Hank had to be carried to the car and was hiccoughing and coughing.

Early in the morning on January 1, 1953, they arrived in Bristol, Virginia, where Carr stopped at an all-night restaurant to eat. He said he asked and Hank said he wasn't hungry. Carr later stopped for gas at a station in Oak Hill, West Virginia, and it was there that he realized that Hank was dead.

The autopsy found that Hank had hemorrhages in the heart and neck. The doctor also said that Hank had recently been severely beaten and kicked in the groin.

Hank was twenty-nine at the time of his death. His funeral took place on January 4th in Montgomery, Alabama. It is estimated that besides the 2,750 mourners filling the auditorium, 15,000 to 25,000 people filed by his silver coffin. He was then buried at the Oakwood Annex in Montgomery.

Hank Williams had a major influence on twentieth-century popular music, mainly country music. The songs he wrote and recorded have been performed by many artists, and have been hits in such musical genres as pop, gospel, and blues.

He has been inducted into several music halls of fame and had several movies made about his life: *Your Cheatin' Heart* starring George Hamilton made in 1964, *Hank Williams: The Man and His Music*, a TV movie made in 1980, and *I'll Never Get Out of This World Alive*, a documentary made in 1993. It was announced in June 2014 that an upcoming biopic, *I Saw the Light*, starring Tom Hiddleston is being made. The movie is based on Colin Escott's 1994 book, Hank Williams: The Biography.

Clyde Bruckman was born on September 20, 1894. He worked with Buster Keaton, writing many of Keaton's most successful films, including *The Navigator*, *The Cameraman*, and *The General*. Bruckman also worked as Assistant Director on *The General*.

Bruckman stopped getting assignments as a director when he became known as an undependable alcoholic. After about 1935, he received nothing but writing jobs.

In spite of Bruckman's problem with alcohol, his years of experience resulted in a job writing for **Columbia Pictures** short-subject department. As Bruckman aged, he began to steal comedy routines from the old silent films on which he had worked. Because of this, Harold Lloyd brought a law suit against Columbia, won $40,000, and Columbia fired Bruckman.

After leaving Columbia, Bruckman went to work for Universal Pictures where he specialized in comedy routines for use in "B" films. Unfortunately he once again began to steal gags for older movies, and once again he was fired.

Depressed, Bruckman shot himself in the head on January 4, 1955. He was buried in Fairhaven Memorial Park in Santa Ana, California.

Ona Munson was born on June 16, 1903 in Portland, Oregon. She moved to New York City at age of twenty, where she found work in the theater. She was given a singing role in *No, No, Nanette* and was acclaimed for it. The song <u>You're the Cream in My Coffee</u> was first sung by her in 1927 when she appeared in *Hold Everything*.

Leaving Broadway for Hollywood, she starred in *Going Wild* (1930), an early talkie. In 1931, she sang in *Hot Heiress*, a comedy. She appeared in *Broadminded* in 1931 and *Five Star Final* in 1931.

The role of Belle, the Madam in 1939's *Gone With the Wind* was first offered to Mae West, but she turned it down, as did Tallulah Bankhead. Munson did not look like the character as described in the popular novel. The character, Belle, was a large, fair-skinned, well-endowed woman, whereas Munson was freckled and thin, but her acting ability was so great that she was given the part. The director, David Selznick said that it was her voice that won him over. She read the part with a sexy, deep, worldly and tired voice.

Unfortunately for Munson, she played Belle so well that she was typecast and had a limited number of parts offered to her during the remainder of her career.

It was two years before she had a good part again, and it was that of another madam, in *The Shanghai Gesture*. Her last film role was in *The Red House* with Edward G. Robinson, released in 1949.

Munson's health began to fail in the early 1950s, and in 1955, she took an overdose of barbiturates. She left a note that read:

<u>This is the only way I know to be free again. Please don't follow me.</u>

She was interred in Ferncliff Cemetery and Mausoleum in Hartsdale, New York.

Philip Loeb was born on March 28, 1891, in Philadelphia, Pennsylvania. He did some acting in high school, served in the army in World War One, and then became a stage manager.

In 1921, he joined the Theater Guild in New York and spent the next eight years acting in various plays produced by the organization. He worked the Actors Equity Association during the 30s.

In 1950, Loeb was publically accused of being a Communist, and General Foods, the sponsors of the radio show that he was starring in (*The Goldbergs*), demanded that the producers of the show drop Loeb because he had become controversial.

Loeb was the sole support of a mentally disturbed son, and was burdened with money worries. This and the black listing probably caused him to commit suicide in 1955 by overdosing on sleeping pills on the day before the FBI officially cleared his name.

He is buried on Mount Sinai Cemetery in Philadelphia, Pennsylvania.

The Conqueror

Two hundred and twenty Hollywood individuals were involved in the making of *The Conqueror,* a fictional account of a love story between Genghis Khan, the Mongol conqueror and the incredibly gorgeous princess Bortai made in 1955. Of those two hundred and twenty, ninety-one had been diagnosed as having cancer by 1980. Forty-six of these ninety-one persons died of cancer, including John Wayne, Susan Hayward, Agnes Moorehead, and Dick Powell. When told that he was dying of cancer, Pedro Armendariz shot himself four years after the film was completed.

Originally the director intended to use Marlon Brando to play Genghis, but John Wayne, quite a Hollywood power at the time, insisted that he was Genghis. Unfortunately, the script was so poorly written that Wayne's typical dead-pan delivery of the dialog was magnified to a point of being comedic. For example: At one point Genghis planned on attacking Princess Bortai's caravan, and his side-kick was opposed to the action.

Wayne's lines to the man, "There are moments fer wisdom, Juh-mooga, then I listen to you--and there are moments fer action — then I listen to my blood. I feel this Tartar wuh-man is fer me, and my blood says, 'TAKE HER!'" were on a par with Tony Curtis' Brooklyn accented portrayal of a Roman slave in *Spartacus*.

The movie was shot in the desert around St. George, Utah where the daily temperature averaged 120 degrees. Unfortunately for the crew and cast, the U. S. Army had tested eleven atomic bombs at Yucca Flats, Nevada just two years earlier in 1953, and clouds of radioactive fallout from these explosions had floated over the area where *The Conqueror* was shot. The crew and cast spent thirteen weeks in this deadly environment, and to make matters worse, Howard Hughes, the producer, had sixty tons of radioactive dirt shipped to Hollywood for use on a retake set. The people involved knew about the radiation, but having no knowledge of the danger, were not concerned. Within thirty years half the residents of St. George had come down with cancer.

Katherine (Kitty) McHugh was born October 3, 1902 in Harmony, Pennsylvania. Although she appeared in more than fifty films including *The Grapes of Wrath* with Henry Fonda, she is most known for her appearances with the **Three Stooges** in their short films, ***Hoi Polloi, Gents in a Jam,*** and *Listen Judge.*

Kitty McHugh committed **suicide** on September 3, 1954 in Hollywood, California. She was fifty-one.

Rebel Without a Cause, released in 1955, .irected by Nicholas Ray

Nicholas Ray married four times. He and Gloria Grahame were married in 1948, and divorced in 1952 after he found her in bed with his son, Tony, who was just thirteen years old at the time.

James Dean was killed at age twenty-four in an auto accident.

Natalie Wood, the female lead**,** was married to Robert Wagner twice. She had an affair with British producer Richard Gregson, and later married him. They divorced two years later after Wood learned that Gregson was involved with his secretary. It is said that she was sexually involved with Nicholas Ray at age sixteen when he was forty-three. On November 29th, 1981, Natalie accidentally drowned. The coroner reported that her blood contained alcohol and drugs at the time.

Sal Mineo was murdered at the age of thirty-six.

Rochelle Hudson: supporting role. Married and divorced four times.

Dennis Hopper: supporting role. Twenty years a drug addict. Married and divorced five times. Married Michelle Phillips, who divorced him two weeks later.

Edward Platt: supporting role. Committed suicide.

Nick Adams: supporting role. Committed suicide.

Dorothy Abbott: supporting role. Committed suicide.

In 1956, the now famous Capitol Records building was constructed on Vine Street.

Sheila Terry (Kay Clark) was born March 10th, 1910 in Warroad, Minnesota.

Terry was brought to Hollywood under contract to Warner Bros.-First National in 1932. She was given small parts in films such as *Week-End Marriage*, and never got out of 'B' films. She is best remembered for westerns playing opposite 'B' stars like Bill Boyd, and John Wayne.

In 1937, Terry married William Magee and up acting. After Magee's death, Terry tried returning to show business, but couldn't find employment, so in 1942, she gave up her dream of screen stardom and moved to New York City, where she worked as a Press Agent.

Terry was found dead in her apartment on January 19, 1957 in New York City. A suicide, she was 46 at the time of her death. She died penniless and was buried in Potter's field.

Dated January 1934, this photograph is marked, "Home of Sheila Terry in Hollywood." Its location is unknown

Doreen Woodbury was born in Sydney, Australia in 1927. She studied dance

and modelling before going to Hollywood and seeking work in the movies. In 1954, she landed a part in *The French Line*, and over the next three years had roles in three more films.

Doreen was said to have been under the patronage of Columbia Pictures head, Harry Cohn. Evidently he saw her as competition for Kim Novak. While in rehearsing for the film, *Pal Joey*, on February 6, 1957, Doreen unexpectedly committed suicide by taking an overdose of prescription drugs. It is believed that her act was caused by a failed love affair. She was cremated and her ashes are in an unknown location.

James Whale was born in Dudley, England on July 22, 1889. When World War One broke out in 1914, Whale was granted a commission as a second lieutenant in the British army. He took part in the Flanders Campaign, and in August 1917, he was captured by the Germans and became a prisoner of war, spending the next two years in a POW camp.

When Whale returned to London in 1919, he began a career as a set designer and actor. Three years later he began a relationship with Doris Zinkeisen that lasted two years, in spite of the fact that Whale had openly displayed he was a homosexual.

After moving to Hollywood in 1929, Whale signed a contract with Paramount Pictures making him dialogue director on a production titled *The Love Doctor*. It only took two weeks to finish the movie. At that point, Whale's contract was not renewed.

Howard Hughes agreed to give Whale the same job he had with Paramount.

His first assignment was to work with the crew busily converting *Hell's Angels* into a talking film. At the end of that project, he was given a five-year contract with Universal Studios, and his next film was *Waterloo Bridge*.

Carl Laemmle, Junior, head of Universal, was so pleased with Whale's work that he offered him any pre-production film in the studio's library. His choice was Mary Shelly's *Frankenstein*. Whale made agreements with Colin Clive and Mae

Clarke to play the leads, and he then took a chance and gave the role of the monster to Boris Karloff, a complete unknown. *Frankenstein* was a great success and has since become a film classic.

Whale's next project was *Bride of Frankenstein*. The film was even a greater success than *Frankenstein* and earned more than two million dollars.

He made a training film for the Army during World War Two.

Whale directed the stage production of *Pagan in the Parlor* in 1951, and that proved to be his last job. The play ran for two weeks in Pasadena and although plans were made to take it to New York that never happened. Whale took a vacation and went to Paris. He hooked up with a bartender there and hired the man to be his driver. The bartender, Pierre Fogel, was thirty-seven years younger than Whale.

Whale went back to California in 1952 with Fogel in tow. Fogel lived with Whale for a few months and then headed back to Paris, but two years later, Fogel returned to Hollywood and became manager of a gas station that Whale owned. The two became full-time lovers, until the spring of 1956. Whale had a stroke, and two months later he had a massive one. While he was in the hospital, Whale became infatuated with one of his male nurses. He hired the man when he left the hospital, and made him his personal live-in nurse. Fogel, of course, was jealous, and without Whale's knowledge, fired the male nurse and replaced him with a female. Whale never regained his full mental facilities following the series of strokes, and he committed suicide on May 29, 1957, by throwing himself into his swimming pool.

The note he left read:

> The future is just old age and illness and pain...I must have peace and this is the only way.

He was buried at Forest Lawn Memorial Park in Glendale, California.

Helen Twelvetrees, born Helen Marie Jurgens on December 25, 1908 in Brooklyn, New York, was a graduate of the American Academy of Dramatic Arts.

Hoping to take advantage of the shortage of performers created when talking film caused many silent stars to be released because their voices were not satisfactory, she moved to Hollywood, where Fox Film gave her a part in their 1929 production of *The Ghost Talks.*

Her first husband had problems with depression and was an alcoholic. Not long after they married, he attempted suicide by leaping from the sixth floor of an office building. He landed on an awning on the second floor and was only slightly injured. Twelvetrees was arrested for attempting to murder him and was not released until her husband was able to explain to the police what had actually happened.

She made three films for Fox in 1929, and then they released her. Undaunted, she signed with Pathé several weeks later, where she co-starred with Spencer Tracy in *Now I'll Tell,* and with Maurice Chevalier in *Bedtime Story,* both made in 1933. In the period of 1929 to 1940, she appeared in thirty-three movies and then returned to New York to work on Broadway.

Her first performance on stage was in *Boudoir* in 1941 which closed after eleven performances causing her to go home to Middletown, Pennsylvania. She acted occasionally in local plays and made one more professional appearance in *A Streetcar Named Desire* when it opened in Sea Cliff, New Jersey.

Subject to bouts of severe depression and an alcoholic, Helen committed suicide on February 13, 1958, by taking a drug overdose. Her ashes were interred in Middletown Cemetery, Middletown, Pennsylvania.

Johnny Stompanato completed his freshman year at Woodstock High School in 1940, and his father then sent him to Kemper Military School for boys in Boonville, Missouri.

In 1947, Stompanato moved to Los Angeles and went to work for mobster Mickey Cohen as a bodyguard. Cohen gave him Lana Turner's phone number, and they began an affair.

Lana Turner broke up with Stompanato after dating him for a year. Not ready to call it quits, he followed her to England, where she was making a film with Sean Connery. It is said that he suspected Lana was having an affair with Connery, and came on the set with a gun. Undaunted, Connery punched him in the face. Whether that is true or not, Stompanato was known to show up in hotels where Lana was staying even after they broke up. On April 4, 1958, while they argued in her house, Stompanato threatened to ruin her face, and therefore end her career.

Lana's fourteen-year-old daughter was listening to the fight from her room. Afraid for her mother, she took a knife from the kitchen and stabbed Stompanato. The knife cut a kidney and punctured an aorta. Stompanato bled out in minutes.

It was decided that the homicide was justifiable based on the fact that Lana's daughter thought she was protecting her mother. No charges were filed.

He is buried in the Oakland Cemetery in Woodstock, Illinois.

730 N. Bedford Drive, Beverly Hills: Lana Turner's home, where Johnny Stompanato was killed.

Pedro Armendariz was born on May 9, 1912 in Mexico City, Mexico. He was born during the Madero Mexican Revolution, and was the son of Pedro Armendáriz García-Conde, a Mexican citizen, and Adele Hastings, an American citizen.

Pedro's family lived in Churubusco, a Mexico City suburb, before moving to Laredo, Texas. After his parents died in 1921, Pedro and his brother became wards of their uncle.

Pedro went on to study at the University of California, where he was a part of the theatre group and learned to love acting. He later graduated with an engineering degree from the California Polytechnic Institute in San Luis Obispo, California.

After graduation, he returned to Mexico City where he went to work for a railroad company. He later became a tourist guide, but it was when movie director Miguel Zacarías heard Pedro reciting Hamlet's monologue to some tourists that his life changed.

Becoming a part in what is known as the Mexican Cinema Golden Era, Pedro's first film appearance was in *Rosario*, a Cooperativa Continental production, released in 1935. He, Dolores del Río and Emilio Fernández, made many of the greatest films of the time, *María Candelaria (Xochimilco),* released in 1944, and *Bugambilia*, released in 1945, for example.

After becoming a friend of John Ford, Pedro worked with him in *The Fugitive*, released in 1947, *Fort Apache* (1948), and *Three Godfathers* (1948).

Pedro and John Wayne in *Fort Apache*

Then in 1954, Pedro landed a part in *The Conqueror*. The film was shot in an area of Utah that was close to the U.S. Army's atomic bomb testing grounds. Exposed to radioactive dust for the time it took to film the movie, ninety-one people who were a part of the large cast and crew were diagnosed with cancer, including the stars, John Wayne (lung) and Susan Hayward (brain).

In 1958, while filming *From Russia with Love,* Pedro, suffering from horrendous pain and ill, was diagnosed with terminal cancer. Although he finished the film and secured his family's financial future, he had to be replaced in the film's final scenes by a double. Unable to endure the pain, Pedro smuggled a gun into the hospital and shot himself in the chest.

His final film *From Russia with Love* was released in 1963. During his career, Pedro appeared in 127 television and film productions between 1935 and 1963.

After Pedro was cremated at Chapel of the Pines Crematory, in Los Angeles, his ashes were sent to Mexico City for burial in Panteon Jardin, Mexico City, Mexico.

The Hollywood Walk of Fame was created in 1958.

Fred Kennedy, a long term bit player who did stunts in order to earn a living, was killed when his horse tripped and fell during the filming of *The Horse Soldiers* in 1959.

Grant Withers, born on January 17, 1905, in Publeo, Colorado. He grew to be 6 feet 8 inches tall; taller than most male Hollywood celebrities. He had a three year career in the films that began in the late 1920s. Early on, he landed lead roles, but over the years his popularity waned and he found himself playing supporting roles in "B" films.

A 1937, a twelve episode serial in which he played Jungle Jim worked out well for him as did a series about Mr. Wong in which he played a police captain.

All in all, Withers made more than sixty movies for Republic Films in the years 1937 through 1957. In his total career, he appeared in more than 200 movies.

Clyde Cook and Withers in *the Headlines* 1929

He starred in *Second Floor Mystery* in 1927, and his co-star was Loretta Young. At age twenty-five, Grant was divorced, had a child, and was becoming an alcoholic. Loretta celebrated her seventeenth birthday on January 12, 1930, and then ran off to Yuma, Arizona with Withers to get married.

Known as a sweet, pure-hearted virginal girl-next-door type, the act was damaging to Loretta's reputation, and it took several years for her public to forget it.

The marriage was not what Loretta expected. She soon discovered that Withers would rather spend his time with "the boys" getting drunk and playing cards than with her.

Young and Withers 1930

In 1931, the Whithers/Young marriage was ended by court decreed annulment.

It is amusing that in the same year, the second film starring the pair was released. It was titled, *Too Young to be Married*.

Loretta Young's reputation for purity nearly took a disastrous plunge in 1935 when she gave birth to a baby girl fathered by Clark Gable. The studios, however, were able to cover the incident up.

Due to the aid of John Wayne and director John Ford, both good friends with Withers, he had roles in nine films between 1948 and 1950. After that, possibly because of his addiction to alcohol, the parts dwindled down to nothing.

In 1959, at the age of fifty-four, Withers committed suicide by overdosing on barbiturates. His suicide note read:

<u>Please forgive me, my Family. I was so unhappy. It's better this way</u>.

He was interred in the Forest Lawn Memorial Park in Glendale, California.

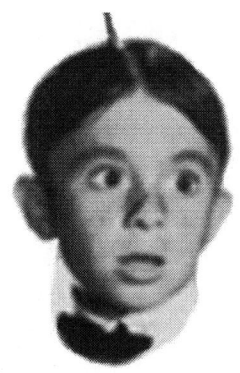

Carl Switzer was born in Paris, Illinois in 1927. When he was seven his family drove to California to visit relatives, and while there, they toured the Hal Roach Studios, where Carl and his older brother, Harold, decided to put on a show in the cafe. Producer Hal Roach was watching, and he gave the brothers parts in the *Our Gang* series.

The Our Gang cast

The Switzer brothers' first appearance was in *Beginner's Luck* (1936). By the end of the year, Carl, as Alfalfa, had become one of the main characters in the *Our Gang* films while Harold's character, Deadpan, failed to catch on.

After Roach sold *Our Gang* to Metro-Goldwyn Mayer in 1938, Switzer became unruly. Once, during filming of *The Big Premiere*, Switzer urinated on the set's lights. The heat filled the set with such a stench that filming had to be stopped for the rest of the day

Switzer's final role was in *The Defiant Ones'* made in 1958. Unable to find acting roles, he quit acting and moved to Kansas, where he worked on a farm. He also worked part-time as a hunting guide and borrowed a dog from Moses Stiltz. The dog was lost, and Switzer offered a fifty dollar reward. When the dog was found, Switzer paid the reward. Several days later Carl demanded that Stiltz give back his fifty dollars. When Stiltz refused, the two began to fight. Stiltz ran into his house and returned with a pistol. Carl allegedly pulled a knife, and Stiltz shot him in the groin. Carl died in the ambulance on January 21, 1959. Stiltz was not charged.

Carl is buried in the Hollywood Forever Cemetery in Hollywood, California.

George Reeves, born on January 5, 1914 in Woolstock, Iowa, acted in high school and college (Pasadena Junior College). In 1939, age twenty-five, Reeves landed a minor role in *Gone With the Wind*.

He was then given a contract with Warner Brothers and worked in many two-reel short films, such as, *Torrid Zone*, and *The Fighting 69th*. He went under contract with Twentieth Century-Fox and worked in several "B" level films such as the Charlie Chan movie *Dead Men Tell*. His next role was as Claudette Colbert's love interest in *So Proudly We Hail!*, released in 1942.

In 1943, the draft called Reeves into the army.

Reeves found that acting jobs were few and far between in Hollywood after World War Two ended, but he did manage to get a part in a Sam Katzman production, *The Adventures of Sir Galahad*.

In 1951, Reeves went to work in television, playing the part of Superman in the new series. Reeves's career as Superman soon made him a national celebrity, but after having played the part for two years, he grew tired of the role and the salary.

In 1953, Reeves was given a minor role in *From Here To Eternity*. The scenes were later cut from many copies of the film. He also landed parts in *Forever Female* and *The Blue Gardenia*. After that role, it seemed he had become so closely associated with the Superman part that he could no longer get roles in films, until Bill Walsh, a producer at Disney Studios and one of Reeves buddies, arranged for Reeves to have a part in *Westward Ho, the Wagons!* in 1956. To get the role, Reeves had to wear a beard and mustache. That was the last time he appeared in a movie.

In spite of his misgivings about being Superman, by mid-1959, he had signed another contract with the promise that the upcoming season would be of the same high quality as the early ones.

Then, on June 16, 1959, Reeves killed himself with a pistol shot in the head. He was buried at Mountain View Cemetery in Altadena, California.

1579 Benedict Canyon Drive, Beverly Hills, California,
where George Reeves died.

Lynn Baggett was born in Wichita Falls, Texas on May 10, 1923, the daughter of a wealthy Texas oil man. A Warner Brothers talent scout saw her on the street in Dallas, Texas in 1941 and gave her three year contract with the studio.

Thrilled, Lynn moved to Hollywood that same year and landed a minor role in the film *Manpower*. In 1943, she was given three unaccredited minor film roles, but then Warner Brothers failed to renew her contract.

Lynn married producer Sam Spiegel, best known for *Lawrence of Arabia* and *Bridge on the River Kwai*, in Las Vegas on April 10th, 1948. Spiegel was twenty years her senior, but Lynn's good friend, Evelyn Keyes and her husband John Huston had played matchmakers and put the unlikely couple together.

In 1950, Lynn was given the part of the wife of Mr. Phillips in *DOA*, and although she only appeared for a few minutes in the film, it turned out to be the largest role she would ever play. Between 1941 and 1951, she appeared in twenty-five films. Her last role was in *The Mob,* a Columbia "B" crime drama starring Broderick Crawford.

In 1951, her husband went to England to work on the film, *The African Queen.* During his absence, Lynn became romantically involved with the writer, Irwin Shaw, who was also married. She then had an affair with John Huston, who turned out to be abusive.

Following a messy divorce filing in 1952, colored with accusations of multiple adulteries, Lynn started teaching at an Arthur Murray dance studio.

In July of 1954, Lynn attended a party given by the British actor Arthur Treacher. While driving herself home, Lynn hit a station wagon packed with young boys on their way home from summer camp. Four of the boys were injured, and Joel Watnick, a nine-year-old, was killed. Lynne drove away from the scene without reporting to the police. Several days later, investigators found the auto she was driving, which was owned by actor George Tobias. He told the police he had loaned the car to Lynn the day of the crash.

Witnesses reported that after the crash, the woman driver got out of the car, looked at the dead boy, and then left. Lynn was acquitted of a manslaughter charge in October, 1954, and sentenced to fifty-days in jail for hit-and-run.

Lynn Baggett and her attorney

After their divorce is final in 1955, Lynn received a settlement. Little is heard from her until on June 7th, 1959, when she overdosed on sleeping pills. Before losing consciousness, she telephoned for help. The police broke down the door to her bedroom and took her to the hospital.

After recovering and returning home, on the 24th of August that same year, a friend found her suffering from malnutrition. Somehow, Lynn had fallen down, and, a folding bed fell on top of her. She was trapped for six days. Once again she is taken to a hospital where she is diagnosed as being chronically depressed and addicted to prescription drugs which has caused her to be partially paralyzed below the knees.

Seven months later, her visiting nurse found her dead in her Hollywood apartment. She had been released from a sanitarium a month and a half before. Lynn was thirty-five.

She is buried at Forest Lawn Memorial Park - Glendale, Graceland section, Lot 992.

Chapter Six: the Sixties

By 1960, Hollywood was a television town. It was reported by Time Magazine that NBC's TV show, *Matinee Theater*, employed 2,400 actors each year, to play speaking characters, whereas, Paramount Studios and Warner Brothers, hired only half that many. The show also required about 250 original scripts each year, which was as many as all of the major movie studios combined. Lucy Ball's Desilu Productions shot more TV footage than five major movie studios.

At the end of the '50s, TV had paid nearly ¼ billion dollars for close to 4000 Hollywood movies.

The first star was placed on the Hollywood Walk of Fame in 1960. It honors Joanne Woodward.

Dorothy Dandridge's parents separated shortly before her birth on November 9, 1922 in Cleveland, Ohio. Ruby Dandridge, her mother then put her two daughters, Vivian and Dorothy, to work in an act that toured for five years.

When the Great Depression ended the duo's touring opportunities, Ruby named the girls "The Dandridge Sisters" and managed to get them work in the Cotton Club and the Apollo Theater in Harlem, New York City.

In 1936, Ruby took the girls to Hollywood where Dorothy was given a small role in one of the *Our Gang* comedies. The following year she was one of the many singers in the Marx Brothers' film *A Day at the Races*. Between 1935 and 1962, Dorothy appeared in thirty-one films. She played the lead in *Carmen Jones* released in 1954. Her last role was in *Cain's Hundred*, released 1962. After that, she worked the nightclub circuit.

She learned in 1962 that her financial manager had stolen her savings and left her with $139,000 in unpaid taxes. After selling her Hollywood home, and placing her daughter, who had suffered with a brain disorder since birth, in a state mental institution, Dandridge moved into a small apartment where she had a nervous breakdown. Alcoholism and drugs became part of her life, and then, in 1965 she entered rehab and cleaned herself up.

Dandridge then landed a job appearing at Manhattan's Basin Street East and was offered film roles in Mexico. The day before she was to board a plane and start her new career, she fell and fractured her ankle. In spite of this and in severe pain she went to Mexico, made the movies, and returned to Los Angeles where she arranged to have her ankle set and placed in a cast on September 9, 1965. On that morning, her manager knocked on her door and got no reply. He broke into the apartment and found Dandridge dead. The coroner ruled her death to have been caused by an accidental overdose of Imipramine. However, a note that was later discovered indicated she had committed suicide.

Eric Fleming (Edward Heddy, Jr.) was born on July 4, 1925 in Santa Paula, California. His father was abusive, and as a result, Eric ran away from home at a young age and lived on the road. When World War Two broke out he joined the U. S. Navy.

After his discharge, Fleming used the G. I. Bill to pay for acting lessons. He later appeared in a number of theatrical productions in Chicago and New York City.

Fleming moved to Hollywood and soon found work in several low-budget films. Among these were *Fright, Curse of the Undead* and *Queen of Outer Space*.

Fleming stood 6 feet 3 ½ inches in height, and this helped him get the starring role as trail boss Gil Favor in the television series *Rawhide* which ran for 202 episodes between 1959 and 1965. He appeared in a total of seventeen television and film productions between 1951 and 1967.

When the Rawhide series ended, he worked in *The Glass Bottom Boat*, released in 1966. His next film, *High Jungle* was made in Peru. While shooting a scene on the Huallaga River, the dugout he was riding in overturned, and Fleming was drowned on September 28, 1966.

He was interred at the University of Peru in Lima, Peru.

Robert (Bobby) Fuller was born in Baytown, Texas in 1942. His family moved to Salt Lake City, Utah while he was a baby where they remained until 1956, when they moved to El Paso, Texas. During the early 1960s, he played in clubs and bars in El Paso, and recorded on independent records.

Fuller and his band, The Bobby Fuller Four relocated to Los Angeles in 1964. At a time when the Beatles and folk rock were dominant in rock, Fuller's group stuck to Buddy Holly's style of classic rock and roll with Tex-Mex flourishes.

Fuller died mysteriously at age twenty-two from gasoline asphyxiation while parked beside a small park near his former apartment at 1776 N Sycamore Ave, around the corner from Grauman's Chinese Theatre.

John Jordan, worked as second unit director. He walked into a helicopter rotor blade during the shooting of *You Only Live Twice* and lost one leg. Later, on April 16, 1969, while working on *Catch 22,* he fell from an observation plane, 2,000 feet to his death, into the Gulf of Mexico.

 Mike Reilly, stunt man, drowned during the filming of *The War Lover,* in 1962.

Camera man **Robert King** drowned during the filming of *Lieutenant Robinson Crusoe, USN* in 1965.

Margaret Sullavan was born in Norfolk, Virginia on May 16, 1909. After graduating Harvard University, in the summer 1929, she appeared opposite Henry Fonda in *The Devil in the Cheese,* her first appearance on Broadway stage.

The following year she was given the lead role in *Strictly Dishonorable*. During the production, she was spotted by a scout working for Lee Shurbert. Shurbert gave her the lead in *A Modern Romance* which opened on Broadway on May 20, 1931. In 1932, she was unfortunate enough to star in four Broadway flops.

In 1933, John Stahl, a Hollywood director gave Sullavan a contract after seeing her perform in *Dinner at Eight*. In May of that year, she moved to Hollywood to begin work on *Only Yesterday*. The next year she played the lead in *Little Man, What Now?* Between 1933 and 1936, Sullavan married and divorced William Wyler and Henry Fonda.

Today, Sullavan is probably best known for working opposite James Stewart in *The Little Shop Around the Corner* released in 1940.

Sullavan stopped working in movies in 1943, moved to New York. For the next eight years she spent most of her time with her family, caring for her three children. She returned to Hollywood in 1950 for *No Sad Songs for Me*. That was her last film appearance.

For two years, 1955 and 1956, Sullavan appeared in 251 performances of *Janus* on Broadway. By this time, she had difficulty hearing and had become severely depressed. She agreed to do *Sweet Love*, which was due to open on February 4. 1960, but on January 1, 1960, Sullavan committed suicide.

Sullavan's daughter Bridget committed suicide by taking an overdose of barbiturates just eight months after Sullavan died. Her son, Bill, also committed suicide in 2008.

She was buried in Saint Mary's Whitechapel Episcopal Churchyard in Lancaster, Virginia.

Phyllis Haver was born on January 6, 1899 in Douglass, Kansas. Her family moved to Los Angeles, California, in 1903. After graduating Los Angeles Polytechnic High, she worked as a piano player accompanying silent films in local theaters.

After Haver had attended an audition call issued by producer Mack Sennett, she was hired to be a Sennett Bathing Beauty. Sennett later gave her roles in some of his comedy two-reelers. In 1927, Haver was given the part of Roxie Hart, a leading character in the film *Chicago*, an adaptation of a popular Broadway play. This was the first time the play was made into a film. Many versions were to follow over the next seventy-five years.

She had a role in *The Battle of the Sexes*, directed by D. W. Griffith and released in 1927, and the next year, she appeared in *The Unholy Three*, released in 1930; Lon Chaney's last film.

Haver committed suicide on November 19, 1960 by taking a barbiturate overdose. She is buried in Grassy Hill Cemetery in Falls Village, Connecticut.

Gail Russell was born Elizabeth L. Russell in Chicago on September 21, 1924. She moved to Los Angeles at the age of seventeen. A Paramount Pictures scout, impressed with her extraordinary beauty, gave her a contract in 1942. Gail had no acting experience, and she was hampered by extreme shyness.

Her first film role was in *Henry Aldrich Gets Glamour*, followed by *The Uninvited* in 1944 where her habit of drinking on the set to bolster her courage began. Then in 1947, she made *The Angel and the Badman* with John Wayne.

Altogether she appeared in nineteen films between 1943 and 1951, but by 1951, her reputation as an undependable alcoholic caused Paramount to refuse to renew her contract.

Her four year marriage to Guy Madison ended in 1954, and she quit acting for the next five years. In 1956, her friend, John Wayne gave her a role in *Six Men From Now*. The following year, she appeared in *The Tattered Dress*, co-starring with Randolph Scott.

Gail was arrested for DUI in 1957, after driving her automobile through the front wall of Jan's Coffee Shop.

She appeared in three more films and made two television appearances over the next five years. On August 26, 1961, her body was discovered in her Brentwood apartment. At the age of thirty-six, she died of cirrhosis of the liver brought on by her extreme alcohol consumption. The coroner's report noted that she was also malnourished. Gail is buried in Valhalla Memorial Park in North

Hollywood.

Clara Blandick was born on June 4, 1880 aboard the USS Willard Mudgett. The ship, in Hong Kong at the time, was captained by her father.

After growing up in Boston, she made acting her career. Her first appearance on stage was in *Richard Lovelace*. In 1900, she moved New York City where she continued to act, appearing on Broadway in 1912 in *Widow by Proxy*. She moved to Hollywood in 1913, and a year later landed her first film role.

Blandick worked as a volunteer for the American Expeditionary Force in France during World War One. Afterward she returned to her career in both stage and film.

She went back to Hollywood in 1929, and soon established a reputation as a dependable and talented supporting actress. In 1930, she played Aunt Polly in *Tom Sawyer*, and the next year she was the same character in *Huckleberry Finn*. Blandick is probably best known for her portrayal of Auntie Em in the 1939 version of *The Wizard of Oz*.

Auntie Em

In 1949, at the age of sixty-nine, she gave up acting. She suffered from several severe health problems and on April 15, 1962, she took an overdose of sleeping pills. She left a note that said:

> I am now about to make the great adventure. I cannot endure this agonizing pain any longer. It is all over my body. Neither can I face the impending blindness. I pray the Lord my soul to take. Amen

She is buried in the Great Mausoleum at Forest Lawn Memorial Park in Glendale, California.

Irene Lentz was born December 8, 1900 in Baker, Montana. She moved to Hollywood in 1920 and landed an unaccredited part in *Molly O'* in 1921. She acted in a total of eight shorts and films between 1921 and 1925, and then studied design at the Wolf school in Los Angeles. She opened her own dress salon in 1928 and received such attention with her designs that the Bullocks Wilshire luxury department store invited her to design for their Ladies Custom Salon. This led to contracts with the movie studios.

In 1937, Irene designed the gowns used by Ginger Rogers in *Shall We Dance*. Between 1937 and 1963, she designed the costumes for 113 movies. She is perhaps best remembered for the wardrobe she designed for Lana Turner in *The Postman Always Rings Twice*, released in 1946.

In 1950, Irene left MGM and opened her own fashion house. Ten years later Doris Day requested that Lentz design the costumes used in Universal Studios production *Midnight Lace,* and Irene received her second Academy Award nomination for her work. Her last film was *A Gathering of Eagles*, released in 1962.

On Nov. 15, 1962, Irene Lentz checked into the Knickerbocker Hotel in Hollywood. After drinking two pints of vodka, she leapt out an eleventh-floor window. A suicide note read:

> "I'm sorry. This is the best way. Get someone very good to design and be happy. I love you all, Irene."

She was buried next to her first husband in the Forest Lawn Memorial Park Cemetery in Glendale, California.

Doris Day wrote in her autobiography that Irene had confided to her that she had loved Gary Cooper for many years. Copper was married and known as a philanderer. He died the year before Lentz killed herself.

Karyn Kupcinet was born Roberta Lynn Kupcinet in Chicago, Illinois (1941).

Her father was Irv Kupcinet, a sportswriter for the Chicago Daily Times. Karyn made her acting debut at age thirteen in *Anniversary Waltz*, and she studied at the Actor's Studio in New York City.

With help from her father and his column in the Chicago Sun-Times, Karyn received an offer from Jerry Lewis to appear in *The Ladies Man* (1961). She was later given a number of roles on television.

In December 1962, she met Andrew Prine, and they began to date. The relationship did not last long because Kupcinet was arrested for shoplifting, and was abusing diet pills and other prescription drugs.

After Kupcinet had an abortion in July, 1963, Prine began dating other women. Karyn then began spying on Prine and his new girlfriend. She also sent threatening and profane messages to Prine.

On the last day of her life, Karyn had dinner with Mark Goddard and his wife at their home on Coldwater Canyon Drive in Beverly Hills. The couple said Kupcinet only toyed with her food during the meal, her voice was funny and she moved her head at odd angles. The Goddards also noticed that Karyn's pupils were constricted. When Goddard confronted Kupcinet about these things, she began to cry.

Karyn apparently went straight home after leaving the Goddards. Freelance writer Edward Stephen Rubin and actor Robert Hathaway came to visit her at around 9:30 pm.

They told detectives the three watched television and drank coffee until Karyn fell asleep on the couch. The men made sure the door was locked behind them before leaving. Hathaway said he and Rubin returned to his place where they were joined by Andrew Prine and watched television until early in the morning.

The Goddards stopped by Karyn's apartment on November 30, because Mark Goddard stated that he had a "funny feeling" that something was wrong. The couple found Karyn's nude body lying on the couch and assumed that she had died from a drug overdose.

While searching Kupcinet's apartment, police found prescriptions for Desoxyn, Miltown, and Amvicel. They also found a note written by Karyn that detailed her issues in life; parents, self-image, and boyfriend problems. The Coroner's report stated that a broken hyoid bone in her throat indicated Karyn had been strangled, and her death was ruled a homicide. The case remains unsolved.

Alan Ladd was born in Hot Springs, Arkansas on September 3, 1913. His father died in 1917, and his mother moved to Hollywood.

After graduating high school, he attended the Universal Pictures acting school for a short time. He was turned out because at the height of 5'6", he was considered too short. He then began a career in radio.

Later he was able to land minor roles in a number of films, including *Citizen Kane*. In 1941, he appeared in a supporting role under his own name in *The Black Cat*. This started a series of films in which he played better and better parts. In 1942, he made *Joan of Paris*, and a few months later, *This Gun for Hire*, co-starring with Veronica Lake.

In 1946, he appeared the classic *Two Years before the Mast*, followed by *The Blue Dahlia*.

He played Gatsby in the 1949 version of *The Great Gatsby*, and in 1953 he made the film that he most known for: *Shane*.

Ladd had three children and apparently had a happy family life, but he was also a part the Hollywood gay society; a group of secretly gay celebrity men that met weekly in George Cukor's home. They had a practice of picking up young men in bars and gyms and bringing them to these get-togethers.

Ladd was found shot in the chest in November of 1962, after a failed suicide attempt.

He performed in the *Carpetbaggers* a few months later, but did not see the film's release as he was discovered in his apartment in Palm Springs on January 29, 1964, dead of an overdose of alcohol and prescription drugs. He is buried in the Forest Lawn Memorial Park Cemetery in Glendale, California.

Sam Cooke was born in Clarksdale, Mississippi in 1931; when he was two years old his family moved to Chicago. There, Cooke sang with his brothers and sisters in a group called The Singing Children. In 1950, Cooke became the lead singer of the landmark gospel group, The Soul Stirrers. The group recorded the hits <u>Peace in the Valley, How Far Am I from Canaan, Jesus Paid the Debt,</u> and <u>One More River</u>, among other gospel songs.

Cooke started his own record label, SAR Records in 1961, created a publishing management firm, and then signed with RCA Victor. One of his first RCA singles was the hit <u>Chain Gang</u>. It reached number two on the Billboard pop chart and was followed by more hits, including <u>Sad Mood, Bring it on Home to Me, Another Saturday Night</u> and <u>Twistin' the Night Away</u>.

Cooke was murdered in 1964, at a motel in Los Angeles. The manager of the motel told police that she killed Cooke in self-defense after he attacked her. The coroner ruled the killing a justifiable homicide.

Sammee Tong was born April 21, 1901 in San Francisco. He worked in forty-six film and television roles between 1934 and 1965.

As a young man, Tong yearned to act. He went to New York City where he made many attempts to find work on the stage during the early years of the Great

Depression but was denied because of his ethnicity. He finally found work singing and performing comedy in Chinese nightclubs in both New York and San Francisco. His first film appearance was in *The Captain Hates The Sea* in 1934. That same year he was given an unaccredited part in *Charlie Chan in Shanghai*. He appeared in the television show, *Bachelor Father* between 1957 and 1962. His last film role was in *Fluffy* made in 1965.

Sammee was heavily addicted to gambling, and as a result had many debts. He was left without income when the television series *Mickey* was cancelled in 1964, and shortly thereafter committed suicide by overdosing on prescription drugs. He is also buried in the Forest Lawn Memorial Park Cemetery in Glendale, California.

Josefina Yolanda Pellicer López de Llergo, born on April 3, 1934 in Mexico, was known in the film industry as **Pina Pellicer**.

Pellicer's first appearance in American films was in *One-Eyed Jacks* where she played opposite Marlon Brando, who directed as well as acted in the production. Stanley Kubrick was originally the director, but he quit, delaying the film's release for two years. Pellicer worked in several Mexican films and appeared in the U.S. television productions, *The Fugitive*, in 1963, and *The Alfred Hitchcock Hour* in 1964.

Pellicer suffered from severe depression, and it is presumed that this fact prompted her to commit suicide on December 4, 1964. She is buried in Mexico City in the Panteon Jardin.

Marie MacDonald was born Cora Marie Frye in Burgin, Kentucky on July 6, 1923. Her mother was a member of the Ziegfeld Follies, and her grandmother was an opera singer. Marie's parents divorced when she was six, and after her mother remarried, the family moved to Yonkers, New York.

Marie won the "Miss New York" contest when she was fifteen, and two years later she appeared in *Earl Carroll's Vanities* on Broadway which led to more Broadway stage work.

After moving to Hollywood, she worked in a chorus line while attempting to land a movie part. Her first singing job was with the Tommy Dorsey Band on his radio show.

She was given a contract by Universal Studios in 1942 and appeared in twenty films over the next nine years. During this time, she married and divorced six times.

Marie's career stalled, primarily because of a lack of talent, and she started drinking and using drugs. In 1951, she stopped acting for three years. She appeared in one television episode of *The Danny Thomas Show* in 1954, and was not seen again until 1958 when she appeared in *The Geisha Boy*. She made another television appearance in 1959, and made her last public appearance in *Promises, Promises* in 1963.

McDonald killed herself in 1965 by taking an overdose of Percodan.

Everett Sloane, born on October 1, 1909 in New York City, attended but did not graduate the University of Pennsylvania, joining a theater company instead.

His stage performances were not well received and for this reason he quit after a few years, and became a Wall Street runner. Then, in 1929, the stock market crashed, depriving him of his job, so he joined Orson Welles' Mercury Theatre.

Welles gave him strong parts in *Citizen Kane* in 1941, *The Lady from Shanghai* in 1948, and in *Prince of Foxes* in 1949. Sloane also worked in radio during the 40s with roles in shows such as *The Inner Sanctum.* Evidently depressed over blindness caused by glaucoma, he committed suicide on August 6, 1965 and is buried in the Angelus-Rosedale Cemetery in Los Angeles.

Carolyn Mitchell was born Barbara Ann Thomason in 1937 in Phoenix, Arizona, to Don and Helen Thomason. While attending Emerson Elementary School in Phoenix, she was known as the prettiest girl in Phoenix. She moved with her family to Inglewood, California in 1951, where she attended Morningside High School and at seventeen, was crowned "Miss Venus."

Early in 1958, car salesman Bill Gardner introduced her to Mickey Rooney, at a nightclub. Rooney, once again a successful actor and married to his fourth wife, bought her a $4,500 fur coat.

On August 7, 1958, Barbara swallowed an overdose of sleeping pills while alone in Rooney's rented home. Mickey left his fourth wife, actress Elaine Devry, bought a house in Sherman Oaks, and Thomason moved in with him. Thomason and Mickey married in Mexico a few months later.

In March of 1959, Thomason, three months pregnant, threatened to commit suicide if Rooney did not get a divorce and marry her legally. On September 13, 1959, she gave birth to a daughter, and Rooney made it public that he and Thomason had married in Mexico. Rooney remarried Thomason in the USA the following year. Over the next four years they had three more children.

In 1963, Barbara and Mickey traveled to Yugoslavia where Mickey had a role in *The Secret Invasion*. Mickey admitted later that he was cheating on her at the time. Barbara went to the set one day when Rooney was working on his new show, *Mickey*. Upon seeing Barbara, Mickey's girlfriend started a fight. By September, 1964, the pair was consulting divorce attorneys. They did not divorce however, and moved from Beverly Hills into a Brentwood house.

Barbara began seeing Alain Delon in the fall of 1964, and Delon introduced Mickey and Barbara to Milos Milosevics.

Mickey went to the Philippines to film a picture, and he stupidly asked Milosevics to look after his wife. Milosevics agreed, and he and Barbara began an affair.

Learning that they were involved when he got home, Mickey moved out of the Brentwood house.

Barbara and Rooney filed for separation in 1965, and Milosevics immediately moved into the Brentwood house where he lived with Barbara and Rooney's four children.

Mickey filed for divorce early the following year, and requested that the court issue a restraining order keeping Milosevics out of the Brentwood house. On January 20, 1966, Barbara went out with Milosevics and her friend Margie Lane for dinner. They returned to Brentwood at 8:30 p.m. The following morning her friend Wilma Catania and Barbara's maid forced open the locked door of the master bedroom. They found the bodies of Barbara and Milosevics; she was lying on her back, shot through the jaw. Milosevics was beside her, face down, a bullet hole in his temple. It appeared that Milosevic had first shot Barbara with Mickey's pistol, and then committed suicide. Some of Barbara's friends are said to have believed that Rooney was involved.

She is buried in Forest Lawn Cemetery in Glendale, California.

Milos Milos (Milos Milosevic) was born on July 1, 1941 in Serbia. In the 1950s, Milos and a buddy became involved in a street fight in Belgrade. As a result, they met Alain Delon, who was filming a movie there at the time. Impressed with the fighting skills demonstrated by the pair, Delon hired both of them as his personal bodyguards. When Delon returned to Hollywood, Milos went with him. It was there that he met a local gangster named Nikola Milinkovich. Nikola paid Milos $200,000 to fight for him in street fights. By placing bets on Milos, Nikola won what was said to be more than $2,000,000.

Through his friendship with Delon, Milos landed a few minor roles in films. Milos appeared in the 1966 comedy *The Russians Are Coming, the Russians Are Coming.*

In 1965, Milos met Barbara Ann Thomason, also known as Carolyn Mitchell, who was Mickey Rooney's wife, and they became romantically involved.

A few months later, on January 30, 1966, Milos and Barbara were found dead in Rooney's Los Angeles home. The police report said that Milos shot Thomason with Mickey Rooney's revolver and then killed himself. Hollywood rumors put another spin on the story; Milos and Barbara were murdered because of their affair.

Jonathan Hale was born on March 21, 1891 in Ontario, Canada. He was probably best known for his portrayal of Mr. Dithers, Dagwood Bumstead's boss in the film series, *Blondie* which ran in the 40s.

He first appeared in *Housewife* in 1934 and had roles in *Alice Adams* with Katherine Hepburn in 1935, as well as 243 other movies made over a period of 31 years.

Hale committed suicide on February 28, 1966, apparently because of severe depression. He is buried in the Valhalla Memorial Park Cemetery in North Hollywood, California.

Montgomery Clift was born on October 17, 1920 in Omaha, Nebraska. His mother took him to New York City when he was fifteen, and when he was twenty, he appeared in *There Shall Be No Night* with Alfred Lunt and Lynn Fontanne. The play won a Pulitzer Prize. Clift worked on the Broadway stage for the next ten years, and then moved to
Hollywood.

Clift's first movie role was in the 1946 production of *Red River* starring John Wayne. He became one of Hollywood's leading male actors in 1951 with the release of *A Place in the Sun,* co-starring with Elizabeth Taylor.

Clift only made sixteen movies, working from 1948 to 1962, with one additional film, *The Defector* in 1966. It is said that Clift hit the top of his acting career with *From Here To Eternity,* which was released in 1953.

Clift and Sinatra in From Here to Eternity

He was supposed to have the male lead in *Sunset Boulevard* (a part that was written specifically for him), but he quit just before shooting began, complaining that the character resembled his actual life too much.

In 1956, Clift had an automobile accident while driving home after attending a party given by Elizabeth Taylor. Serious damage was done to one side of his face, and he was left with chronic pain that increased his dependency on drugs. In addition, his appearance was much altered for the worse. He spent two months convalescing and then returned to finish the film. Pain caused him to rely heavily on drugs and alcohol, and his health began to fail.

Acting teacher Robert Lewis called the remaining years of Clift's acting career "the longest suicide in Hollywood history."

He made six movies over the next four years, but his drug and alcohol abuse became so destructive that it was becoming almost impossible for him to continue acting. Universal Studios sued him for cost over-runs that resulted from Clift's many absences during film shooting of *Freud: The Secret Passion* released in 1962.

On July 22, 1966, Clift was found dead in his New York City apartment bedroom by his live-in personal secretary. His death is attributed to drug and alcohol abuse.

Montgomery Clift was known to be bisexual, and it is believed that the moral code of the 1940s and 50s in Hollywood contributed to his abusive lifestyle.

He is buried in the Friends Quaker Cemetery in Brooklyn, New York.

Lennie Bruce (Leonard Alfred Schneider) was born on October 13th, 1925 in Mineola, Long Island, New York. His father was a shoe clerk, and his mother, a professional dancer. After his parents divorced, his mother farmed him out to relatives.

Shortly after the start of World War Two, Lennie quit school and joined the Navy. Unable to contend with life in the military, he pretended to be homosexual and was discharged.

Lennie's mother got him gigs in night clubs doing a comedy act, and in 1948, he appeared on the television show, *Arthur Godfrey's Talent Scouts*. As a result, he was able to get an agent and better club bookings.

He married Honey Harlow, a strip-tease artist, and in 1953, the pair left New York for Los Angeles. The marriage lasted five years, and produced one child, a daughter they named Kitty. After Harlow went to prison for drug possession, Lennie won custody of their daughter.

Needing money, Lennie developed what became known as the Brother Mathias Foundation scam. He went to Florida where he stole some clergy clothing and solicited donations for a leper colony in British Guyana. He was arrested in Miami and charged with impersonating a priest. Lennie was found not guilty as he had actually charted the foundation in the state of New York, and the fact that there actually was a Guiana leper colony. Lennie claimed to have collected $8,000 in a period of three weeks, and maintained that he sent $2,500 to the leper colony.

Lennie developed an act that was unlike that of other comedians, ridiculing newsworthy events of the day and well-known personalities. He also used language that was generally unacceptable, and in many locations illegal. Reviews and news articles brought him a great amount of publicity, and this led to work in better clubs as well as a great deal more money. Popularity, wealth, and association with drug users soon made him an addict.

Lennie was first arrested in San Francisco in 1961. He was charged with public obscenity and found not guilty by a sympathetic jury. Following that incident, he found himself the target of religious groups and law enforcement everywhere he appeared.

He was arrested again in 1964 in New York City, again for breaking laws covering the use of obscenity. Even though Lennie received support from many politicians, writers, and teachers, he was sentenced to prison, and served three months. Constant police harassment, lawyer's fees, and criminal trials drove him into deep depression and increased dependency on drugs; as a result, he was bankrupt by 1965. The police began to threaten club owners with the loss of their liquor license if they hired Lennie and this pretty much ended his career as a comedian.

Lennie was hired to appear in a Los Angeles club in 1966. The audience was small, and the police were present. He went on-stage unshaven, dressed in nothing but a rain-coat, and obviously drugged, spoke unevenly about free speech and constitutional rights, and staggered off. On August 3rd of the same year he was found dead in his home at 8825 West Hollywood Blvd., Los Angeles, of a drug overdose. He was forty years old. He is buried in Eden Memorial Park Cemetery in Mission Hills, California.

Lennie is credited with writing six screen plays, acting in four movies, and directing one movie short.

8825 Hollywood Blvd. in West Hollywood, where Lenny Bruce died.

Barbara Payton was born Barbara Lee Redfield on November 16, 1927 in Cloquet, Minnesota. When she was eleven, her family moved to Odessa, Texas where her parents opened "The Antler's Inn," a tourist court. Her parents were alcoholics and her father abused her mother. After an impulsive act of teenage rebellion and an annulled elopement, she quit high school in the eleventh grade. The next year, in 1944, Payton married a second time. Now wed to a decorated combat pilot, she moved to Los Angeles so he could attend USC on the G.I. Bill.

In L.A., Barbara took up modelling. She was very successful, but as her career grew and they welcomed their new son, John Lee, the marriage floundered. They separated four years later.

Barbara became known as a notorious party girl in the Hollywood nightclub scene. When she was spotted in one of those Hollywood clubs by a Universal Studios' representative, she was signed to a movie contract that resulted in a role in *Trapped*, released in 1949. In 1950, the Paytons divorced and Warner Brothers picked up her contract. She was given a part in *Kiss Tomorrow Goodbye* and that turned out to be her best known film.

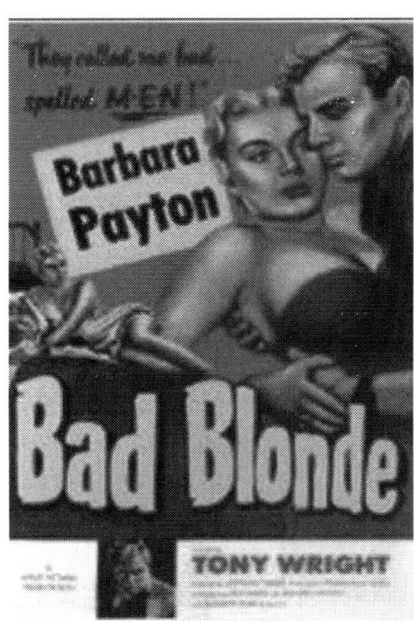

Barbara eventually lost custody of her son in 1956, when her ex-husband brought charges against her, claiming that she exposed John Lee to "profane language, immoral conduct, notoriety, unwholesome activities" and failed to provide the boy with a "moral education".

Between 1949 and 1963, Barbara appeared in fifteen movies. Her film career hit the skids after *Murder is My Beat* (1955), and she became known as an undependable alcoholic involved in multiple affairs. She married four times over the following six years. At one point, she was dating both Franchot Tone and Tom Neal at the same time. Eventually, Neal and Tone got into a fight after running into each other in Payton's apartment. Tone wound up in a hospital with a broken nose, cracked cheek bone, and a concussion. He remained in a coma for eighteen hours.

The incident resulted in headlines, and Payton took advantage by marrying Tone immediately. Two months later, she left him and moved in with Neal. This incident destroyed both Payton and Neal's hope of ever working in Hollywood again, so they toured for four years in various plays and then divorced.

Payton's abuse of alcohol and drugs, coupled with a wild lifestyle, diminished her beauty and she became depressed. After being arrested as a prostitute, she lived on the streets.

In 1967, she moved to San Diego to live with her parents, where she died of liver and heart failure attributed to alcoholism. Barbara was cremated and is interred at Cypress View Mausoleum and Crematory in San Diego, California

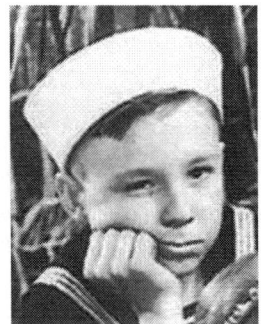

Harold "Slim" Switzer was born on January 16th, 1925, in Paris, Illinois. He was Carl Switzer's older brother. Carl was commonly known as Alfalfa, one of Hal Roach's *Our Gang* members. Harold also had a part in the *Our Gang* series. He was known as Deadpan.

Harold and Carl were known around Paris for their mastery of musical instruments, and singing ability. In 1934, when Harold was nine, his parents took the family on a trip to California to visit relatives. One of their sight-seeing excursions took them to the Hal Roach Studios.

The family toured the facilities, and ended up having lunch in the Our Gang Café where Harold, age eight, and Carl, age six, decided to do some entertaining. Mr. Roach witnessed the impromptu show, and immediately signed both boys to contracts to appear in the *Our Gang* shorts. Their first film was *Beginner's Luck*, released in 1935.

Carl won immediate popularity as Alfalfa, but Harold's character, Deadpan, didn't catch on, and he remained a background member of the gang.

Carl earned 125 television and film credits between 1935 and 1958, but Harold's career ended with the short, *The New Pupil*, released in 1940.

Harold owned a clothes washer and dryer service company in 1967. He became involved in a dispute with one of his customers, stabbed the man to death, and then got into his car, drove to a remote spot near Glendale, and committed suicide.

He is buried in the Hollywood Forever Cemetery in Hollywood, California.

His brother, Carl, got into an argument with a friend on January 21st, 1959, near Mission Hills, California. The argument ended when Carl pulled a knife, and the friend shot and killed him.

Albert Dekker was born Albert Van Ecke on December 20, 1905 in Brooklyn, New York. He graduated Bowdoin College and then worked with a Cincinnati stock company.

In 1927, Dekker had a major part on the Broadway stage in *Marco Millions*. After spending nearly ten years on Broadway, he was offered a film role in *The Great Garrick* and moved to Hollywood.

Dekker appeared in some 106 film and television presentations from the 1930s to the 1960s. He is probably best known for playing the title role in *Dr. Cyclops*, which was released in 1940.

Dekker was discovered dead on May 5, 1968, in his Hollywood home. He was naked, kneeling in his bathtub, blindfolded, a rope tied tightly around his neck, and a gag in his mouth. His wrists were handcuffed, and he had two hypodermic needles stuck in his arms. Explicit words of sexual connotation were scrawled on his body, a woman's vagina was illustrated on his stomach, and both of his nipples had been enhanced with sun rays. The coroner ascribed his death to accidental autoerotic asphyxiation.

Bobby Driscoll was born on March 3, 1937 in Cedar Rapids, Iowa. That same year his parents moved to Des Moines, Iowa where the family lived for six years. They then relocated to Los Angeles in the hope that the California climate would help Bobby's father's pulmonary disease.

Bobby won an audition at MGM when he was six, and was hired to play in *Lost Angel*, which premiered in 1943. His next role was in *The Fighting Sullivans* made the following year. Between 1943 and 1960 Bobby appeared in forty-nine film and television roles. He is probably most remembered for his work with Disney in films like *Song of the South*. He won an academy award for being the outstanding juvenile actor of 1949.

Bobby Driscoll and Robert Newton in *Treasure Island*

When Bobby turned sixteen in 1953, severe facial acne and a rough voice hurt his career in film, and most of his appearances after 1953 were on television; his final screen appearances were in *The Scarlet Coat* (1957) and *The Party Crashers*

(1958).

Bobby remarked that when he entered public high school following his last job with Disney he had plenty of money and started taking drugs, mostly heroin. In 1956, he was arrested for the first time; the charge was possession of marijuana. Later that year, he and his girlfriend ran off to Mexico where they were married. After having three children together, they divorced in 1960. Late in 1961, at age twenty-four, he was sent to prison on drug charges.

When Driscoll was released in 1962, he was unable to find work as an actor in films or television. In 1965, a year after his parole expired, he moved to New York, hoping to work on the Broadway stage. Unsuccessful at that, he became part of Andy Warhol's Greenwich Village art community, known as The Factory, a hangout for hip artsy types, homosexuals, and drug users, and famed for its erotic parties.

Penniless, Bobby left The Factory in late 1967 and disappeared into Manhattan's underground. On March 30, 1968, his body was found in a deserted tenement. The coroner's report said that he died of heart failure caused by long-time drug abuse. He was buried in an unmarked pauper's grave, and where he remains today.

Nick Adams was born Nicholas Aloysius Adamshock on July 10, 1931 in Nanticoke, Pennsylvania, where his father worked in the coal mines. Nick was five when his uncle was killed working in the mines, and Nick's father abruptly moved the family to Jersey City, New Jersey. After graduating high school in 1948, Nick moved to New York City.

Out of work and broke, he went to an audition for the stage play, *The Silver Tassie*, where he met the actor, Jack Palance. Palance put him in touch with a junior theater group where he was given a paying role in their production of *Tom Sawyer*.

A year later, Adams hitched his way to Los Angeles where he adopted the name Nick Adams, taking it from the protagonist of two dozen short stories written in the 1920s and 30s by American author Ernest Hemingway.

Adams had the naive belief he would be spotted by a studio agent or a director if he worked at the Warner's Theater in Beverly Hills, so he took a job there doing janitorial and maintenance work. Ordered to change the marquee lettering one day, he thought it would be good public relations to put his own name up. He was promptly fired.

He then landed an acting job at the Las Palmas Theater in a play titled, *Mr. Big Shot*. The job paid sixty dollars a week, but after he paid the $175 membership fee for an Actors Equity card he was required to have, he still had no money.

In 1952, to avoid being drafted into the Army, Adams joined the United States Coast Guard. His ship docked in Long Beach, California in June of 1954, and Nick hopped a bus to Hollywood where he managed to get an audition with director John Ford. Nick then took leave from the Coast Guard and was given an uncredited part in the 1955 film version of *Mister Roberts*.

In 1955, after being discharged, he was given a minor role in *Rebel without a Cause*, and that same year he had another small role in *Picnic* starring William Holden and Kim Novak.

Adams and his good friend, Elvis Presley

Over a period of sixteen years, Adams appeared in a total of sixty-two film and television roles. He was best known for his leading role in the television production of *The Rebel*, a series that ran from 1959 to 1961. From that point on his acting career hit the skids.

In 1959, Adams married Carol Nugent, an actress he met in an episode of *The Rebel*. They had two children, and then, separated in 1967.

In 1963, Adams spent over $8000 dollars to advertise himself, hoping to win an Academy Award nomination for his role in *Twilight of Honor*. He did manage to win a nomination, but the Oscar went to Melvyn Douglas.

Adams used his own money to pay for an airline ticket to Rome in 1968, hoping to get a part in a "B" film titled *Murder in the Third Dimension*, only to learn upon arriving that the film had been cancelled.

After Nick returned to Hollywood, he was found dead in his apartment at age thirty-six. The coroner's report found paraldehyde mixed with sedatives and other drugs in his organs. No prescription bottle or needle marks were discovered. Paraldehyde is a depressant is used as a sedative.

The official cause of death was suicide; however the circumstances have caused many to wonder.

2126 El Roble Lane, Beverly Hills, the house where Nick Adams died.
He is buried in SS. Cyril and Methodius Cemetery in Berwick, Pennsylvania. His headstone reads:

Nick Adams-the rebel-actor of Hollywood scenes

Scotty Beckett was born on October 4, 1929, in Oakland, California. His family moved to Los Angeles when he was three. Scotty's father became seriously ill, and when Scotty was visiting him in the hospital one day, he sang a song for his dad. A studio casting director heard Scotty singing and arranged for an audition. This got Scotty a role in the film *Gallant Lady,* which was released in 1933. His father died soon after.

Scotty became part of the *Our Gang* group in 1934 and appeared as a regular in the series for a year. Between 1933 and 1957, Beckett appeared in 103 film and television roles. His parts in later years were mostly unaccredited.

He was arrested in 1948 on DUI charges, and in 1949 he married, but that marriage only lasted five months. He spent time in jail in 1954 for passing bad checks and carrying a pistol. That same year he worked in thirty-four episodes of the television show *Rocky Jones, Space Ranger*; this was his last role of any importance.

Beckett was arrested in 1957 by customs officers when he attempted to smuggle drugs into the United States. By then he had married again and claimed his wife had severe mental problems and needed the drugs. But the fact was that she was in a state hospital being treated for alcoholism. When his wife divorced him a few months later, Beckett tried to kill himself by ingesting sleeping pills. Failing at that, and realizing he would never work again as an actor, he took a job selling used cars.

In 1959, Beckett was involved in an automobile accident while driving under the influence. His skull was fractured, his hip broken, and he was left crippled for life. He attempted suicide in 1962 by slashing his wrists. The attempt failed.

He was arrested in 1963 on charges of assault with a deadly weapon after trying to stab a man. He again attempted suicide when released.

On May 8, 1968, only thirty-nine years old, he was brought to a Hollywood nursing home seriously injured in what was thought to be a drug related fight. He died there a few days later. It is reported that he had overdosed on barbiturates and/or alcohol.

Scotty is buried in San Fernando Mission Cemetery in Mission Hills, California.

Al Mulock was born on June 30, 1925, in London, England. He went to New York to study at the Actors Studio, returned to London, and organized the "The London Studio," teaching Lee Strasberg's Method to British would-be actors. He appeared in numerous British films and television productions throughout the 1950s and 60s. In the '60s, he became involved in the popular Italian Spaghetti Westerns, and is best known for roles in *The Good, the Bad, and the Ugly*, and *Once Upon a Time in the West*.

In May, 1968, screenwriter Mickey Knox, and production manager Claudio Mancini, both of whom were working on *Once Upon a Time in the West* in Guadix, Spain, saw Mulock's body fall past their hotel room window as they sat, drinking coffee and discussing an upcoming sequence of the film.

It is said that Mulock was not killed in his suicide attempt but that he died as a result of an extremely bumpy automobile trip to the hospital. His left lung was pierced by a broken rib.

Fellow actors reported that Mulock was heavily addicted to cocaine. When he was unable to purchase any in the small village, he gave up and leaped from the hotel roof.

William Lennon was the father of Diane, Peggy, Kathy, and Janet, the famous *Lennon Sisters*. Lennon, father of eleven children, worked as a pro at the Westchester Golf Course, Marina Del Rey driving range's golf shop. He was president of the Santa Monica Chamber of Commerce.

On August 12, 1969, he got into an argument with a man on the golf course parking lot. The man, later identified as Chet Young, was a delusional stalker who believed Mr. Lennon was standing in the way of his marriage to Peggy Lennon. Young went to his car and removed a rifle from the trunk. When William attempted to run, Young shot him in the back. He then walked up to William and shot him again, in the head.

Two months later, Young used the same weapon to kill himself.

Born in Durango, Mexico in 1899 to a prominent Mexican family and moving to Los Angeles in 1913 to escape the Mexican Revolution, Jose Ramón Gil Samaniego grew up to be **Novarro**, MGM's "Latin Lover" and top Latin star after Rudolph Valentino died. He began to work in the cinema in 1917 as a bit player. His role in *Scaramouche* in 1923 made him star.

In the late 1920s and early 1930s, he was earning more than $100,000 per film. He invested some of his income in real estate, and his Hollywood Hills residence is one of the renowned designs by architect Lloyd Wright. Due to his wise investments when his movie career ended, he was able to live comfortably.

Novarro had been troubled all his life as a result of his conflicting views over his Roman Catholic religion and his homosexuality. His life-long struggle with alcoholism is often traced to these issues. He was a pal of Richard Halliburton, who was also a closeted homosexual. In 1968, Novarro was murdered by two brothers, Paul and Tom Ferguson (aged twenty-two and seventeen, respectively). Novarro had hired the two men from an agency to come to his Laurel Canyon home for sex. According to the prosecution in the murder case, the two young men believed that a large sum of money was hidden in Novarro's house, but they left with just twenty dollars they took from his bathrobe pocket.

The men had scrawled, "Us girls are better than those faggots," on a bathroom mirror. When police checked Novarro's phone records, they found that a call had been made to Chicago during the time in question. They called the number and a woman answered. She turned out to be Tom's girlfriend, and she told police that Tom had described what he and his brother had done to Novarro. The brothers were sentenced to life in prison, but in time were released on probation.

Novarro allegedly died as a result of asphyxiation, choking to death on his own blood after being brutally beaten. He is buried in the Calvary Cemetery in East Los Angeles, California.

Dorothy Abbott was born in Kansas City, Missouri on December 16, 1920. She grew up in Kansas City and, after graduating high school, went to work as a stenographer. In 1945, perhaps struck by the national excitement that followed the ending of World War Two, Dorothy packed her bags and moved to Hollywood with the intent of finding work in the entertainment field.

She got a job dancing in the chorus of the Los Angeles based revue produced by the famous theatrical entrepreneur, Earl Carroll. Carroll opened a theatre on Sunset Blvd in Hollywood in 1938, where he featured lightly clad beauties in shows that earned him the title, "The Troubadour of the Nude." Dorothy, for some unknown reason, was publicised as "The Girl with the Golden Arm." Carroll died in the crash of United Airlines flight 624 in 1948, just three years after Dorothy joined his show, but she had moved on by then.

A Paramount Studios agent spotted the beautiful, dusky-voiced, Dorothy, in 1946, and she was signed to a $150 a week contract. Her first screen appearance was an uncredited part in *The Razor's Edge,* which starred Tyrone Power, and was released in 1946. She played the part of a show girl, and had no lines.

Over the next two years, she appeared in two more Paramount productions, again in uncredited, non-speaking roles. Finally, in 1948, she was given one line in *Night Has a Thousand Eyes*, but no credit.

In 1949, Dorothy met a Los Angeles Narcotics officer named, Adolph Rudy Diaz. Diaz was well known in Los Angeles, as he had taken part in several high profile arrests, including Robert Mitchum for marijuana possession. Diaz was descended from a Native American Apache tribe, and was handsome in a rough, swarthy way. Dorothy fell deeply in love with Diaz, and they married almost immediately.

Rudy Diaz

Dorothy continued to act in small, uncredited roles, adding to the family income by working part-time as a real estate sales person. In 1953, she was given a part in the television police drama *Dragnet,* playing of Joe Friday's (Jack Webb) girlfriend, and appeared in six episodes over the next two years. This connection resulted in the producers of *Dragnet* dramatizing several of her husband's experiences. As a result, Diaz quit his police job in 1968, and became an actor.

Dorothy appeared in fifty movies and television productions during the eighteen years between 1946 and 1964. She is probably best known for her nineteen appearances in the television series, *The Adventures of Ozzie and Harriet,* during the years 1956 to 1964. She landed a part as a detective in the film, *Pal Joey,* in 1957. Six years later, gossip columnists were reporting an affair between her husband and actress Ann Sothern.

In 1968, Dorothy divorced Diaz. Just a few months after the divorce was finalized, on December 15th, Dorothy committed suicide. It was said that she did so while in a state of severe depression over the failure of her marriage.

Dorothy is buried in Rose Hills Memorial Park in Whittier, California.

Diaz continued to act for another fifteen years, usually appearing as an American Indian, or a Mexican. During that time, he appeared in forty-one television and film roles, including Clint Eastwood's, *Coogan's Bluff,* released in 1968, two episodes of The *Rockford Files,* between 1974 and 1977, and his last role, *Painted Desert,* released in 1993.

Diaz died in Los Angeles on December 5th, 2006.

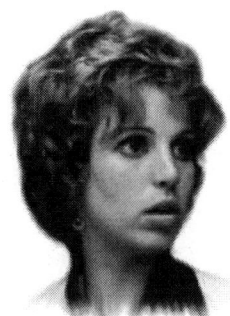

Diane Linkletter was the daughter of television host Art Linkletter. In 1965, at age seventeen, she ran away from home and got married; her father had her brought home and then had the marriage annulled.

At age twenty, Diane committed suicide by jumping from the seventh floor of a high-rise apartment building. Her father blamed her death on a reaction to ingesting LSD, but statements made by her friends seem to indicate that she was in a state of severe depression and that she had in fact, committed suicide.

She was dating a man named Edward Durston, and he was with her at the time of her death. Durston took actress Carol Wayne to Mexico fifteen years later. After the two had an argument that was witnessed by others, Wayne's body was discovered floating in the nearby ocean.

Diane is buried in the Forest Lawn Memorial Park Cemetery in Glendale, California.

Diana Blanche Barrymore (Diana Blythe) was born on March 3, 1921, in New York City. Her father was the well-known actor, John Barrymore, and she was the half-sister of John Jr., niece of Lionel and Ethyl, and aunt of Drew Barrymore.

Her parents divorced when Diana was four years old. When she and her mother moved to Europe, Diana was enrolled in a Paris boarding school. Diana did not see either of her parents while she attended school, but in 1934 when she was fourteen, John showed up a visit. He took Diana and her seventeen-year-old friend to dinner and a movie, got drunk, and made a sexual pass at Diana's schoolmate.

In 1938, she was given a screen test for the part of Scarlett O'Hara in *Gone With the Wind*. Obviously she did not get the part. The following year she did summer stock in Maine for ten dollars a week. By 1940, her salary had increased to $150 per week when she appeared in *Outward Bound* in the Harris Theatre in Chicago.

Diana; cover of Life, 1939

She moved to Hollywood in 1942 after producer Walter Wanger promised her $1,000 a week to work for him. She was given parts in two of his films: *Eagle Squadron*, released in 1942, and *Ladies Courageous*, released two years later. Between 1941 and 1951 she appeared in eleven movie productions. The last was *The Mob*, completed in 1951.

Because she became involved with drugs when she was a teenager, her addiction had a negative effect on her work in films and her reputation. In 1955, she attempted suicide while living in Boston. She swallowed twenty-seven sleeping pills and washed them down with whiskey.

Diana's autobiography, *Too Much, Too Soon* was made into a movie in 1958. Time Magazine, April 15th, 1957: "If a former glamour girl is down about, shaken by the DTs, and degraded by three nightmare marriages plus numerous vulgar affairs, how can she rehabilitate herself? She simply writes a book about it all."

Diana committed suicide on January 25, 1969 by taking a lethal combination of sleeping pills and alcohol. She is buried next to her mother in the Woodlawn Cemetery in the Bronx, New York Plot: Division 20, between E. Border Avenue and Chapel Hill.

Barbara Bates was born in Denver, Colorado on August 6, 1925. She worked as a model while still a teenager and later won a beauty contest. Her prize was train fare to Hollywood.

Barbara signed a contract with Universal in 1945 and appeared that same year in minor roles in six films. During this period, she became involved in an affair with an agent who was married; a short while later the agent divorced his wife and married Barbara.

Between 1946 and 1948, Barbara had unaccredited minor roles in eight films, and did some photo modeling for magazines. Warner Brothers saw some of these photos and gave her a contract. As a result, her acting career took off, and she was given credited parts in major films such as *The Inspector General* with Danny Kaye, but when Barbara refused to go on a promotional tour for the *Inspector General*, Warner Brothers fired her.

Barbara and Danny Kaye in *The Inspector General*

She then signed with 20th Century Fox, and in 1950 was given a major role in *All About Eve*. Her work in this film established her as a star and she later co-starred in *Cheaper by the Dozen*.

In spite of this sudden spring into success, or perhaps as a result of it, Barbara sank into severe depression and bad health.

She took a television role in 1954 in the NBC show *It's a Great Life*, but because of her mental and physical problems, NBC fired her.

After that happened, she moved to London seeking work and was hired by the Rank Organization. Still crippled by depression, she began and then quit two leading roles in a period of just four weeks. In 1957 Rank canceled her contract. In 1960, she returned to Hollywood only to learn a few months later her husband had cancer. The events overwhelmed her and as a result she cut her wrists in an attempt at suicide.

Between 1945 and 1962, Barbara appeared in thirty-six television and film productions.

Six years later, her husband died and she left Hollywood to return to her childhood home in Denver. There she worked first as a secretary and later as a nurse's aide.

She remarried in 1968, but despite these seemingly good changes in her life, on March 18, 1969, she committed suicide. She is buried in Crown Hill Cemetery in Wheat Ridge, Colorado.

Judy Garland was born on June 10, 1922, in Grand Rapids, Minnesota, where her parents operated and appeared in a vaudeville theatre. When she was two-years-old, Judy first performed there with her two sisters.

Under a cloud of rumors accusing her father of making sexual advances toward the boys working as ushers in his theater, the family relocated to Lancaster, California. When Judy was four, her father began to try to find the sisters work in the movies.

They were seen in the film *Bubbles* in 1930, and made their last film together in 1935, performing in a short titled, *La Fiesta de Santa Barbara*.

Metro-Goldwyn-Mayer put Judy under contract in 1935, and in 1936, she appeared in *Pigskin Parade*.

Between 1936 and 1969 she appeared on film and television fifty times. Among her most memorable parts was *Broadway Melody of 1938*, in which she sang <u>You Made Me Love You</u> to a photo of Clark Gable. *The Wizard of Oz* followed in 1939, and *Meet Me in St. Louis* in 1944.

Garland was working so many hours in film production that the studio gave her amphetamines to help her sleep. She later blamed this fact on her lifelong addiction to drugs

While working on *The Pirate* in 1947, Judy had a nervous breakdown. She entered a psychiatric hospital in Stockbridge, Massachusetts for rest and treatment, and attempted suicide shortly thereafter.

Judy made three additional films for MGM but because of her drug use, headaches, and alcoholism she was suspended after being cast in *The Barkleys of Broadway*.

Garland was later cast in the film adaptation of *Annie Oakley*, but once again her undependable work habits caused MGM to suspend her contract.

When June Allyson became pregnant in 1950, Garland's contract was renewed and she took over June's role in *Royal Wedding*. Again, she missed work on many occasions and was suspended.

In 1954, Garland and her husband, working through their company, Transconia Enterprises, decided to produce a remake of *A Star is Born* with Judy playing the lead. The movie proved to be a big hit, but because of Judy's many personal problems during filming, the project went over-budget, lost money, and Judy failed to solve her financial difficulties as she had hoped.

Her popularity rose over the following few years, but in 1964, after only forty-five minutes on stage, Judy fell apart during a concert in Melbourne, Australia.

She continued to perform sporadically over the next five years and on June 22, 1969, she was discovered in her house in London dead of a drug overdose.

Carol Thurston was born on September 27, 1923 in North Dakota. She began

her acting career in her father's repertory company at the age of twelve. After graduating High School, she worked for a while in the Billings Montana Civic Theater. Later, her father took a job with Lockheed Aircraft, and they moved to Los Angeles.

Cecil B. DeMille gave Carol a role in his film, *The Story of Dr. Wassell* in 1943. Two years later, Thurston married an Air Force lieutenant colonel.

In 1948, Thurston won a part in Universal Picture's film, *Rogue's Regiment.* This led to a series of parts through the years '49 to '55, including *Pearl of the South Pacific.* She performed in a total of forty-four film and television productions over a period of nineteen years. From 1956 to 1962, Carol acted in the television series, *The Life and Legend of Wyatt Earp.*

On December 31, 1969, at age forty-nine, Thurston committed suicide in Los Angeles.

Sharon Tate was born in Dallas, Texas in 1943. In 1959, at age sixteen, she won the title Miss Richland. Her father was transferred to Italy that same year.

While in Italy, Tate watched some of the filming of *Adventures of a Young Man,* and was given a part as an extra. Noticing Sharon, the film's director introduced himself and encouraged the teenager to take up acting. The next year, she landed a job with Pat Boone, and appeared with him in a television special he was making in Venice, Italy.

Later that same year, Sharon was hired as an extra in *Barabbas* which was being shot near Verona. Jack Palance liked what he saw and he set up a screen test for her in Rome.

After she then returned to the United States alone, she told her family she wanted to go back to school. Instead, she began to look for work in the movies. A few months later, her mother suffered a nervous breakdown, and Sharon went back to Italy.

Tate's family returned to the United States in 1962, and Sharon went back to Los Angeles where she signed on with an agent.

In 1963, she signed a six-year contract and began to get small parts in popular television shows. The following year she met Jay Sebring, a popular Hollywood hair stylist.

She landed roles in *The Americanization of Emily* and *The Sandpiper*, and in 1965, she was given her first major role in *Eye of the Devil*.

Sebring accompanied Sharon when she went to London to shoot the film, and after the movie was completed she stayed on in London. It was at this time that she met Roman Polanski.

Polanski was busy planning *The Fearless Vampire Killers*, and after meeting Sharon, he decided she would be good in the leading role in the film. The film company went to Italy, and they began a relationship. Tate moved in with Polanski in his London apartment after filming ended.

Tate returned to the United States to begin filming the role of Malibu in *Don't Make Waves*. Polanski returned to the United States shortly thereafter to direct and write the screenplay for *Rosemary's Baby*.

In late 1967, Tate and Polanski returned to London where they married. They then returned to Los Angeles and leased Patty Duke's home in Beverly Hills.

In the summer of 1968, Tate began work on *The Wrecking Crew*. She became pregnant, and she and Polanski moved to Benedict Canyon. Tate's next film was *The 13 Chairs* and in March, 1969, she went to Italy for filming. Polanski began work on *The Day of the Dolphin* in London. Sharon returned to Los Angeles on July 20, 1969. Polanski was not due to return until a month later.

On August 8, 1969, just two weeks before she was due to give birth, Sharon went to dinner with Sebring, Frykowski and Folger. After returning home, they were murdered by members of Charles Manson's "Family". Police also found the body of Steven Parent, shot to death in his car, which was parked in the driveway.

10050 Cielo Drive, Beverly Hills, where Sharon Tate and others were murdered by the Manson family.

Sharon and her baby boy, Paul Polanski, are buried in the Holy Cross Cemetery in Culver City, California.

Sue Williams was born Karen Susan Hamilton on November 14, 1945 in Glendale, California. She became a model shortly after graduating high school. A local photographer submitted some shots he had made of Sue to Playboy magazine, and she was hired. At 4'11, she was one of the shortest women ever selected to appear as a Playmate in Playboy.

Because of the Playboy spread, she was able to win acting jobs and appeared in several films and on television. She was seen in *How to Stuff a Wild Bikini* credited by the name Sue Hamilton.

Williams shot herself in the chest on September 2, 1969 and is buried in Forest Lawn Memorial Pa

Chapter Seven: the Seventies

Hollywood was clearly in a depression at the beginning of the '70s. Income was down as was creativity. Even so, the '70s proved to be a memorial decade in movie creativity.

Prior restrictions on language, sexual content and, violence had been loosened. The hippie and civil rights movements, the growth of rock and roll music, and openness about drug use had a great effect

Hollywood was freer, ready to take risks and to listen to the ideas of young film makers, while the older professionals and studio heads died out.

Although the 50s and 60s were known for wide-screen epics displayed on CinemaScopic screens, the 70s were noted for creative writing and subjects that reflected the questioning spirit and truth of the times.

1970s uncertainty gave rise to some of the finest, boldest, and most commercially-successful films ever made, such as *The Godfather* (1972), *The Exorcist* (1973), *Jaws* (1975), *Close Encounters of the Third Kind* (1977), and *Star Wars* (1977).

In the 70s, the had-been-powerful MGM Studios sold off large amounts of its assets, got out of the movie-making business, and moved into other businesses such as hotels and casinos.

The '70s became a period of high-priced tickets and food. Films could become more expensive, like *Jaws,* which grew in cost from $4 million to $9 million during production, but still became the highest grossing film in history -until *Star Wars* came along. *Jaws* and Star Wars were the movies to earn more than $100 million in rentals. *Jaws* was give a TV marketing campaign that cost $700,000 for three nights of nationwide prime-time TV ads on all the networks.

In 1977, George Atkinson of Los Angeles advertised the rental of 50 Magnetic Video titles in the *Los Angeles Times*. He then opened the first video rental store, Video Station, on Wilshire Boulevard. Heb rented videos for $10 a day. Within 5 years, he had sold franchises to more than 400 Video Station stores across the nation.

Chester Morris was born in New York City on February 16, 1901. His mother and father were stage actors.

His first appearance on Broadway was in *The Copperhead*. He was sixteen at the time

The following year he had a part in the silent film, *The Amateur Orphan*, produced by the Thanhouser Film Corporation. His role in *Alibi*, released in 1929 brought him a nomination for best actor.

He appeared in a total of 126 film and television productions between 1917 and 1970.

Although he was in his forties when World War Two started, he still took the time to perform hundreds of shows for the U.S.O, military hospitals, and various bond drives around the country.

When Chester learned that he was dying of cancer in 1970, he decided to commit suicide by taking an overdose of barbiturates. He was cremated and his ashes scattered.

Inger Stevens was born Inger Stensland in Stockholm, Sweden on October 18, 1934.

At the age of nine, following her parents' divorce, Inger moved with her father to New York City. When she was thirteen, she and her father moved to Manhattan, Kansas, where she attended Manhattan High School, and when she turned sixteen, she began to dance in burlesque shows in Kansas City. Two years later, she moved back to New York City and began to study acting at the Actor's Studio while working as a chorus girl.

Inger took minor roles in various television and theatre productions until she auditioned and won a part in *Man on Fire*, released in 1957. She attempted suicide in 1959 as a result of unhappy affairs with Bing Crosby, James Mason, and Harry Belafonte, among others.

All in all, she had roles in fifty-three film and television productions between 1954 and 1970, appearing in one hundred and one episodes of *The Farmer's Daughter*, between 1963 and 1966.

In 1961, she married Ike Jones, an African-American producer, actor, and screenwriter, but they kept the marriage secret because of public attitudes toward mixed marriages at the time.

Inger was discovered on April 30, 1970, lying on her kitchen floor, dead of an overdose of prescription drugs combined with alcohol. She was cremated and her ashes were scattered in the Pacific Ocean.

Janis Joplin was born on January 19, 1943 in Port Arthur, Texas. She attended Thomas Jefferson high school, and it was there that she first began singing blues and folk music.

After graduating, she enrolled at Lamar State College of Technology in Beaumont, Texas, in 1960; later transferring to the University of Texas at Austin.

Janis then moved to San Francisco in early 1963, where she became part of the hippie movement in Haight-Ashbury. Jorma Kaukonen, who would later play guitar for the Jefferson Airplane group, recorded several pieces with Joplin in 1964, but by this time, Janis was already a serious drinker and a drug user.

John Gilmore in his book <u>Laid Bare: A Memoir of Wrecked Lives and the Hollywood Death Trip</u>, said "Back then, nobody knew or cared who she was-a lump-faced kid with sores on her skin, frumpy like someone working a hot-dog stand."

Between staying stoned and singing the blues or folk music for tips, Janis said the only other thing she wanted was to be laid three times a day.

At the insistence of friends concerned that she was damaging her health through the use of amphetamines, Janis went home to Port Arthur in 1965. It is reported that she managed to withdraw from drugs, and quit drinking while attending Lamar University for a year.

In 1966, Joplin's singing style attracted the attention of the rock band, Big Brother and the Holding Company. They invited Janis to join them in 1966, and she made her first appearance in the group at the Avalon Ballroom in San Francisco.

In August, 1966, they moved to Lagunitas, California, where they shared a house with the Grateful Dead. Once again, Janis began using drugs. Friends report that within three years, Joplin had developed a serious addiction to heroin and was spending as much as $200 a day on the drug.

Joplin toured with the Kozmic Blues Band in 1969 and performed at Woodstock that August, where she continued using large amounts of drugs and alcohol.

Janis wrote and performed in fifty-three television and film productions between 1968 and 1970. When she failed to show up for a recording session on October 3, 1970, the group's road manager went looking for her. He discovered her body in her motel room. The autopsy reported that she died of an overdose of heroin mixed with alcohol.

Janis was cremated and her ashes were scattered on the Pacific.

Frank Wolff was born on May 11, 1928 in San Francisco. He graduated UCLA with a degree in the arts. Between 1957 and 1973, he appeared in sixty-one television and film roles.

Frank performed in two films for Roger Corman: *I Mobster* and *The Wasp Woman*. Following Corman's advice, he began to work in Europe where he appeared in over fifty films, mostly Italian-made.

He is probably best known for his part in *Once Upon a Time in the West*, released in 1968.

Suffering from severe depression over a belief that his acting career was waning, Wolff committed suicide in his hotel room in Rome, Italy on December 12, 1971. His burial site is unknown.

Stunt pilot **Charles Boddington** died when his plane crashed during filming of *The Red Baron* (1971).

Barbara Colby was born in New York City in 1939 and grew up in New Orleans. She graduated high school in 1957 and received a scholarship to Bard College in New York City.

Barbara first acted on stage in 1964 in *Six Characters in Search of an Author*, appeared in *The Devils* on Broadway the following year, and spent the remainder of the 1960s working in the New York theater.

Her first television role was in an episode of *Columbo* in 1971. That was followed by parts in *The Odd Couple*, *McMillan and Wife*, *Gunsmoke* and a number of other television shows. She might be best remembered for her portrayal of Sherry, a prostitute, in a 1974 jail cell episode of the Mary Tyler Moore series.

Colby's film appearances included *California Split*, released in 1974, and *Memory of Us*, also released in 1974.

On July 24, 1975, Barbara and her boyfriend, James Kiernan, were walking to their car in Venice, California, when two men shot them. Barbara was killed. Kiernan described the men to police before he also died, and said the shooting happened without any reason or provocation. Police reported that nothing was stolen from the couple. The killers have not been caught.

Bella Darvi's birth name was Bayla Wegier. She was born on Oct 23, 1928 in Poland.

After living through World War Two in a Nazi concentration camp, Bella went to Monaco where she became part of a society of high rollers. She soon became an addicted gambler and was well on her way to alcoholism.

Darryl F. Zanuck and his wife Virginia Fox, met Bella in a casino and Virginia was impressed with Bell's foreign allure. At his wife's insistence, Zanuck took Bella in tow, paid off her gambling debts, and flew her to Hollywood. The name Darvi was a combination of Darryl and Virginia.

Zanuck gave Darvi a part in *The Egyptian*, and *Hell and High Water*, both released in 1954, and *The Racers*, released the following year. Critics were quick to point out Darvi's lack of acting skill; this, combined with a slightly cross-eyed expression, a lisp, and her heavy accent did not help her career.

Between 1954 and 1971, Darvi appeared in sixteen film and television productions.

Within a short time, Zanuck left his wife for Darvi, but then left her when he discovered that Bella was either a lesbian or bisexual. This ended Darvi's special treatment in Hollywood, and her job opportunities dried up.

After returning to Europe, she publicly dated both men and women. She resumed her addiction to gambling and heavy drinking, and generally fell apart. She was given a few minor roles in "B" films, but she soon found herself heavily in debt.

She attempted suicide several times, and in 1971 was successful. She turned on the gas in her apartment, took some sleeping pills, and quietly died. She is buried in Cimetiere de Bagneux in Ile-de-France, France.

Andrea Feldman was born on April 1, 1948 in New York City. After attending Quintano's School for Young Professionals, a high school for the performing arts, she starred in three Andy Warhol films; *Imitation of Christ*, *Trash*, and *Heat*. She was also featured in a documentary film called *Groupie*, made in 1970.

Addicted to amphetamines and in and out of state hospitals due to multiple nervous breakdowns, Andrea often referred to herself as "Crazy Andy."

On August 8, 1972, Andrea called her ex-boyfriends to her New York City apartment to see what she said would be her "final starring role."

She left this note:

"I'm headed for the big time. I'm on my way up there with James Dean and Marilyn Monroe."

Then, holding a Bible in one hand and a crucifix in the other, Andrea jumped to her death from her fourteenth floor apartment. She was twenty-four.

Anissa Jones was born on March 11, 1958 in West Lafayette, Indiana. Her parents moved to Playa Del Rey, California, soon after. Anissa's mother took her to a commercial audition when she was six, and as a result, she made her first appearance on television. Two years later Anissa won the role of Buffy in the television series *Family Affair*. She appeared in 138 episodes between 1966 and 1971. She was thirteen years old when *Family Affair* went off the air and was unable to find other parts to play. At age eighteen, Anissa was given control of a trust fund that amounted to $180,000. That same year, on August 27, 1976, she attended a party at Oceanside. Her dead body was found the next morning. According to the coroner's report, she had ingested cocaine, PCP, Quaaludes, and Seconal. Anissa's ashes were scattered at sea.

Jack Cassidy was born in Richmond Hill, New York on March 5, 1927. After a long and successful career on Broadway, he moved to Hollywood in 1952 to begin an even longer career in television.

Between 1952 and 1977, he appeared in seventy-four television productions.

Jack married Shirley Jones in 1956, and they worked together in the television series, *The Partridge Family*, before divorcing in 1974. He and Shirley had three sons.

Jack and Shirley 1956

David Cassidy wrote that his father was an alcoholic suffering from mental problems. After the divorce, Jack was seen watering his lawn one afternoon in the nude. Shirley reported that he once told her he was Christ. He spent two days in a psychiatric hospital in December. 1974, and it was then that Shirley learned that Jack was bipolar.

Jack lived alone for several years and on December 1, 1976 he fell asleep with a lit cigarette in his hand and died in the resulting fire.

Jack was cremated and his ashes scattered in the Pacific Ocean.

Christa Helm was born Sandra Clements in Milwaukee, Wisconsin in 1949. She left home at age seventeen hoping to become a go-go dancer. She married at eighteen, gave birth to a daughter and allowed the child to be adopted. Moving to New York, she found work as a fashion model. It was there that she met Lea and Perrin heir, Stuart Duncan. Duncan produced the film, Let's Go for Broke, and made Helm the star.

Later, Helm moved to Hollywood where she used her sexual attractions as a vehicle into films. She had little success, landing only a small part in a Starsky and Hutch episode and one commercial.

Helm became involved with narcotics. She eventually ran upon hard times and took employment as a waitress.

On her way to visit a boyfriend on February 12, 1977, Christa was attacked by unknown assailants, stabbed numerous times, and beaten savagely to death with a blunt object.

Stunt man **Jim Sheppard** died during the filming of *Comes a Horseman* (1978), when he hit his head on a fence post while being dragged by a horse.

Katherine Walsh was born on April 11th, 1947 in Kenton County, Kentucky. A witty and talented child, she is said to have wanted to be an actress from childhood. Her first starring role was Alice in her school's production of *Alice in Wonderland*.

In 1963, Katherine's mother moved Katherine and three of her four siblings to Beverly Hills, where Katherine signed a contract with the William Morris Agency, and then with Columbia Pictures.

Katherine was attending the Royal Academy of Dramatic Art in London, when in 1965, her father, Thomas Walsh, the President of the Atlantic Underwriters Association, died in the crash of an American Airline's commercial flight.

In 1966, Katherine appeared in the Columbia Pictures production of *The Chase*, which stars Marlon Brando, Robert Redford, and Jane Fonda.

In 1966 and 1967, she appeared in two movies, and three television productions. She is probably best known for her role in *The Trip*, written by Jack Nicholson, in which she played the part of Lulu.

Shortly after her work in *The Trip*, Katherine returned to London. On October 7, 1970, her body was discovered in her rented flat in Kensington. He police labeled her death murder, but the crime has never been solved.

Katherine Walsh in a scene from the film, *The Trip*.

During the filming of *Zeppelin*, in 1970, a plane and a helicopter collided. **Butch Williams**, Assistant-director, **Skeets Kelly**, camera man, and pilots **Jim Liddy** and **Gilbert Chomat**, were killed.

Star Wars, released in 1977, earned $193.8 million in one year, and it marked the beginning of mass merchandising based on a movie. Lucas sold his *Star Wars* logo on toys, games, lunchboxes and even clothing.

Jim Morrison was born James Douglas Morrison on December 8, 1943 in Melbourne, Florida, the son of a naval officer. He moved to Los Angeles in 1964, where he earned a degree at UCLA.

After graduating, he took up residence in Venice, adopting the popular hippie life style by living on the roof of a friend's building. It was there, while under the influence of LSD, he met the men that became The Doors.

In 1967, Morrison's group was given a recording contract by Elektra Records Their release of <u>Light My Fire</u> was number one on the Billboard Hot 100 for three weeks. When the group released their second album, <u>Strange Days</u>, they became one of the nation's most popular rock bands.

In 1968, *The Doors* performed in London. It is reported that Morrison was an alcoholic by that time.

In 1971, Morrison moved to Paris with his girlfriend. According to her, on July 3, 1971, Jim inhaled heroin, thinking it was cocaine. She fell asleep instead of calling for medical aid, and Morrison bled to death. She overdosed on heroin three years later.

Jim is buried in Paris in the Pere Lachaise Cemetery, which is one of the city's most popular tourist attractions.

Pete Duel was born in Rochester, New York on February 24, 1940. He grew up in Penfield and after taking some courses at St. Lawrence University in Canton, he moved to New York where he appeared in a touring production of *Take Her, She's Mine*.

He and his mother traveled from New York to Hollywood in 1963, sleeping in a tent at roadside parks at night in order to conserve funds. There, he landed television roles in shows like *Gomer Pyle, USMC, Channing*, and *Combat!* before getting a starring role *Love on a Rooftop* in 1966. He is probably best known for his role in the television series, *Alias Smith and Jones*, which ran for thirty-three episodes from 1971 through 1972.

He appeared in a total of 208 film and television productions between 1962 and 1973.

In the early hours of December 31, 1971, Duel died at his Hollywood Hills home of a self-inflicted gunshot wound to the head. According to police, Duel's friends and family said he was depressed about his addiction to alcohol. He had been arrested and pleaded guilty to a DUI accident that injured two people the previous June. Duel's death was later ruled a suicide.

2552 Glen Green Terrace in the Hollywood Hills, where Pete Duel died.

Duel was buried in the Oakwood Cemetery in Penfield, New York.

Edie Sedgewick was born in Santa Barbara, California on April 20, 1943.

Despite the fact that her family was wealthy, and that she grew up in luxury, she had psychological difficulties due to her father's tendency to narcissism, physical abuse, and a controlling personality. He also had affairs and made no attempt to keep them secret. Sedgewick said that, as a child, she saw him having sex with a strange woman.

She became anorexic before she was fifteen, and it was a lifelong problem. Edie's mother had her committed to the Silver Hill Hospital in New Canaan, Connecticut in the fall of 1962. A fellow patient has said that there was little control exercised in the hospital, and as a result, Edie changed her ways very little, dropping in weight to just ninety pounds.

In March 1965, Sedgwick met artist Andy Warhol and began spending a great deal of time at the Warhol "Factory". Warhol gave Sedgwick a part in *Vinyl*, a film he was making at the time. He also put her in *Horse*. Audiences expressed interest in Sedgwick, and Warhol decided to write a film that would star her and created *Poor Little Rich Girl*.

Warhol starred Sedgwick in three more of his films in 1965. These were *Outer and Inner Space*, *Prison*, and *Lupe and Chelsea Girls*. By the end of the year, Sedgwick and Warhol were estranged, and Sedgwick asked him to stop showing her films.

After abandoning the Warhol group, Sedgwick became close to Bob Dylan. That relationship ended when she learned that Dylan was married to Sara Lownds.

In 1966, Sedgwick became addicted to barbiturates. Her health began to fail, and she returned to California to be with her family. She was arrested in August of 1969 for drug possession and placed in the psychiatric ward of Cottage Hospital.

In 1971, Sedgwick's doctor prescribed pain medication for her due to a physical illness. Not long after that her husband gave her the medication just before he went to bed. The next morning he discovered that she had died during the night.

The coroner called Sedgwick's death a suicide resulting from ethanol intoxication. She is buried in Oak Hill Cemetery in Ballard, California.

Pier Angeli was born Anna Maria Pierangeli on June 19, 1932 in Cagliari, Sardinia, Italy. Her twin sister, Marisa, would become known as the actress, Marisa Pavan.

In 1948, while studying Art in Rome, Pier was discovered by director Leónide Moguy, who promptly signed the beautiful Pier to a contract. After playing a role in *Tomorrow is Too Late*, released in 1949, she was signed by MGM; and at eighteen, given the title role in the MGM production of *Teresa*, playing opposite John Ericson.

In that time of her life, Pier was very busy. She appeared with Gene Kelly in another MGM film, *The Devil Makes Three*, followed by MGM's *Sombrero*, co-starring Ricardo Montalban, and then appearing in *The Story of Three Loves* with Kirk Douglas.

Pier then starred with Paul Newman in *The Silver Chalice*, released in 1954

Pier and Paul Newman in *The Silver Chalice*

It was on this set that she met James Dean. He was making *East of Eden* at the time. Pier and James dated, and Pier soon fell in love with the brash young actor. James, however, proved to be unwilling to enter into a serious relationship.

Pier's next romance was with Vic Damone who also worked for MGM. They were both Catholic and within a few months were engaged. On November 24th, 1954, Pier and Vic were married at a church in Beverly Hills and had a son the following year.

In 1956, now twenty-four, Pier won the female lead in the major film, *Somebody Up There Likes Me*, once more, playing opposite Paul Newman.

Struggling in her personal life, Pier's marriage failed and they divorced in 1958. Four years later, she again married, this time to composer Armando Trovajoli. They had a son, but then separated in 1965.

After appearing in thirty-three films, Pier made her last film in 1971, a disaster titled *Octaman*.

Said to be depressed and lonely, she died on September 10, 1971 of a barbiturate overdose. She is buried in the Cimetière des Bulvis, in France.

George Sanders was born in Saint Petersburg, Imperial Russia on July 3, 1906 to English parents. In 1917, when the Russian Revolution began, his family returned to England, where he went to Brighton College. He was employed by an advertising agency after graduation. It was there he met a secretary named Greer Garson, who advised him to become an actor.

Sanders worked in British films until 1936, when he moved to Hollywood and was given a role in *Lloyds of London*, released that same year. Between 1936 and 1973, he performed in 133 television and film roles. In 1950, Sanders won an Academy Award for Best Supporting Actor for his performance in *All about Eve*.

He was married to Susan Larson from 1940 until 1949. After divorcing her, he married Zsa Zsa Gabor. In 1970, he married Zsa Zsa's sister, Magda. This last marriage lasted six weeks.

A heavy drinker, in his later years Sanders was in poor health, had dementia, and suffered emotional problems. This was apparent in his last movie roles.

On 25 April 1972, Sanders was found dead, in a hotel room in a coastal town near Barcelona, Spain. His death was the result of ingesting five bottles of Nembutal.

He left behind three suicide notes saying:

<u>Dear World, I am leaving because I am bored. I feel I have lived long enough. I am leaving you with your worries in this sweet cesspool. Good luck.</u>

George Sanders was cremated and his ashes were scattered in the English Channel.

Gia Scala was born Giovanna Scoglio in Liverpool, England on March 3, 1934 and grew up in Rome. In 1948, she moved to New York City, where she graduated Bayside High School. Gia then took a job as a file clerk, later becoming a reservation clerk for Scandinavian Airlines. She studied acting at night and made several appearances on radio and television.

In 1954, Columbia Pictures gave her a contract, and she moved to Hollywood.

Between 1955 and 1969, Gia appeared in thirty-one film and television roles. She is perhaps best remembered for her portrayal of Anna, in the film, *The Guns of Navarone*, released in 1961.

Gia was never at ease playing the part of a glamorous starlet. As a result, she became an alcoholic and lost her contract with Universal due to unreliability. Following this, she sought work in Europe.

After her husband left her, Gia attempted suicide by jumping into the Thames River. She was saved by a passing cab driver. She was arrested several times after that for being drunk and became deeply depressed. In 1971, she decided to return to Hollywood, but her problems continued. In April of 1971, she was arrested over a dispute over fifty cents with a parking lot attendant that turned violent. Then July of '71, she wrecked her sports car while intoxicated. In May of '71, her friend, actress Anna Kashfi, took legal custody of her while she was in acute mental depression and undergoing psychiatric care.

On April 30, 1972, she was found dead in her Hollywood home. An autopsy showed that she had died of an overdose of drugs and alcohol, which authorities ruled a suicide.

Gia is buried in Holy Cross Cemetery in Culver City, California.

Peggie Castle was born Peggy Blair in Appalachia, Virginia on December 22, 1927. She grew up in Hollywood, where she went to Hollywood High School. Stories have it that she was spotted by a talent scout while having lunch in a Beverly Hills restaurant (the fact that her father managed the Goldwyn Studio may have helped). Peggie had minor roles in several films, and due to some sexy publicity photos, she was named "Miss Classy Chassis" by the UAW, and "Miss Cheesecake" by the Pacific Restaurant Association.

Between 1947 and 1966, Peggie appeared in fifty-five television and film roles. For three years, starting in 1959, she had a role in the television series *Lawman*, as a dance hall hostess. Peggie was married four times, divorced three, and widowed once. When her career began to fade, she became an alcoholic and died of cirrhosis of the liver brought on by alcoholism in 1972.

Peggy was cremated and her ashes scattered.

Veronica Lake was born Constance Frances Marie Ockelman on November 14, 1922 in Brooklyn, New York. Her father died in an explosion in 1932. Her mother then married Anthony Keane, and Veronica was bundled off to a boarding school in Montreal. She went to Miami Senior High School in Miami, Florida following a family move. Her mother later stated that Veronica was placed under a psychiatrist's care at that time because of behavioural problems and was diagnosed as schizophrenic.

Lake's family relocated to Beverly Hills in 1938, and Veronica attended the Bliss-Hayden School of Acting. This led to an RKO contract and a minor role in

Sorority House, released in 1939. While she was still a teenager, Paramount producer Arthur Hornblow Jr., took an interest in her career and changed her name to Veronica Lake. When RKO cancelled her contract, she married John S. Detlie, an art director, who was 14 years older than her.

She was given a small role in *Forty Little Mothers*, in 1941, and her performance impressed Paramount Pictures so much that they gave her a long-term contract. She starred in *Sullivan's Travels*, released in 1941, and then appeared in *I Wanted Wings* that same year. Her performance was acclaimed and *Hold Back the Dawn* followed later that same year.

She worked with Alan Ladd in four films. It is said that the only reason they were paired was because Lake was the only Paramount actress short enough to match Ladd's diminutive 5 feet 5 inches. Lake was 4 feet 11 ½ inches tall.

Lake developed a reputation for being a difficult acting partner. According to Eddie Bracken, "She was known as 'The Bitch' and she deserved the title." Joel McCrea, who worked with her in *Sullivan's Travels*, was said to have refused a co-starring role in *I Married a Witch* because, "Life's too short for two films with Veronica Lake."

She played a Nazi in *The Hour Before the Dawn*, released in 1944 and received scathing reviews. It was said that her German accent was "unconvincing".

Lake began to use alcohol heavily during the 1940s, and except for *The Blue Dahlia*, released in 1946, the films she made during that period are mostly forgotten. Paramount cancelled her contract in 1948. Her career was pretty much over following the release of *Slattery's Hurricane* in 1949.

After the IRS had taken all of her assets for unpaid taxes, she filed for bankruptcy, divorced her husband, and began to look for television parts.

Lake ceased acting in 1959 and moved to New York City where she lived in cheap hotels. She was arrested for public drunkenness and disorderly conduct several times.

A newspaper reporter discovered her working behind a bar at the Martha Washington Hotel. She tried to convince him that she was just helping a friend, but later admitted that she had lied. The ensuing story garnered her a few television appearances and several stage parts in off-Broadway productions, but her physical and mental health was declining rapidly. By the late '60s, she had apparently become paranoiac and claimed the FBI was stalking her.

On July 7, 1973 Veronica died of complications caused by her acute alcoholism. She was cremated and her ashes were scattered at sea.

Michael Dunn was born a dwarf in Shattuck, Oklahoma on October 20, 1934. He stopped growing at a height of three feet-ten inches. His family moved to Dearborn, Michigan when he was four. Dunn possessed a high IQ and began to read at age three. In 1947, he won the Detroit News Spelling Bee. He finished Redford High School in 1947 and in 1951, graduated from the University of Michigan at the age of sixteen.

After moving to New York City, he landed a minor role in the stage production of *Two by Saroyan*, in 1962. His first movie role was in *Without Each Other*, released in 1962. All total, he appeared in thirty movie and television roles between 1962 and 1974.

Between 1965 and 1968, he worked in the television production, *The Wild, Wild West*.

Dunn was awarded the New York critics' Circle Award for best supporting actor in *The Ballad of the Sad Café* in 1963. He was nominated for an Oscar for his supporting part in *Ship of Fools* released in 1965.

Dunn was found dead in his hotel room in London, on August 30, 1973. He was in London to work on *The Abdication*. Dunn suffered from severe physical problems, including deformed hip joints. The cause of death was not established, but it is believed that he took his own life. He was buried in Fort Lauderdale, Florida, but was later moved to Sunset Memorial Park in Norman, Oklahoma where his parents were buried.

Judd Holdren was born near Villisca, Iowa on October 16, 1915. He quit high school, and then moved to Omaha, Nebraska, where he studied at the Omaha Playhouse. He was in the Coast Guard during World War Two, and after the war ended, he moved to Hollywood.

Among his early films were *All the King's Men* in 1949, and *Purple Heart Diary* in 1951. Between 1949 and 1960, Holdren appeared in forty-one film and television roles. Between 1960 and 1963, he landed just one small part, and as a result, gave up acting and went into the insurance business. Although he was often seen escorting many different Hollywood beauties during his Hollywood days, he never married.

Suffering from extreme depression, Holdren shot himself in the head on March 11, 1974. He is buried at Valhalla Memorial Park in North Hollywood.

Patricia Cutts was born in London, England, on July 20, 1926. Her father, Graham Cutts was a film director, and her mother, Robin Coles was an actress. Patricia was given her first film role when she was two years old.

In 1940, at age fourteen, Cutts ran away and joined a stage company. Under the name Patricia Wayne, she appeared in a few British films in the early 1950s.

She moved to New York City in 1955 where she worked in television. The New York critics did not give her much praise. In 1957, Ruth Gordon and her husband saw Cutts in a stage production and were impressed enough to offer a role in the Broadway production, *The Matchmaker*. She only had one role in 1961, and one in 1962. It was two years before she appeared again on the *Alfred Hitchcock Hour*.

In October, 1962, she married William Nichols, a television producer and divorced him one year later.

Cutts returned to London in 1967, where she appeared in several television productions. In 1974, she killed herself with an overdose of barbiturates. It is not known where she is buried.

Edward Platt was born in Staten Island, New York on February 14, 1916. He attended Northwood, a private school in Lake Placid before going to the Juilliard School of Music, and then landing a part in the Broadway production of *Allegro*.

Platt served as a radio operator in the army during World War Two.

He moved to Hollywood after a friend, Jose Ferrer, helped him get a part in the film version of *The Shrike*. Platt appeared in 121 television and film roles between 1949 and 1974 and is probably best remembered for his portrayal of "The Chief" in the long-running television production, *Get Smart* appearing in 135 episodes between 1965 and 1970.

Platt suffered for many years from severe depression and in the later part of his life, had financial difficulties. He committed suicide on March 19, 1974. He was cremated and his ashes scattered into the Pacific Ocean.

Judith Rawlins was born in Milwaukee, Wisconsin on June 24, 1936. Her family moved to Sherman Oaks, California while she was a child.

Rawlins took courses at the Valley Community Players and did animation work for Walt Disney Studios on such films as *101 Dalmatians*, and *Lady and the Tramp*. She later worked as a secretary for Vic Damone, and they married in 1963. She appeared in seven television and film roles between 1960 and 1963. Rawlins divorced Damone in 1970.

In 1974, Damone became engaged to Becky Jones, an heiress to the Houston oil family. Perhaps because of this, Rawlins was found dead on March 28, 1974 from an overdose of the pain killer, Darvon. The coroner, however, ruled her death the result of an accident.

She is interred as Judith Riedel Rawlins at San Fernando Mission Cemetery, Mission Hills, California.

David Knowles, a photographer, fell from a mountain and died during filming of *The Eiger Sanction* in 1975.

Sal Mineo was born in The Bronx in 1939, the son of Sicilian coffin makers. His first appearance on stage was in *The Rose Tattoo* in 1951, and he performed with Yul Brynner in *The King and I*. He is probably best known for his parts in *Rebel without a Cause*, and *Giant* which was released in 1956.

In the early 1960s, in his 20s, he was considered too old to continue to play roles of the type that had made him popular and he stopped getting offers. He was turned down when he auditioned for *Lawrence of Arabia* and began to show signs of depression.

He told one reporter, "One minute it seemed I had more movie offers than I could handle, the next, no one wanted me."

It is said that he camped out on Francis Ford Coppola's front lawn, pleading for the part of Fredo in *The Godfather* but was denied that also.

By 1976, his popularity appeared to have improved. He landed the part of a bisexual burglar in the stage production of *P.S. Your Cat Is Dead* in San Francisco and followed the play to Los Angeles.

At the age of 37, he was stabbed to death on February 12, 1976, behind his apartment building when returning home after a rehearsal. His homosexual activities are thought to have played a part in the murder.

He is buried in the Gate of Heaven Cemetery in Hawthorne, New York.

Freddy Prinze was born Frederick Karl Pruetzel to a German father and a Puerto Rican mother in New York City on June 22, 1954. In 1973, he made his first television appearance on *The Jack Paar Show*. In December of that same year, Prinze began playing the role of Chico in the television series, *Chico and the Man*, a part that lasted from 1974 to 1977.

In October of 1975, Prinze married Katherine Cochran, and they had a son, Freddy Prinze, Jr. When Freddy Sr. was arrested in 1976 on a charge of DUI, his wife filed suit to divorce him, claiming his drug addiction was endangering Freddy Jr. That same year, he starred in the television film, *The Million Dollar Rip-Off*.

Prinze became deeply depressed over problems at work, the divorce, and the loss of his son, and in January, 1977, just twenty-two, he shot himself in the head. Freddy is buried at Forest Lawn Memorial Park in Glendale, California.

Elvis Presley, the fan-proclaimed King of Rock and Roll, was born on January 8, 1935 in Tupelo, Mississippi. His family took him to Memphis in 1948.

Sam Phillips, owner of Sun Records, arranged for Elvis to work with guitarist Scotty Moore and bassist Bill Black, and the result was rockabilly, a combination of country and rhythm and blues. RCA Victor took over his contract in a deal arranged by Colonel Tom Parker, who became Presley's manager. Their first release, *Heartbreak Hotel* was recorded in 1956, and it became an immediate success. Elvis went to Hollywood in November of 1956, to make *Love Me Tender*, and between 1956 and 1969, he appeared in thirty-one movies.

According to journalist Tony Scherman, at age forty-two, Elvis was fat, and dull-witted, as a result of the pills he swallowed every day.

On August 16, 1977, he was discovered unconscious. He was later pronounced dead at the hospital. Elvis suffered from glaucoma, an enlarged colon, a bad liver, and high blood pressure, all probably the result of his abuse of drugs.

Elvis was buried at his home, Graceland, in Memphis, Tennessee, but after someone tried to steal his body, Elvis was moved to the Graceland Meditation Garden.

Gig Young was born Byron Elsworth Barr on November 4, 1913 in St. Cloud, Minnesota. He grew up in Washington D.C., where he was active in high school theatrical productions. This resulted in a scholarship to the Pasadena Community Playhouse in Los Angeles. He and George Reeves were seen by a Warner Brothers scout while performing in a play, and they were both given contracts.

Young used his real name in his early pictures, but in 1942, he played the part of a character named Gig Young in *The Gay Sisters*, and adopted the name.

Until he was given the part in *The Gay Sisters*, he was earning so little money that he worked part-time in a gas station in order to pay bills.

Young performed in sixteen films between 1940 and 1943. In 1943, after World War Two broke out, he enlisted in the Coast Guard, and worked as a pharmacist's mate until the war ended in 1945.

After returning to Hollywood, he got a small part in *Escape Me Never* in 1947. Between 1948 and 1978 he worked in seventy film and television productions. He won an Academy Award in 1969 for Best Supporting Actor in *They Shoot Horses Don't They?* The award apparently harmed his career as he never received another starring role. The fact that he had become an alcoholic did not help.

Mel Brooks fired him on his first day at work on the film, *Blazing Saddles* because he went into withdrawal tremors while shooting.

Young married five times; the last time in 1978 to Kim Schmidt, who was forty-four years younger than him. For reasons unknown, Young shot and killed his wife three weeks after their marriage, and then committed suicide by shooting himself in the head. He is buried using his real name, Byron Barr, in Green Hill Cemetery in Waynesville, North Carolina.

Charles Boyer was born in Figeac, Lot, Midi-Pyrénées, France on August 28, 1899. He studied at the **Sorbonne** for a short while, and then in 1920, he was spotted by an MGM scout while performing on the Paris stage. MGM took him to Hollywood where he was given a minor role in *Red-Headed Woman*, released in 1932. His first lead was in the 1934 version of *Caravan*. Boyer appeared in a total of ninety television and film roles between 1920 and 1976. He is probably best known for his part as Pepe le Moko in *Algiers*, released in 1938.

Gaslight with Charles Boyer and Ingrid Bergman

Boyer, like many Hollywood leading men, was short in stature. He developed a pot gut and began going bald at an early age. Later in life, he had roles in such films as: *Around the World in 80 Days*, released in 1956, *How to Steal a Million* and *Is Paris Burning*, both released in 1966, and *Casino Royale*, released in 1967. He co-starred with Katharine Hepburn in the 1969 film version of *The Madwoman of Chaillot*, and his last role was as the High Lama in a poorly received musical version of *Lost Horizon*, released in 1973.

Boyer's only child, Michael Charles Boyer was twenty-one when he committed suicide playing Russian roulette after separating from his girlfriend.

Two days after his wife died of cancer in 1978, Boyer killed himself by overdosing on Seconal. He was buried in Holy Cross Cemetery, Culver City, California beside his wife and son.

Marguerite (Maggie) McNamara was born in New York City on June 18, 1928. In 1951, she replaced Barbara Bel Geddes in the Broadway production of *The Moon Is Blue*, and later that same year, she landed a part in *The King of Friday's Men*.

When the film version of *The Moon Is Blue* was produced in 1953, she was given the role of Patty O'Neil, and as a result, she won an Academy Award nomination for Best Actress.

She then appeared in *Three Coins in a Fountain*, released in 1954.

McNamara ceased acting after her last onscreen role; a 1964 television episode of *The Alfred Hitchcock Hour* entitled "The Body in the Barn". She spent her later years working as a typist in New York City.

In February 18, 1978, she was found dead in her New York apartment after she had taken a deliberate overdose of sleeping pills and tranquilizers. She is buried in St. Charles Cemetery in Farmington, New York.

Deborah "Debbie" Weems was born in Houston, Texas on February 3, 1951. She studied acting at the Interlochen Arts Academy in Michigan, and appeared in local productions of *Annie Get Your Gun* and *The Miracle Worker*.

Between 1968 and 1970, Weems studied at the Boston Conservatory of Music. She then moved to New York City, where she landed a part in *Godspell*.

Beginning in 1973 she had a regular role in the television production, *Captain Kangaroo*. This led to typecasting, making it difficult for Weems to find work in films or television.

She was given a minor role in the film *Between the Lines* in 1977. Suffering from depression, a few months later, on February 22, 1978, she committed suicide by leaping from the sixteenth floor of her apartment building. Her death was ruled a suicide, and she was buried in Calvary Cemetery in Marlin, Texas.

Alan Scott Newman was born in Cleveland, Ohio on September 23, 1950.

His parents, actor Paul and Jackie Newman took him to New York City when he was one-year-old. His father left his family in NYC when he moved to Hollywood. By the time Alan was eight, his parents had divorced.

Paul then married Joanne Woodward. This created emotional problems for Alan.

In 1968, Alan went to Hollywood where he worked as a stuntman in his father's films. He refused offers of assistance in his career made by his father, and became a heavy drinker, leading to related arrests.

In the two year period, 1975 to 1977, Alan worked in six television and film productions; all minor roles, but due to his alcoholism, Alan wound up doing manual labor.

Alan was involved in a motorcycle accident in 1978, and began using pain killers. He killed himself on November 19, 1978, by overdosing on Valium and other drugs, mixed with alcohol.

Later, Paul said when his children were growing up, he wasn't around much, and when he was there, he was inconsistent. He believed that fact made it hard for them to find balance in their lives. After his son died, he said that was the saddest day in his life and he would never get past the guilt he felt.

In 1980, Paul founded the Scott Newman Center to help health care professionals and teachers educate children about the dangers of alcohol and drug use. That led to the Rowdt Ridge Gang Camp, summer camps for families on the road to recovery after dealing with the problems of drug use.

Kim Winona, born in Nebraska as Constance Elaine Mackey on October 10, 1930, was a Sioux Native American. She grew up on the Rosebud reservation in South Dakota.

Winona married another Native American when she was seventeen, and she and her husband moved to Los Angeles. Her husband, a printer, opened a small business, while Kim went to work as a secretary in a commercial art business and did modeling part-time.

She was given a screen test after her photos were seen by a movie scout. This led to a job touring the nation as "Miss Apache", promoting the film, *The Last Hunt*. Winona then appeared in twenty-six episodes of the television production, *Brave Eagle* during 1955 and 1956.

Kim married three times and had two daughters. Apparently depressed by marriage failures and receiving no additional acting offers, Winona committed suicide in June of 1978 by shooting herself in the head. There seems to be no record of where she is buried.

Bob Crane was born in Waterbury, Connecticut in 1928, but he spent his childhood and teenage years in Stamford, Connecticut. He joined the National Guard in 1948, and in 1949, he married Anne Terzian. They had three children. After Bob and his wife divorced, he married Patricia Olsen, and they had a son.

In 1950, Crane started his broadcasting career in New York. He later moved his family to California to host a morning show in Hollywood.

In Hollywood, Crane began substituting for Johnny Carson on the daytime game show *Who Do You Trust?* and also appeared on *The Twilight Zone, Alfred Hitchcock Presents*, and *General Electric Theater*. When Carl Reiner gave him a guest shot on *The Dick Van Dyke Show*, Bob was noticed by Donna Reed and landed the role of her neighbor in her popular sitcom.

In 1965, Crane was offered the starring role in *Hogan's Heroes* which became a hit and finished in the Top 10 in its first year on the air. *Hogan's Heroes* ran for six seasons between 1965 and 1975. The series won two Primetime Emmys.

During the run of *Hogan's Heroes*, Richard Dawson introduced Crane to John Henry Carpenter, who had access to video tape recorders. Carpenter then began photographing Crane's sexual escapades with various women.

In 1973, Crane purchased *Beginner's Luck*, a play that he starred in, directed, and took on tour around the country. Stage manager Tom McCluskey had this to say about Crane's opening of his production at the Clearwater, Florida Showboat Dinner Theatre in 1974 "First day, he walks into rehearsal and says: 'Hey, I need to know where the gay clubs are'.

I just kind of looked at him. He said: 'No, I'm straight. I just videotape kinky stuff.' It was kind of embarrassing, if you want to know the truth. It was almost like talking about athlete's foot or something. He was pretty open about this (topic)."

Crane evidently telephoned Carpenter on the night of June 28, 1978, and told him that he was ending their friendship. The following day, Crane was discovered beaten to death in Scottsdale, Arizona. Robert Graysmith's book *The Murder of Bob Crane* states that investigators found semen on Crane's dead body, indicating that the murderer may have ejaculated on him after killing him.

John Henry Carpenter

The car Carpenter had rented the previous day was impounded, and in it, blood was found that matched Crane's blood type, and in spite of this, the Maricopa County Attorney declined to file charges, stating that there was insufficient evidence.

Fourteen years later Carpenter was arrested, charged with murdering Crane, and found not guilty.

Kim Schmidt was born in Germany in 1957. She came to Hollywood in 1976, landed a minor role in the television production *Spectre* in 1977, and married Gig Young that same year. (Young was forty-four years older than her). She was murdered by Young on October 19, 1978 for unknown reasons, and he then committed suicide.

Jean Dorothy Seberg was born in Marshalltown, Iowa, on November 13, 1938.

Otto Preminger ran a contest in 1956, seeking someone to play the title role in *Saint Joan*. Seberg won and was taken to Hollywood. *Saint Joan* was not a popular film, nor was *Bonjour Tristesse*, her next film, which was released in 1958. Because of these failures, she decided she would do better by moving to France. Two years later, she landed the leading role in *Breathless*.

Seberg married novelist Romain Gary in 1962, who was twenty-four years older than Jean.

After coming back to the U. S. in 1964, she co-starred with Warren Beatty in *Lilith*, appeared in *Paint Your Wagon* in 1969, and then starred in *Airport* the following year.

During the late 1960s, Seberg supported the NAACP, Native American groups, and the Black Panther Party. This activity led to FBI investigations. It is reported that the FBI attacked her with false stories planted in Newsweek magazine. Among other allegations of sexual misbehavior and infidelity, it was said that her son was not fathered by her husband but by a member of the Black Panther Party.

After appearing in the film *Mousey* released in 1974, she returned to Europe.

Jean died in Paris in August, 1979 in an automobile crash. The coroner's report said the cause of the crash was caused by the massive overdose of barbiturates and alcohol Jean had ingested. Probable suicide was ruled the official cause of death.

Some people questioned this ruling, suspecting foul-play. They pointed out that there was so much alcohol in her system that they did not believe she could have driven a car. Also, she needed glasses to drive but was not wearing them. The following year, her ex-husband committed suicide. She is buried in Cimetiere de Montparnasse in Paris, France.

Victor Kilian was born in Jersey City, New Jersey in 1891 and began his career at the age of eighteen by joining a vaudeville company. In the mid-1920s, he was performing in Broadway plays, and 1930 had made his debut in motion pictures. For the next twenty years he worked as a character actor in films such as *The Adventures of Tom Sawyer*, released in 1938. While working out a fight scene in *Reap the Wild Wind*, Kilian lost one of his eyes.

In the '50s, Kilian was blacklisted, but the Actors' Equity Association refused to honor the ban and he was able to continue working on the stage. He is best known for his role as Grandpa Larkin in the television soap opera spoof *Mary Hartman, Mary Hartman*, which aired in 1976.

In 1961, Kilian's wife, Daisy Johnson died. He was living alone, when in 1979, he was beaten to death by robbers who burglarized his apartment.

Gordon Parks, Jr., Director, **Peter Gilfillian**, camera man, and two others, were killed when their plane cra lming of *Revenge* in 1979.

During the filming of *Steel* (1979), stunt man **A. J. Bakunas** died while performing a 300 foot fall. The air bag split.

Laurie Bird was born in Long Island, New York on September 26, 1953. Her mother committed suicide when Laurie was three years old.

Bird was working as a model when the director of *Two-Lane Blacktop*, released in 1971, chose her for a part in the film. Bird only appeared in two more movies, *Cockfighter*, released in 1974, and *Annie Hall*, released in 1975.

Bird gave up acting to become a photographer, became romantically with director Monte Hellman who starred her in some of his films, and later with Art Garfunkel, who allowed her to do the photography for several of his albums.

For reasons unknown, Bird committed suicide in Art Garfunkel's New York apartment June 15, 1979. She is buried in the Flushing Cemetery in Flushing, New York.

Jon Hall was born Charles Felix Locher in Fresno, California on Feb 23, 1915, but he grew up in Tahiti, the son of an actor and a Tahitian princess. Hall moved to Hollywood in 1934, where he was given a contract by Goldwyn Productions.

He had nine bit parts between 1935 and 1937, and then won the lead role in *Hurricane*. His uncle, James Norman Hall, wrote the book. Altogether Hall played in a total of forty-six film and television productions between 1934 and 1965. Most of these were romantic adventure films such as *Aloma of the South Seas*, released in 1941.

Hall married singer-actress Frances Langford in 1938, and they divorced in 1955.

He is probably best known for his title role in the television series, *Ramar of the Jungle*, in which he appeared in fifty-two episodes between 1952 and 1954.

Hall was not only an actor; he was also a pilot and a boat designer. He worked on projects for the U. S. Navy, including a shark-killing device and an underwater camera. He and his father co-developed the Locher-Hall Telecurve map, an advanced map making device.

Because of pain caused by bladder cancer, Hall committed suicide in North Hollywood, California on December 13, 1979. He is buried in Forest Lawn Memorial Park in the Hollywood Hills. His marker:

<u>Charles F. Locher</u>

<u>"Jon Hall"</u>

<u>Beloved Son and Brother</u>

<u>1915-1979</u>

Chapter Seven: the Seventies

Chapter Eight: the Eighties

Frank Christi, born in 1929 in Brooklyn, often played tough guys in movies and television shows, and he had criminal record in real life.

He had movie roles, playing a villain, in a number of films, including *The Godfather,* and *Terminal Island.* He also played supporting roles in *Beretta,* and *The Rockford Files.*

According to Los Angeles police, while acting he worked part-time as a real counterfeiter and forger.

Christi was shot and killed in his carport on July 9, 1982 just outside of Studio City. A neighbor reported seeing two men fighting with Christi. Two of Christi's friends were also murdered that same morning.

He is buried in Saint John Cemetery in Middle Village, New York.

Lindsay Harry Crosby was born in Los Angeles County on January 5, 1938. His father was Bing Crosby. Lindsey was married three times and fathered five children. Between 1945 and 1987 he appeared in fourteen television and film productions. He also sang in a trio with his brothers.

Said to have suffered depression as a result of having been physically and mentally abused by his father, he killed himself on December 11, 1989. Because of his suicide and simular depression, his brother, Dennis, also committed suicide three years later. Lindsay, Dennis, their brother Philip, and their mother Dixie Lee Crosby are buried in Holy Cross Cemetery in Culver City, California.

James Timothy "Tim" Hardin was born in Eugene, Oregon on December 23, 1941.

In 1959, at age eighteen, he quit school and joined the Marines. While serving as an advisor in 1959 in Vietnam, Hardin became addicted to heroin.

Hardin moved to New York City after being discharged, and studied at the American Academy of Dramatic Arts. After being suspended for truancy, he did some solo musical appearances in Greenwich Village.

He was noticed by record producer Erik Jacobsen after moving to Boston in 1963, and Jacobsen got him a contract with Columbia Records.

The following year he returned to Greenwich Village where he made a few records for Columbia. Columbia was not satisfied with his work and released him from his contract.

Because of his heroin addiction, by 1973 his work was so erratic that he ceased getting offers. He overdosed on drugs and died on December 29, 1980.

Mary Elizabeth Hartman was born in Youngstown, Ohio, on December 23, 1943. She appeared in fourteen movie and television roles between 1965 and 1982, the most notable being the role of a blind girl in *A Patch of Blue*, released in 1965, for which she received a Golden Globe award and an Academy Award nomination for Best Actress. In 1973, she was given a starring part in *Walking Tall*, playing the wife of Sheriff Buford Pusser.

Hartman is said to have suffered from depression and other mental problems, and as a result, gave up acting and moved to Pittsburgh to live with her family.

She died in a fall from her fifth floor apartment on June 10, 1987 after calling her psychiatrist with a complaint of depression. Her death is considered to have been a suicide. She was buried in the Forest Lawn Memorial Park Cemetery in her hometown.

James Hayden, born on November 25, 1953, performed on Broadway, but is most likely better known for his role in the movie *Once Upon a Time in America.*

He served as a medic in the army during the Vietnam War, and after his discharge returned to New York City where he studied at the American Academy of Dramatic Arts.

He played the role of a heroin addict in *American Buffalo* in 1983, and died that year after taking an overdose of heroin.

Walter Slezak was born in Vienna, Austria on May 3rd, 1902. When he was twenty years old, the Hungarian director Mihaly Kertesz (later named Michael Curtiz) offered him a role in *Sodom und Gomorrah*, released in 1922.

After coming to the U. S. in 1930, he immediately landed parts on the New York stage. By 1950, he was a Broadway star. Slezak won acclaim for his appearance in the film, *Lifeboat* in 1944. Between 1922 and 1980 he appeared in ninety-six television and film roles.

He was the father of Erica Slezak, the award-winning actress on the popular daytime soap opera, *One Life To Live.*

Depressed over numerous health problems, shortly before his 81st birthday,

Slezak shot and killed himself on April 21, 1983. He is buried in the Bavarian village Rottach-Egern.

Carol Wayne was a comedienne and actress probably best known for playing the *Matinee Lady* in the '60s, sharing comedy routines with Johnny Carson on *The Tonight Show.*

She worked with Peter Sellers in *The Party* in 1968, and married television producer Burt Sugarman in 1975. For the next five years, she appeared on Sugarman's various game shows.

Wayne and Sugarman divorced five years later, and with the help of Lee Majors, she worked in several episodes of *The Fall Guy.*

In 1984, Carol appeared in the nude in the February issue of Playboy. By that time, Carol had a serious drug habit.

In December of 1984, Carol went to Manzanillo, Mexico with Ed Durston. Two weeks later the pair missed their flight to LAX. When they tried to get rooms in the same hotel they had been staying in, the clerk told them that there were no vacancies, and recommended that they try the Playa de Santiago. Carol reportedly shouted that she "would not be caught dead in that dump" and left the hotel lobby alone.

Durston went to the Santiago and registered for two rooms in both names. The next morning he checked them both out, took his and her luggage, and took a cab to the airport. He left Carol's luggage at the airline desk, saying that she would pick it up shortly, and flew back to Los Angeles.

On January 13th 1985, Carol's body was discovered in Santiago Bay by a local fisherman. She was cremated and the location of her ashes is unknown.

While filming a high speed chase in *For Your Eyes Only* (1981), the four-man team came out of the bobsled run at the wrong place and hit a tree. One of them, **Paolo Rigon**, a stuntman, was killed.

On November 21, 1986, on the set of the film *Million Dollar Mystery*, **Dar**

Robinson rode his stunt motorcycle off a cliff to his death.

Stunt pilot, **Art Scholl** died on September 16, 1985, when working on, *Top Gun.* He was unable to pull out of a spin.

While performing a 78 foot fall during the filming of *The Sword and the Sorcerer* in 1981, stunt man **Jack Tyree** was killed when he hit an airbag off center.

Rodney Mitchell, Assistant Camera man, was killed when a camera truck flipped over during the filming of *The Dukes of Hazzard* in 1980.

Rob Van Der Kar, camera man, was killed when a helicopter crashed during the filming of *Magnum, P. I.* in 1980.

During the filming of *The Five of Me* in 1981, a driverless auto hit and killed **Jack Tandberg,** assistant camera man.

Bruce Ingram, assistant camera man, was killed during the filming of *The Wraith* (1986), when a camera car crashed.

On September 19, 1988, actor, **Roy Kinnear**, fell from a horse during filming of, *The Return of the Three Musketeers.* He broke his pelvis and died the next day from complications.

Don (Red) Barry was born on January 11th, 1911 in Houston, Texas. Although some say his last name was de Acosta, Don chose to use Barry, his mother's last name. There is no official record of his father's name, however, this statement was made in June, 2009, by one Linda Poinboeuf Denyer: "Don was my first cousin. His father and my dad, Julius Joseph Poinboeuf, were brothers. Don's real name was Milton Poimboeuf, and his dad was Leonce. Our fathers were the first generation to be born in the U.S. Our grandfather, Jules, was from France. Our grandmother, Regina Acosta, was from Barcelona, Spain."

When Don grew up, he played football at the Texas School of Mines before moving to Hollywood.

Barry appeared in 246 film and television parts between 1933 and 1981. His first western role, made for Republic in 1939, was *Saga of Death Valley.*

The following year he was chosen to play Red Ryder in the Republic serial,

Adventures of Red Ryder. It was this role that gave him the nickname "Red".

Don Barry as Red Ryder with Tommy Cook as Little Beaver.

The Studio Chief at Republic decided Barry could be their version of James Cagney because Barry was short, scrappy, and had a feisty personality. Barry's acting abilities were proved in the World War Two film, *The Purple Heart*, released in 1944. However, his combative attitude and huge ego resulted in many of the casts and crews he worked with detesting him. Republic Director William Witney once called him "the midget". Director John English worked with him once and refused to work with him again.

Barry worked mostly in "B" westerns in the 40s and 50s, acting in roles that got smaller and smaller. One more or less typical example of his work was as a black-clad gunfighter in a 1961 episode of the western television series *Maverick*.

On July 17, 1980, police officers showed up at his North Hollywood home following a call regarding a fight between Don and his wife, Barbara. Barry came out of his house, pointed a pistol at his head, and pulled the trigger. He is buried in forest Lawn Memorial Park in the Hollywood Hills.

Dorothy Stratten (Dorothy Ruth Hoogstraten) was born in a Salvation Army hospital in Vancouver, British Columbia in 1960. At age seventeen, while attending Centennial High School in Coquitlam she met a pimp named Paul Snider. Snider talked her into having nude photos made, and he sent them to Playboy magazine. She later married him.

The two moved to Los Angeles where she was made Playboy's Miss August in 1979. She then went to work as a bunny at the Century City Playboy Club. She later she landed parts in the television series *Buck Rogers* and had a minor role in *Skatetown, U.S.A.*

Stratten and Peter Bogdanovich became involved when he directed her in *They All Laughed*. That turned out to be her first and only part in a major film. She and Bogdanovich planned to marry as soon as she could divorce Snider.

Shortly after noon on August 14, 1980 Snider met Stratten at his home on August 14, 1980 to discuss the divorce; instead, he killed her and himself with a shotgun.

Dorothy is buried in Westwood Memorial Cemetery in Los Angeles, California.

10881 Clarkson Road, West Los Angeles where Dorothy Stratten was murdered.

Rachel Roberts was born in Llanelli, Carmarthenshire, Wales, on September 20, 1927. She moved to London, where she did some stage work. Between 1953 and 1980, she appeared in forty-four film and television roles. She is most remembered for her portrayal of Mrs Appleyard in *Picnic at Hanging Rock*.

In her personal life, she met and married Alan Dobie in 1955. They divorced in 1961. She then married Rex Harrison in 1962, but they divorced in 1971.

Broken hearted and hoping to start a new life, she moved to Hollywood in 1975. When she made one more attempt to win Harrison back in 1980, but that failed. Devastated, she committed suicide on 26 November 1980, at her home in Los Angeles.

It was reported that she died as a result swallowing lye, alkali, or some other unidentified caustic substance, as well as having ingested barbiturates and alcohol. The corrosive effect of the poisonous agent was an immediate cause of her death. Her death was ruled a suicide. She was fifty-three years old.

Rachel was cremated at the Chapel of the Pines Crematory in Los Angeles. In 1992, her ashes were scattered on the banks of the River Thames in London.

Jenny Maxwell born in 1941, was a distant relative of Marilyn Monroe. She played Ellie Corbett in *Blue Hawaii* opposite Elvis Presley.

In 1981, Maxwell was shot and killed outside of her Beverly Hills condo during a botched robbery.

Boris Sagal was born in Yekaterinoslav, Soviet Union on October 18, 1923. He went to the Yale School of Drama after emigrating to the U. S. He then moved to Hollywood where he directed ninety-six movies, including *Omega Man* starring Charlton Heston. He is the father of actors Katie, Joe, Jean and Liz Sagal.

While working on the television miniseries, *World War III*, on May 22, 1981, he apparently turned the wrong way when exiting a helicopter and walked into the moving tail rotor. Partially decapitated, he died five hours later in a Portland hospital.

Boris is buried in Forest Lawn Memorial Park-Hollywood Hills in Los Angeles.

William Holden was born William Franklin Beedle, Jr. in O'Fallon, Illinois on April 17, 1918. In 1921, Holden's family moved to South Pasadena where he graduated South Pasadena High School.

Holden was signed by Paramount Pictures in 1937 after a scout heard his performance in a Pasadena radio broadcast. Columbia Pictures shared Holden's contract, and he worked in thirteen "B" films between 1938 and 1943, before joining the Air Force. At the end of World War Two, he returned to acting and appeared in sixty-one more films before his death. He is probably best known for his portrayal of Joe Gillis in the 1950 release of *Sunset Blvd*, but he also gave outstanding performances in *Picnic*, released in 1955, and *The Bridge On the River Kwai* released in 1957.Between 1938 and 1981, Holden appeared in a total of seventy-four films.

Holden was married to Brenda Marshall for thirty years. He had a short affair with Audrey Hepburn in 1954. They planned to marry, but Hepburn, who wanted children, learned that Holden had had a vasectomy, and broke off their relationship.

Holden was involved in an automobile accident in Italy in 1966. He was drunk at the time, and the other driver died. He received a suspended sentence.

Holden's body was found in his apartment on November 16, 1981. He evidently fell against a table while drunk, cut his head, and bled to death.

535 Ocean Ave., Santa Monica, California
The Shorecliff Towers where William Holden died.

He was cremated and his ashes were scattered in the Pacific Ocean.

Natalie Wood was born Natalia Nikolaevna Zakharenko in San Francisco on July 20, 1938. Later that year, Natalie's family moved to Santa Rosa. It was there that she received a contract offer after being seen while watching a movie being shot.

She and her mother moved to Hollywood, and at age four, Natalie was given a part in the film, *Happy Land*, released in 1943. Her most popular role as a child came in 1947, when, at age nine, she portrayed Susan Walker in *Miracle On 42nd Street*.

Natalie 1946

Natalie performed in seventy television and film parts between 1943 and 1983.

When she was sixteen. Natalie became involved in a sexual relationship with director Nicholas Ray. Ray, known to be bisexual, was forty-three years old at the time. He should have been charged with statutory rape, but the studio covered the crime up

In 1957, Natalie married Robert Wagner. She was eighteen, and he was twenty-seven. In 1996, Natalie divorced Wagner after discovering him having sex with another man. She attempted suicide in 1966, underwent psychological treatment and retired from acting.

In 1969, she married producer Richard Gregson. They separated in 1971 when she learned that he was having an affair. They divorced in 1972, and she remarried Wagner.

Natalie's last acting role was in *Brainstorm*, released after her death. She invited her co-star, Christopher Walken to spend a weekend with her and Wagner aboard their yacht. On November 28, 1981, while the boat was moored off Catalina Island, Natalie, intoxicated, attempted to board a dinghy, fell into the water, and drowned. The cause and circumstance remain a mystery.

She is buried in Westwood Memorial Park in Los Angeles, California.

On July 7, 2012, Los Angeles County Coroner announced that he had altered Natalie's death certificate; the cause now reads "undetermined", instead of "accident". This resulted from what detectives said was new evidence.

John Adam Belushi was born in Chicago on January 24, 1949, the son of a restaurant operator. He went to Wheaton Central High School, and then joined The Second City comedy troupe in 1971. The following year National Lampoon gave him a part in *Lemmings*, an Off-Broadway production.

He moved to New York in '73 and had a continuing part there in *The National Lampoon Radio Hour* for two years. John's next job was on *Saturday Night Live*. That lasted until 1979, and it was in that period that he appeared in *Animal House*.

Belushi moved to Hollywood after leaving *Saturday Night Live*, with the intention of becoming a film actor. Between 1979 and 1982 he starred in *Neighbors, The Blues Brothers*, and two other movies.

On March 5, 1982, Belushi spent that evening with Robin Williams, Robert DeNiro, and another friend, Catherine Smith. After Williams and DeNiro left, he killed himself by accidentally taking cocaine and heroin together (known as a speedball).

Smith later told a National Enquirer reporter that she had given Belushi the drugs that killed him. As a result, she was extradited from Toronto and charged with first-degree murder. The charge was later lowered to involuntary manslaughter, and she served fifteen months in prison.

8221 Sunset Blvd., West Hollywood, the Chateau Marmont Hotel, where John Belushi died.

Belushi is buried in Elmwood Cemetery and Mausoleum, River Grove, Illinois.

Brenda Benet was born Brenda Ann Nelson on August 14, 1945 in **Hollywood, California**. In 1964, Brenda first appeared on television in such shows as *Shindig!* She was very much in demand as a television actress throughout 60s and the 70s and also appeared in the film *Walking Tall* in 1973. But she is probably best remembered for her performances from 1979-1982 in the daytime soap opera, *Days of our Lives*.

After two failed marriages, first to actor Paul Peterson and then to Bill Bixby, with whom she had a son, Brenda entered into a lesbian relationship. She stayed with **Tammy Bruce**, a Republican political pundit, until two weeks before her death.

Brenda sank into severe depression after her only son died, and on April 7, 1982, she shot herself in the head and died. Brenda was thirty-six.

Romy Schneider was born Rosemarie Magdalena Albach in Nazi-era Vienna on September 23, 1938. She appeared in sixty-two movies between 1953 and 1982, after making her first film at the age of fifteen. Romy spent a few years in Hollywood in the middle 1960s. She appeared in the 1964 film, *Good Neighbor Sam*, and then in *What's New Pussycat,* which was released in 1965.

Romy married Harry Meyen, a German director and actor in 1966. He committed suicide thirteen years later. Their son, David Christopher, born on

December 3, 1966, was killed when he was fourteen, while attempting to climb a spiked fence. He severed an artery and bled to death.

After her son had died, Romy began to drink heavily, and on May 29, 1982, she committed suicide by ingesting a mixture of alcohol and sleeping pills. She is buried in the Canton of the Monfort-l'Amaury. Her tombstone bears the name of Rosemarie Albach. Her long-time friend, actor Alain Delon, arranged for her son, David, to be buried in the same grave.

Vic Morrow was born Victor Morozoff on February 14, 1929 in the Bronx, New York.

He dropped out of school at seventeen to join the U. S.. Navy. After the Navy, he used his G.I. benefits to go to college. It was there, after taking part in a college drama production, he realized he wanted to act, so he moved to New York City and enrolled in the Actor's Workshop. His first movie role was playing a street punk in the 1955 film, *Blackboard Jungle*. He continued to act in various television and film productions, until in 1962 when he was cast in the television World War Two hit, *Combat*. When the series ended, he appeared in mostly made-for-TV and "B" movies.

Then in 1982, he landed a role in *Twilight Zone: The Movie*, a science fiction film that was released in 1983. It was written to be a reproduction of the very popular television series *The Twilight Zone*.

The first segment concerns a big-mouthed bigot played by Vic. During filming, Morrow and two children were killed when a helicopter spun out of control and landed on top of them. All three died instantly; decapitated by the helicopter's blades. It was later learned that the two children were employed contrary to California child-labor laws, which forbade children to work an hour past curfew.

Vic is buried in the Hillside Memorial Park in Culver City California.

Dominique Dunne was born in Santa Monica, California in 1959. Her first performance was in the television production of *Diary of a Teenage Hitchhiker* in 1979. In the 1980s, she played minor roles in *Family, Hart to Hart,* and *Fame.* In 1982, she landed a part in *Poltergeist.* That same year she began living with John Thomas Sweeney, who was sous-chef at the restaurant Ma Maison in Los Angeles. Sweeney turned out to be a wife beater, and she left him. On October 30, just two weeks later, Sweeney strangled Dunne in front of her home. Taken to a hospital she lived five days, and then died on November 4.

8723 Rangely Ave., West Hollywood: where Dominique died.

She was interred in the Westwood Memorial Park in Los Angeles.

Tennessee Williams was born Thomas Lanier Williams III in Columbus, Mississippi on March 26, 1911. He spent his early years in his grandfather's home in Clarksdale.

Williams studied journalism at the University of Missouri from 1929 to 1931 and graduated the University of Iowa, in 1938.

He had a few heterosexual relationships as a young man, but by the late 1930s he had settled into homosexual life style and became part of a gay group in New York. Williams began an affair with Kip Kiernan, a young dancer in 1940, but Kiernan left him and married a woman. This left Williams depressed, and that state of mind increased when he heard that Kiernan had died.

Williams met Pancho Rodriguez y Gonzales in Taos, New Mexico in 1945; Gonzales was a Mexican hotel clerk. The next year Rodriguez moved to New Orleans to be with Williams, and remained there for two years.

Williams next fell in love with Frank Merlo in 1948, and they remained together for the next fifteen years.

Between 1948 and 1983, Williams wrote eighty-one plays, screenplays, and short stories. By 1960, Williams was an alcoholic and drug abuser. As a result, his writings during the 1960s and '70s were not up to the level of his original efforts.

Williams' depression became so severe that he was hospitalized several times. His doctor kept injecting him with larger and larger doses of amphetamines to fight his depression, and later gave him Seconal for his insomnia. Williams never overcame his addiction to these drugs.

1995 stamp issue

Williams died in his hotel room, in New York, on February 25, 1983. He had a peculiar habit; when he used eye drops, he placed the bottle cap in his mouth, leaned his head back, and injected the drop. That night, the cap became lodged in his throat and strangled him.

He is buried in Calvary Cemetery in St. Louis, Missouri.

Doodles Weaver was born Winstead Sheffield Glenndenning Dixon Weaver to a wealthy family in Los Angeles on May 11, 1912. His older brother was the president of NBC during the 1950s; and he was Sigourney Weaver's uncle.

Weaver worked in radio during the 1930s and 1940s, and appeared in his first film role in 1936. Between 1936 and 1981 he had 139 roles in television and film.

Weaver is probably best remembered for his work with Spike Jones, particularly for his role as Professor Feetlebaum. He was given his own series *A Day With Doodles* in 1964, but it only aired nine times.

Weaver became an alcoholic, and as a result, ceased getting work in television or film. His health failing, he died from two self-inflicted gunshots to his chest in 1983. He is buried in the Avalon Cemetery on Santa Catalina Island.

Peter Scott Ivers was born on September 20th, 1946 in Illinois, and grew up on the outskirts of Boston, Massachusetts. He majored in language at Harvard University, and is perhaps best known for hosting the TV show, *New Wave Theater.*

Ivers began his musical career in 1969 with the release of his composition, Knight of the Blue Communion, published by Epic. Take It Out On Me, published by Epic in 1971 failed to be popular, and Ives then signed a contract with Warner Bros.

In 1976, David Lynch hired Ivers to write some music for use in the cult classic film, *Eraserhead*. Ivers wrote the song sang by the lady in the radiator, *In Heaven*.

In 1981, Ivers accepted the position of Host of the television show, *New Wave Theater* in Los Angeles. Two years later, he was discovered in his apartment beaten to death by someone using a hammer. No one was ever charged with the crime.

Ivers is credited with five television and film soundtracks, three musical scores for TV and film, and acting in one film.

Joseph Svec, stunt man, was killed in 1983 while making *The Right Stuff*. For an unknown reason, he failed to open his parachute after jumping from a plane.

Three men, **Nigel Thornton**, pilot, **Jaron Anderson**, mechanic, and **David Perrin**, stunt pilot, were killed while filming *High Road to China* in 1983, when their helicopter crashed.

A race car swerved off the track while *Midnight Spares* was being filmed in 1983. The car hit and killed Focus-puller **David Brostoff.**

Dennis Carl Wilson was born in Hawthorne, California on December 4, 1944. He and his two brothers formed the Beach Boys in 1961. Dennis had no musical talent so his brother Brian assigned the drums to him. Dennis soon mastered the drums and later added the guitar and piano to his musical skills. His first musical composition was <u>Little Bird</u>. Dennis' music appeared in seven soundtracks between 1979 and 2010.

Dennis picked up two female hitchhikers in 1968. Later he picked the same girls up again and drove them to his home. He left them there while he attended to some business, and when he returned he discovered that his house was full of strangers. Among this mixed group was Charles Manson. Dennis was taken with the Manson family and allowed them to live with him, paying their expenses for some time. When Dennis finally recognized the madness that Manson's group shared, he moved away and left them.

Manson's musical writing ability had impressed Dennis so much that he introduced Manson to Terry Melcher who was in the music publishing business. Roman Polanski rented Melcher's home shortly thereafter, and it was here that Manson's people brutally murdered Polanski's wife, Sharon Tate and several others in August, 1969.

Dennis appeared in one movie, *The Mechanic* released in 1971.

Wilson married Carole Freedman, and they had a daughter. When they divorced he married Barbara Charren. The marriage produced two sons. He married Karen Lamm twice.

Dennis' last marriage was to Shawn Love who was said to be Mike Love's illegitimate daughter. Mike was one of the Beach Boys. Over the years, Wilson became an alcoholic and drug abuser. He drowned on December 28, 1983 while swimming off his boat at Marina Del Rey.

On January 4, 1984, he was buried at sea off the California coast by the U.S. Coast Guard.

Marvin Gaye was born in Washington, D.C in 1939. His father was a minister at the House of God. Gaye started playing musical instruments while still a teenager. After entering high school, he started running away from home in order to attend R&B concerts.

He joined the Air Force when he was sixteen and proved to be a poor military man. His refusal to obey orders resulted in an honorable discharge for medical reasons.

After he returned home he went to work as a dishwasher, and joined up with a four member musical group known as the Marquees.

Bo Diddley signed the Marquees to a contract with Okeh Records in 1958, and later that same year Harvey Fuqua made them part of his group, The New Moonglows. They also made background vocals for Chuck Berry and Etta James.

In late 1959, Gaye was arrested for possession of marijuana.

Gaye signed on with Motown, and his first job was road drummer for The Miracles. He made a single, **Pride & Joy** in 1963, and it became a hit, selling closed to one million copies. That same year his **Can I Get a Witness** was in the top 30. This was followed by **Ain't No Mountain High Enough.** He recorded **I Heard It through the Grapevine** in April, 1967, before Gladys Knight and the Pips performed the song.

In 1972, Gaye left Detroit and moved to Los Angeles. Six years later he began to appear on talk shows circuits such as *Dinah Shore & Friends*, and he went on tours in the U. S., England, and Japan. By that time, he was using drugs on a regular basis.

He later moved in with his parents in Los Angeles. His friends have said that his mental and physical condition deteriorated severely and that he threatened suicide several times because of his poor relationship with his father.

Gaye's father killed him on April 1, 1984, when Marvin intervened in an argument his father was having with his mother.

2101 S. Gramercy Place, Los Angeles, where Marvin Gaye was murdered.

He was cremated and his ashes scattered in the Pacific Ocean.

Truman Capote was born on September 30, 1924 in New Orleans. His mother left him with relatives, who raised him until he was fourteen when he was returned to her in New York City. At the age of sixteen, he quit school and went to work for *The New Yorker*, thus beginning his writing career.

He published his first novel, *Other Voices, Other Rooms,* in 1948 and won immediate recognition for his writing talent. His novel, *Breakfast at Tiffany's*, and the subsequent film adaptation, released in 1961 made him a national figure.

Capote worked on *In Cold Blood* from 1959 to 1966. Its publication made him a millionaire. Between 1953 and 2002 he wrote twenty-five short stories, books, and television and movie scripts.

Capote then started work on a book titled *Answered Prayers*. Early chapters were published by *Esquire* in 1965, and the revelation of intimate details about his friends caused a negative backlash that drove him to alcoholism and drug addiction.

Capote spent the remainder of his life sponging off admirers while spending book advances paid against *Answered Prayers* that he never earned.

He died in 1984 at age fifty-nine from cirrhosis of the liver brought on by alcoholism and drug addiction.

Truman was interred in the Westwood Memorial Park in Los Angeles.

Gary Vinson was born in Los Angeles on October 22, 1936. He took up acting as a career at the age of twenty-one, appearing in minor roles in television shows such as *Perry Mason* and *Gunsmoke.*

Vinson had parts in a total of sixty-nine television and films between 1957 and 1983.

It is rumored, Vinson was facing charges of child molestation when he killed himself on October 15, 1984. He is buried in the Evergreen Cemetery in Los Angeles, California.

Jon-Erik Hexum was born in Englewood, New Jersey on November 5, 1957. Between 1982 and 1984, Jon appeared in six television and movie roles. He played the part of Phineas Bogg in twenty episodes of the television series *Voyagers* in 1982 and 1983.

While Hexum was working on a scene in the film, *Cover Up* in 1984, his character had to remove the bullets from a 44-calibre pistol, and reload blanks in their place. To pass time while waiting for everything to be arranged he started playing Russian roulette with the weapon. He loaded three empty cartridges and two blank cartridges into the chambers, pointed the gun at his temple, and pulled the trigger.

Blank cartridges have paper wadding in them. When he pulled the trigger the wadding fractured his skull, and part of the resulting bone fragments penetrated his brain. He was operated on, but on October 18, 1984, he was declared brain dead.

Richard Burton was born on November 10, 1925 in the village of Pontrhydyfen, Neath Port Talbot, Wales. He was two years old when his mother died giving birth to her thirteenth child. He then went to live with his sister's family in the nearby town of Port Talbot. During World War Two, he served in the RAF as a navigator. After the war, he worked in England both on stage and in motion pictures.

Burton's first appearance in a movie took place in the 1947 release of *The Last Days of Dolwyn*. He met his first wife there, and after two children, they divorced in 1963 as a result of his public affair with Elizabeth Taylor. Burton had supporting roles in *Now Barabbas Was a Robber*, released in 1950, and the 1951 production, *The Woman with No Name*.

Burton moved to Hollywood in 1952, when he landed the lead in *My Cousin Rachel*. His next part was in *Desert Rats*, which was made the following year.

He became a major star in 1954 following his performance in *The Robe*. His next film appearance was in *Cleopatra*, released in 1963, and it was at this time that he became romantically involved with Elizabeth Taylor. They married in 1964.

Burton and Taylor in *Cleopatra*

Burton admitted in interviews that he had experimented with homosexual liaisons. According to Taylor, he had once been involved with Laurence Olivier and had attempted to start an affair with Eddie Fisher.

Burton was known to be an alcoholic and addicted to pain medication. He is said to have smoked as many as one hundred cigarettes a day.

On August 5, 1984, Burton suffered a brain hemorrhage. His health was poor due to cirrhosis of the liver probably resulting from his addictions.

Special Effects man, **Cliff Wenger, Jr.**, was killed in 1985 while working on the film *Rambo, First Blood Part II*, when an explosion went bad.

While filming *Runaway Train* (1985), a helicopter crashed, killing pilot **Rick Holley.**

Gian-Carlo Coppola was born in Los Angeles, California on September 17, 1963. He was director Francis Ford Coppola's son. Between 1972 and 1983 he appeared in five film and television roles.

On May 26, 1986, Gian-Carlo was a passenger in a speed-boat being piloted by Ryan O'Neal's son, Griffin O'Neal. Not seeing that a boat in front of them was towing the boat behind it, Griffin steered the boat between them. Griffin ducked the towline, but Gian-Carlo was decapitated.

O'Neal pleaded guilty to a charge of negligent operation of a boat and received a year-and-a- half of probation. Failing to do community service as ordered by the judge, he served eighteen days in jail.

Susan Cabot was born Harriet Shapiro in Boston, Massachusetts in 1927. Her early jobs included nightclub singer and reading radio ads. She did some television work, and through that Columbia Pictures gave her a short contract. After the contract expired, Universal signed her to an exclusive contract. Her first roles were in "B" westerns. Growing tired of the monotony, she asked for and was given a release from her contract.

Returning to New York, she landed a role in *A Stone for Danny Fisher* and was once again offered work in Hollywood. In 1960, she appeared in *The Wasp Woman*, and that turned out to be her last movie part. She was 33 years old when she quit acting.

She married Michael Roman in 1968 and gave birth to a son before they divorced in 1983. The boy was a dwarf, and he had serious mental problems. On

December 10, 1986, he beat Susan to death with a piece of weight lifting equipment. He was given a three-year suspended sentence on a charge of manslaughter.

Susan was interred in the Hillside Memorial Park, Culver City, California.

Victor Magnotta, stunt man, drove a car off a pier and into the Hudson River in 1987 while shooting *The Squeeze*. He failed to escape the vehicle and drowned.

Dar Robinson, stunt man, died when he drove a motorcycle off a cliff during filming of *Million Dollar Mystery* in 1987.

Joyce Jameson was born in Chicago, Illinois on September 26, 1932. Her first film role was in *Show Boat*, released in 1951. She appeared in 112 television and film parts between 1951 and 1984, including the part of Rose in *The Outlaw Jose Wales*, released in 1976.

Although she was often typecast as the floozy-type, she was educated and well-read.

Jamison is said to have suffered from insomnia and depression for which she took Miltowns. She overdosed on prescription drugs in 1987. After cremation, her ashes were scattered at sea.

Edgar Rosenberg was born on September 21st, 1925 in Bavaria, Germany. His parents, Jews, moved him to Denmark, and later to South Africa, in order to escape Nazi anti-Semitism.

Edgar was educated at Cambridge, England, and after graduating, moved to Los Angeles, California, where he went to work for NBC. He eventually attained the position of Assistant to Emanuel Sacks, Vice-president in charge of Entertainment.

Edgar was badly injured in a traffic accident, and was unable to work for nearly a year. NBC fired him, and he worked for a while as Night Clerk in a Los Angeles book store.

In the early '60s, he went to work for the public relations company.

Edgar married Joan Rivers in July 1965, just four days after hiring her to assist him to rewrite a screenplay for a joint movie deal made with his friend Peter Sellers. He served as his wife's manager for most of their marriage and was producer of *The Late Show,* which starred her. They had one daughter, Melissa Rivers.

Edgar formed a production company, Telsun Foundations, which released five movies.

Edgar suffered a major heart attack in 1984, had open heart surgery, and was said to be deeply depressed afterward.

In August of 1987, Joan was fired by Fox, the producer of *The Late Show*, and she and Edgar separated shortly thereafter. In early August, 1987, Edgar went to Philadelphia to visit Tom Pileggi, a man that he called his closest friend. They were often partners in real estate ventures. On August 14th, Edgar committed suicide in a Philadelphia hotel room by overdosing on the prescription drug Valium, combined with alcohol. He was just sixty-two years old. Edgar's daughter, Melissa, age nineteen at the time, was notified of her father's death, and it became her responsibility to tell Joan. Edgar left suicide notes to both his wife and daughter.

Judith Barsi, born in 1978, grew up in Los Angeles. She was discovered by a talent scout at the age of five while she was roller skating. Barsi appeared to be at least two years younger than she actually was. For this reason she became a popular child actress, and appeared in more than seventy television commercials.

Barsi was earning approximately $100,000 a year by the time she was in the 4th grade. This fact evidently created psychological problems for her father as he became extremely abusive and paranoid, threatening suicide on several occasions, as well as making death threats against his daughter.

Barsi was given a role in *Jaws, The Revenge*, and before she left to go on location, her mother reported that her father told the girl, "If you decide not to come back, I will cut your throat." Fear of her father caused Barsi to have a mental breakdown. On Barsi's agent's advice, her mother took her to a psychologist who reported the father's abuse to Child Protective Services.

Barsi's mother promised CPS employees that she would divorce her husband and move into separate living quarters. She did not keep her promise.

On July 25, 1988, Barsi was murdered by her father. He shot her while she slept, and then killed his wife. After pouring gasoline on the bodies, and setting them afire, he committed suicide.

Judith is buried in Forest Lawn Memorial Park (Hollywood Hill) in Los Angeles, California.

Richard Quine, an American stage, film, and radio actor, was born in Detroit on November 12, 1920. He first appeared in the Broadway production of *Very Warm for May* in 1939, followed by *My Sister Eileen* the following year.

He served in the Coast Guard during World War Two and married actress Susan Peters in 1943. In 1945, his wife was paralyzed from the waist down in a hunting accident. They divorced three years later, and she died of anorexia three years after that. He was engaged for a short time to Kim Novak and later married and divorced three additional times.

He appeared in a total of forty-two film and television roles between 1948 and 1980.

Quine suffered from depression and other health related problems and killed himself with a pistol on June 10, 1989. He is buried in Westwood Memorial Park in Los Angeles, California.

John Daniel "Tooz" Matuszak was born on October 25th, 1950, in Oak Creek, Wisconsin. He was always big for his age. When he eventually became a professional football player, he stood 6 feet 8 inches tall and weighed over 280 pounds. John attended the University of Tampa, where he was the star of their football team. One of his UT teammates was future professional wrestler Paul Orndorff.

When he turned pro, John was the first draft pick of 1973 by the Houston Oilers of the NFL. He spent the end of his career playing for the Oakland Raiders, and retired after winning his second Super Bowl in 1981. Matuszak placed ninth when he took part in the 1978 *World's Strongest Man* competition,

In his autobiography, John said that he took many painkillers as well as other narcotics while playing professional football. Because of this admission, Sports Illustrated, in 2005, named him one of the top five all-time "bad boys" of the NFL.

In the summer of 1976, while a member of the Kansas City Chiefs, John was taken by auto to a hospital after drinking beer and wine and taking sleeping pills. Paul Wiggin, then the coach of the Chiefs, drove Matuszak to the hospital and pounded on the player's chest after his heart had stopped beating.

Matuszak took up acting in the 1980s, working in both movies and television. His first major role was in *The North Dallas Forty*, released in 1979. He played a football player. He later had parts in *Caveman* (1981), *The Ice Pirates* (1984), and *One Man Force* (1989, but is perhaps best remembered for his role as the deformed, captive Sloth in *The Goonies*.

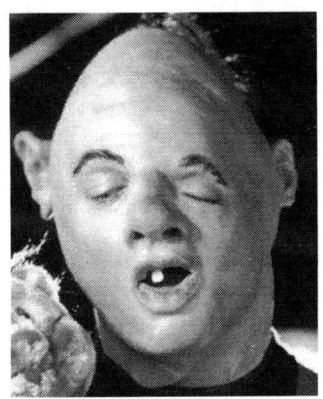

John as the Sloth

John made many guest appearances on television shows such as *Perfect Strangers, M*A*S*H, The Dukes of Hazzard, Hunter, Silver Spoons, The A-Team, 1st & Ten, Miami Vice* and *Cheers*. He appeared in thirty-three movie and television roles between 1979 and 1990.

John died on June 17, 1989 in Burbank, California. The Los Angeles County Coroner's Office reported that his death was the result of acute propoxyphene intoxication. Propoxyphene is the generic name of the narcotic ingredient used in the prescription pain medicines Darvon and Darvocet. The report also said that John had cocaine in his blood at the time of his death.

Rebecca Schaeffer, born in 1989, was the only child of a child psychologist and a writer. As a teen, she began modeling, appeared in television commercials, and as an extra in a television movie. After appearing on the cover of *16 Magazine*, she was given the part of Patti Russell in the television series *My Sister Sam*.

On July 18, 1989, a stalker fan, Robert Bardo rang her door front intercom. It was not working properly, and she had to go to the door. As she opened the door, Bardo shot her and ran. Schaeffer was killed instantly. After shooting Schaeffer, Bardo returned home to Tucson by bus. In Tucson, he was arrested for walking in traffic on a freeway; perhaps attempting to commit suicide.

A female relative of Bardo's called the Los Angeles Police while Bardo was being held in a Tucson jail, and told them Bardo had told her he was going to Los Angeles to visit Schaeffer the day before the murder. He was sentenced to life in prison without possibility of parole.

120 Sweetzer Ave. in North Hollywood, where Rebecca Schaeffer was murdered.

She is buried in Ahavai Sholom Cemetery in Portland, Oregon.

Chapter Nine: the Nineties

Movie attendance was high in most of the 1990s. Multi-screen theaters were popular all across the U. S. The average movie cost almost $53 million to produce by 1998, and a large percentage ran as high as $100 million or more. In the early part of the decade, box-office revenues had dropped because of the economic recession of 1991. They were back up by 1993 and increased for the remainder of the year. The average ticket price ranged from around $4.25 at the beginning of the year, to about $5 by the end. While the number of multi-screen theaters increased from 23,000 in 1990 to 35,600 in 2000, the number of drive-ins dropped from 910 in 1990 to 667 in 2000.

In the mid-1990s, demands made by the highest-paid movie stars such as Tom Cruise, Mel Gibson, Eddie Murphy, Kevin Costner, Harrison Ford, Robin Williams, and many others, were incredibly expensive. Jack Nicholson wouldn't agree to filming during LA Lakers' basketball home games, and Harrison Ford, Kevin Costner and Tom Cruise required that movie studios pay for their private jets.

When promoting *Ghost,* released in 1990, Demi Moore traveled with an assistant, bodyguard, masseuse, hair stylist, cosmetician, fashion consultant, and a second assistant to help the first.

Warren Beatty's *Dick Tracy* (1990) was the *first* 35 mm feature film with a digital soundtrack.

Warner Communications and Time Inc. merged to form Time/Warner in 1990, the largest communications merger to date, at a cost of $14 billion.

Forrest Gump, released in 1994, used digital photo trickery to insert a person into historical footage, to erase the legs of amputee Gary Sinese, and to enhance the ping-pong game.

One of the trends that ran in the late '80s and early '90s was that many of the movies that were produced went directly to video, either laserdisc, DVD, or cable, with no theatrical release at all.

Japanese corporation Matsushita Industrial, Inc. acquired the entertainment conglomerate MCA/Universal for $6.1 billion in 1994.

While making *Mary Reilly*, released in 1996, Julia Roberts demanded a $10 million salary, and had the movie studio keep a jet ready in London to fly her from Pinewood Studios back to the United States.

Viacom bought Paramount Pictures in 1994 after a bidding war with USA Networks/QVC.

Disney became the first studio to gross $1 billion at the box office in 1994. Showtime Networks and Castle Rock Entertainment entered into a multi-year, 50-picture exclusive output deal in 1994.

It was significant that the first new Hollywood studio in many decades, DreamWorks (SKG), was formed in October 1994 as the brainchild of director-producer Steven Spielberg, ex-Disney executive producer Jeffrey Katzenberg, and film producer/music industry giant David Geffen.

Their first real hit was also their first film to be nominated for Best Picture, *Saving Private Ryan,* released in 1998.

By decade's end, DreamWorks had three consecutive Best Picture winners, these were Sam Mendes' suburban satire *American Beauty,* released in 1999, Ridley Scott's sword and sandal epic *Gladiator*, released in 2000, and Ron Howard's biopic *A Beautiful Mind*, released in 2001.

Seagram bought MCA/Universal from Matsushita for $5.7 billion in 1995 and renamed it Universal Studios.
Disney bought the ABC Network in 1995.
Time/Warner acquired Ted Turner's Turner Broadcasting System (TBS) in 1996, including its cable TV stations and its extensive film library.

Orion Pictures was sold to MGM in 1997.

Miramax Studios, was established by brothers and co-chairmen Harvey and Bob Weinstein in 1979. The organization produced and distributed independent movies, both foreign and domestic, and even mainstream films. Miramax became known by producing what are called "art" films; the small independent and foreign language movies that other studios refused to make. Among these are *Working Girls*, released in 1987, Italy's *Cinema Paradiso*, released in 1988, *My Left Foot*, released in 1989, and the winner written by former video store clerk Quentin Tarantino, Reservoir Dogs, released in 1992.

In 1993, Walt Disney Studio Entertainment purchased Miramax for $65 million dollars.

The best-paid female actress of the '90s was Julia Roberts. Her first movie was *Mystic Pizza,* released in 1988, followed by *Steel Magnolias,* released in 1989. She was nominated for Best Supporting Actress for this one. After doing *Pretty Woman* in 1990, she began to earn a million dollars per movie.

The best paid male star of the '90s was Tom Cruise, due to the popularity of films like *Days of Thunder*, released in 1990, *A Few Good Men*, released in 1992, *The*

Firm, released in 1993, *Interview with the Vampire*, released in 1994, *Mission: Impossible*, released in 1996, and *Eyes Wide Shut*, released in 1999.

Soon before its bankruptcy in 1991, Orion Pictures distributed the three-hour western, *Dances with Wolves*, released in 1990. The movie won Best Picture in that year's Academy Awards, as well as six other Oscars. Dances With Wolves was the first "western" to win Best Picture since *Cimarron*, which was released in 1931.

Ennis Cosby was the son of Bill Cosby. Ennis was driving down the 405 on January 16, 1997 intending to visit a friend. His car had a flat, and he pulled off on the Mulholland Drive exit where he was killed by a drive-by shooter.
Mikail "Michael" Markhasev, described as a "wannabe" gang member was charged for the murder, tried, found guilty and sentenced to life in prison.

Dennis Michael Crosby was born in the Los Angeles area on July 13, 1934; his father was Bing Crosby. Dennis graduated Bellarmine College in 1952, and was then drafted into the army.

In 1958, Crosby married a Las Vegas showgirl who had been Miss San Francisco of 1950, and Playmate of the month for October 1958. His father had once dated the same woman.

Dennis was sued in 1958 by Marilyn Scott, who claimed that he was the father of her daughter, Denise. The court ordered Dennis to pay for Denise's support. When Denise was nineteen, her grandfather, Bing Crosby, died; she had never been given an opportunity to meet him.

Between 1945 and 1965, Dennis appeared in five television and film roles. He also appeared in various television shows as himself.

It is reported that Bing Crosby was both physically and mentally abusive to his sons, and this might partially explain why Dennis' younger brother, Lindsay shot himself with a shotgun on December 11, 1989, and Dennis did the same on May 7, 1991. He is buried in the Holy Cross Cemetery in Culver City, California.

Robert Creel "Brad" Davis was born on November 6, 1949 in Tallahassee, Florida. Brad won a musical talent contest in 1965, and began his acting career by working at Theater Atlanta. He moved to New York City, where he studied at the American Academy of Dramatic Arts while working at the American Place Theater. He won a part in the television series *Roots,* in 1976, and followed that with a starring role in the film *Sybil.* Brad is best known for playing the lead role in the film, *Midnight Express*, released in 1978, which won him the Golden Globe Award for New Star of the Year.

Brad revealed to a reporter that he was bisexual, and in 1985 discovered that he had AIDS. He kept the fact secret until 1990.

On September 8th, 1991, Brad committed suicide by taking a drug overdose. He is buried at Forest Lawn Memorial Park (Hollywood Hills).

John Denver was born in Roswell, New Mexico on December 31, 1943. He received a guitar on his eleventh birthday, taught himself to play it, and picked up spending money by performing locally while a student at Texas Tech University.

In 1965, he moved to Los Angeles where he first earned his living singing in hippie coffee shops. Later that year he became a member of the Chad Mitchell Trio. John cut an album for RCA in 1969. One of the songs was *Leaving on A Jet Plane* which was picked up by Peter, Paul, and Mary, became number one on the Billboard Hot 100.

Between 1973 and 2009 John appeared in thirteen film and television productions. He is probably best known for playing Jerry Landers in the 1977 film, *Oh, God!*

John admitted in his autobiography that he used marijuana, cocaine, and LSD, and had attempted suicide once. The FAA revoked John's pilot's license in 1996 because of his continued heavy use of alcohol.

He died in 1997 after crashing his experimental airplane. He did not have a pilot's license, or a medical certification.

Denver's plane

Chris Farley was born in Madison, Wisconsin on February 15, 1964. He graduated Marquette University in 1986, and then began to work as a professional comedian at the Ark Improv Theatre, later moving to the Improv Olympic theater in Chicago.

In 1990, Farley joined the cast of *Saturday Night Live*. In 1992, Farley was given a minor role in *Wayne's World,* and between 1992 and 1998, he appeared in fifteen television and film roles.

Farley became an alcoholic and drug addict in Hollywood, and this caused him problems with his acting career. He went through rehab sixteen times.

He was found dead on December 18, 1997. The autopsy report indicated that he had overdosed on a combination of cocaine and morphine.

Edward Flanders was born in Minneapolis, Minnesota on December 29, 1934. After appearing in several Off-Broadway productions, Flanders began to work in television. Between 1967 and 1995 he appeared in fifty-six television and film roles, including 120 episodes of *St. Elsewhere*.

After experiencing two divorces, and severe financial difficulties, Flanders, suffering from depression, killed himself with a pistol on February 22, 1995. His ashes were given to family or a friend.

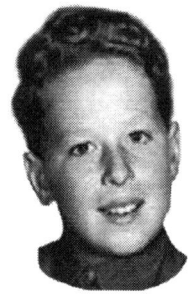

Rusty Hamer was born in Tenafly, New Jersey on February 15, 1947. At age five, he was given the role of Rusty in the television production, *Make Room for Daddy*. Between 1953 and 1971, he appeared in twelve television and film productions;

the role of Rusty being the best known. *Make Room for Daddy* ran for eleven seasons, and at its conclusion, Hammer, age seventeen found himself unable to get acting jobs. In 1970, he made a final effort, appearing in *Make Room for Granddaddy*, which ran for just one season.

Having spent most of his formative years in front of the camera, in 1972, when he gave up and moved to DeRidder, Louisiana, Rusty found he was mostly unable to transition out of the Hollywood life. He took jobs as an oil-rig worker and then as a short order cook.

Broke, depressed, and an alcoholic, he killed himself with a gunshot to the head on January 18, 1990. Rusty was cremated and his ashes scattered at sea.

Paul Peterson, another former child actor who was on *The Donna Reed Show*, was so moved by Rusty's suicide, he established a support group. "A Minor Consideration" works to improve working conditions for today's child actors and to assist former child stars to make the transition from childhood fame to adult life.

Rodney Harvey was born in Philadelphia, Pennsylvania, on July 31, 1967.

Film director Paul Morrissey gave Harvey roles in two of his films, *Mixed Blood*, released in 1985, and *Spike of Bensonhurst*, released in 1988. He also appeared in the television production, *The Outsiders* in 1990, and made a guest star appearance on *Twin Peaks*. He is known for his role in *My Own Private Idaho*. His last film role was in *God's Lonely Man*, released in 1996.

Harvey became a heroin addict while working on *My Own Private Idaho*, and after being sentenced to jail several times, he died of an overdose of heroin and cocaine on April 10, 1998 in Los Angeles.

Lois Hamilton was born Lois Aurino in Philadelphia, Pennsylvania on October 14, 1943. Hamilton moved to Hollywood after working as a model for several years, where she immediately found work on television.

Between 1972 and 2004, she appeared in twenty-three television and film roles, including five episodes of the television series, *The Ropers*, during 1979 and 1980.

She was also a successful artist, showing her sculpture and paintings in one-man shows in the Los Angeles area.

Hamilton was injured in an automobile accident in 1999 and suffered from on-going pain as a result. A few months after the accident, she flew to Rio de Janeiro,

Brazil, where she is said to have overdosed on sleeping pills. She is buried in the Valhalla Memorial Park in North Hollywood, California.

Phyllis Linda Hyman was born in Philadelphia on July 6, 1949. In 1975, Hyman was given a contract by Sid Maurer to sing on the Roadshow Records label. Between then and 1983, she recorded for several companies, including Arista. It was in this period that Hyman became addicted to cocaine.

Hyman appeared in three Hollywood productions between 1974 and 1989. She overdosed on Pentobarbital and Secobarbital in her New York apartment on June 30, 1995, a few hours before an appearance at the Apollo Theatre. The note she left read:

"I'm tired. I'm tired. Those of you that I love know who you are. May God bless you."

Phyllis was cremated and her ashes given to her family or a friend.

Luigi Pistilli was born in Grosetto, Italy on July 19, 1929. Between 1957 and 1995, he appeared in seventy-one U. S. and Italian television and film roles. He is probably best known for his parts in spaghetti westerns such as *The Good, the Bad, and the Ugly* released in 1966.

Pistilli appeared in *Tosca* in 1996, and his performances were harshly criticized. This and the end of a four year relationship with singer/actress Milva, threw him into a state of deep depression. On April 21, 1996, he took a dose of barbiturates and hung himself. He was buried in Cimitero di Cori Alto in Lazio, Italy beside his mother and son.

Robin Rochelle Stille was born in Philadelphia, Pennsylvania on November 24, 1961. After moving to Los Angeles, she graduated high school in Garden Grove, California in 1979. She began her acting career in *The Slumber Party Massacre*, which was released in 1982, and only appeared in a total of eight film and television roles between 1982 and 1990.

Said to have been an alcoholic and unable to find acting parts, Robin committed suicide in 1996. She is buried in Rose Hill Memorial Park in Whittier, California.

David Strickland Jr. was born on October 14, 1969 in Glen Cove, Long Island, New York. He appeared in eleven film and television roles between 1994 and 1999. Strickland is probably best known for his performances in the television series, *Suddenly Susan* which ran for seventy-one episodes between 1996 and 1999.

Strickland took lithium because of bipolar disorder, and he abused alcohol and drugs.

Charged with possession of cocaine in 1998, he was sentenced to three years probation. It has been reported that he ceased taking lithium as prescribed before he committed suicide by hanging himself with a bed sheet on March 22, 1999. He was cremated and his ashes given to his family or a friend.

On December 20, 1995, during the filming a Disney comedy, a boat flew off a ramp upside-down. It crashed into two other boats and killed a woman.

lint C. Carpenter, stuntman, died during the filming of *Hired to Kill* (1992).

During the filming of *Love Serenade* (1996), stuntman **Collin Dragsbaek** died when he fell from the top of a grain elevator onto a faulty airbag.

Sonja Davis, a stunt double, fell to her death while filming *Vampire in Brooklyn* (1995).

Del Shannon, born Charles Weedon Westover on December 30, 1934 in Grand Rapids, Michigan, he grew up in Coopersville, where he learned to play the guitar. He was sent to Germany in 1954 after being drafted into the army, where he played guitar in a band called The Cool Flames.

Shannon's first record was the classic <u>Runaway</u>, released in 1961. His last big hit <u>Keep Searchin'</u>, was released four years later.

Between 1962 and 2011, Shannon wrote and performed music for thirty-three television and film productions. His hit, <u>Runaway</u>, was used in several films after his death, such as *Cowboys and Angels* and *Good Will Hunting* between 1994 and 2000.

Depressed by his failing career, Shannon shot himself with a rifle in Santa Clarita, California on February 8, 1990. He was cremated and his ashes were scattered at sea.

Del Shannon was inducted into the Rock and Roll Hall of Fame in 1999.

Capucine was born Germaine Lefebvre in Toulon, France on January 6, 1933. When she was seventeen, she began modeling for the Givenchy and Christian Dior fashion houses. There she met the American actress Audrey Hepburn, and they became life-long friends.

Spotted by a movie producer while modeling in New York City in 1957, Capucine was signed to a contract by Columbia Pictures and given lessons in the English language.

Her first film role was in *Song Without End*, released in 1960. Between 1960 and 1986, she appeared in forty-two U. S. film and television productions.

When she met William Holden, who was married, while working in *The 7th Dawn*, they began a two year affair.

Capucine left Hollywood in 1962 to take up residence in Switzerland to be near her close friend, Audrey Hepburn. Unfortunately, Capucine was a manic-depressive and is said to have been saved from suicide attempts on several occasions by Hepburn.

She took her life on March 17, 1990 by leaping from the eighth floor of her apartment building.

Capucine was cremated and her ashes scattered.

Albert Salmi was born in Brooklyn, New York on March 11, 1928. He enlisted in the army during World War Two, and at the end of the war used the G. I. Bill to study acting under Lee Strasberg. Salmi won the lead in the Broadway production of *Bus Stop* in 1955, co-starring with Peggy Ann Garner. They fell in love and were married on May 16, 1956.

In 1957, he moved to Hollywood to work in *The Brothers Karamazov*, which was released in 1958. Between 1958 and 1989, he appeared in 158 television and movie productions.

He and Garner divorced in 1963, and Salmi immediately married Roberta Pollack.

Salmi went into semi-retirement in 1982 and moved with his wife to Washington State. It is reported that he suffered from clinical depression brought on by a belief that he was no longer wanted by the film industry.

On April 23, 1990, Salmi shot and killed his wife, and then turned the weapon on himself. He is buried in the Greenwood Memorial Terrace in Spokane, Washington.

David Stephen Rappaport was born with dwarfism in London, England on November 23, 1951. Growing to a height of less than four feet, he took a degree in psychology at the University of Bristol, played the drums professionally for a while, married, and then became a teacher. After his wife left him, he decided to take up acting, and in 1981 landed a major role in *Time Bandits*. Between 1973 and 1991, he appeared in thirty-four film and television productions.

Rappaport was another actor that suffered from bouts of severe depression, and on May 2, 1990, he drove to Laurel Canyon Park and shot himself in the chest. He is buried in the Waltham Abbey Jewish Cemetery in Essex, England.

In 1990, while filming *Delta Force 2*, **Jojo Imperiale,** pilot, **Gadi Danzig**, camera man, **Mike Graham**, key grip, **Geoff Brewer**, actor, and **Don Marshall,** gaffer, were all killed when their helicopter crashed.

Born on December 24th, 1941 in Los Angeles, California, **David Arkin** studied acting at UCLA, and then worked with Rob Reiner as a member of The Session Improvisational comedy troupe on the *Tonight Show*, the *Steve Allen Show*, and others. He later performed in *Second City*, and on television in *Hawaii 5-0*, and *Storefront Lawyers*. David also appeared in a number of Robert Altman films, including *MASH*, released in 1970, *The Long Goodbye*, released in 1973, *Nashville*, released in 1975, and *Popeye*, released in 1980. All told, he had fourteen film and television credits between 1965 and 1980.

David Arkin as S. Sgt Volmer in MASH

At the time *The Long Goodbye* was being cast, Arkin introduced his friend Arnold Schwarzenegger to Robert Altman, and this began Schwarzenegger's career in film.

Arkin married Lynn Gillham in 1965. They divorced in 1967. He then married Deborah Lubin in 1978, and they divorced in 1981. His final marriage was to Anne Curry in 1982. They were still married at the time of his death.

Said to have been suffering from depression, Arkin killed himself in Los Angeles on January 14th, 1991. He was forty-nine.

In1991, stuntman **Jay Currin** dove off a fifty foot cliff and was killed when he missed the air bag. The movie being filmed was *Bikini Island*.

Arcadia Lake, was born Michelle M. Carpenter, place unknown, on September 3, 1958. Other than her work in pornographic films (Tammy in the 1978 film *Debbie Does Dallas,* for example), little is known about the life of Lake.

Lake was a drug addict before she began her career in porno. Eric Edwards, who met her in 1978, helped her through a series of detox programs, and then introduced her to his occupation, starring in twenty-five pornographic films between 1968 and 1983.

She left Eric Edwards and disappeared from public view in 1983.

It is reported that she returned to drug use, and died of an overdose in 1991.

Max Cantor was born on May 15, 1959. His father, Arthur Cantor, was a theatrical producer. He spent his childhood in New York City, graduated Buxton School in Williamstown, MA, and Harvard University.

He appeared in the television production of *Diner* in 1983, in the film *Dirty Dancing* in 1987, and in *Fear, Anxiety & Depression* in 1989.

While researching addicts in New York for a film role, he became addicted to heroin and died from an overdose at the age of thirty-two.

One of the crew working on the film *The Bodyguard* (1992), was crushed to death between two lighting cranes.

Todd Armstrong (John Harris Armstrong) was born on July 25th, 1937 in St. Louis, Missouri, where he graduated Ladue High School in 1956. His father was a famous St Louis architect, who designed many of the cities well-known buildings.

Todd moved to California in the late '50s, where he studied acting at the Pasadena Playhouse. Unable to find steady employment as an actor, he worked part-time as a landscape gardener.

He was working at Gloria Henry's home in 1961 when his luck changed. MS Henry was a film and television actress under contract to Columbia Pictures. In 1958, she had appeared in Charles Bronson's film, *Gang War*, and was in her second year playing Alice Mitchell, the mother of the title character on the popular CBS television series, *Dennis the Menace*. MS Henry was so impressed with Todd's good-looks that she arranged for him to test at Columbia.

Todd was given a recurring role in the television show *Manhunt*, which starred Victor Jory. Todd appeared in thirteen episodes during the 1961 season.

Changing his name to Todd Anderson in 1962, he first appeared on film in director Edward Dmytryk's drama, *Walk on the Wild Side*, which starred Laurence Harvey and Jane Fonda. When he was given a part in the Daniel Mann-directed film, *Five Finger Exercise*, he changed his name back to Armstrong.

In1963, Todd won his first starring role as the lead in *Jason and the Argonauts*. The film was directed by Don Chaffey. Todd won accolades for his portrayal of Jason, but unfortunately, because he was an American in a mostly English cast, his voice was dubbed by British actor Tim Turner.

Jason and the Argo's crew

Columbia Picture's publicity department failed to position *Jason and the Argonauts* in the movie marketplace in such a way as to separate the film the many Italian Hercules-inspired fantasy pictures released in 1963, and the film was unable to find an audience.

Two years later, in 1965, Todd co-starred with George Segal and Tom Courtenay in the World War Two POW film, *King Rat*. He found work in ten more television and film productions over the next twelve years, and then gave it up.

Little information is available regarding Todd's final ten years of life. It is rumored that he became an alcoholic living on his wife's income.

On November 17th, 1992, Todd, living in Butte, California, committed suicide by shooting himself. It is believed that he did this after learning that he had contracted AIDS.

Andre René Roussimoff was born in France on May 19, 1946.

André had a hormonal disorder that resulted in excess growth hormone. As a result, he stood 6' 3" tall at age twelve and reached 7' 4" as an adult. He worked as a wrestler for thirty years, and began acting in 1956.

Between 1956 and 1993, he appeared in twelve television and movie roles. He is probably best known for his portrayal of Fezzek in *The Princess Bride*, released in 1986.

Because of his disease, Andre was in constant and intense pain, and his heart was weakened by the excess load of his size. He became an alcoholic and became known as "The Greatest Drunk on Earth" after drinking 119 pints of beer in six hours. Andre died of congestive heart failure and alcoholism on January 27. 1993. He was cremated, and his ashes were buried in his favorite garden on his North Carolina ranch.

Brandon Bruce Lee was born in Oakland, California on February 1, 1965. He was the son of actor Bruce Lee and Linda Emery. His family moved to Hollywood shortly after his birth, and moved back to Hong Kong in 1965 after his father ceased to be popular.

Brandon's father died of a cerebral edema when Brandon was eight, and his mother took him back to the United States where they lived for a short period in his mother's hometown, Seattle, Washington. In 1974, they returned to the Los Angeles area, where Lee grew up.

He went to the Chadwick School, but while in his senior year was expelled for insubordination. After earning a GED in 1983, he enrolled in Emerson College in

Boston and majored in theater. He then moved to New York City and studied acting under Lee Strasberg.

In 1985, Lee returned to Los Angeles and went to work for Ruddy Morgan Productions as a script reader. His first acting role was in *Kung Fu: The Movie*, a television production. Lee's first major part came later that year in *Legacy of Rage*.

He starred in *Showdown in Little Tokyo* in 1991 and signed a contract with 20th Century Fox shortly afterward. His first role for 20th Century was in *Rapid Fire*, released in 1992.

The next year he was given the lead in *The Crow*, and on March 31, 1993, while filming a scene in which his character was supposed to have a pistol fired at him, there was a mistake in the loading of the blank cartridge and a bullet remained in the pistol's barrel. When it struck Lee in the stomach, it penetrated all the way to his spine. Following a 6-hour operation to remove the bullet, Lee died.

He is buried in Lake View Cemetery in Seattle, Washington.

Herve Villechaize was born in Paris, France on April 23, 1942. He studied art in Paris, and then, in 1964, at age twenty-one, moved to New York City where he learned English by watching television.

Herve, a dwarf, worked as a photographer in New York, while acting part-time in theatre. Between 1966 and 1992, he appeared in nineteen television and film roles, and was best known for his role as Tattoo in the 132 episodes of *Fantasy Island* that ran from 1977 through 1983.

Herve caused many problems while working in the *Fantasy Island* cast. He made indecent proposals to the female actors, and argued with the director and producers. When he threatened to quit unless his salary was increased to match that of Ricardo Montalban, the male lead, he was fired.

Losing his job sent him into a deep depression. It is said that he made it a practice to sit in a dark room each night, drinking heavily, watching reruns of the show, and screaming obscene remarks at the actors. His agent claimed that Herve pulled a pistol on him in a restaurant, cursing him, and making impossible demands.

Herve's problems were evidently a result of physical pain caused by the fact that his internal organs had continued to grow to normal size in spite of his small body. The internal pressure reached a point where he could no longer sleep in a prone position, but had to kneel while asleep in order to breathe normally.

Herve shot himself in the temple on September 4, 1993. After cremation, his ashes were scattered off Point Fermin in California.

River Phoenix was born River Jude Bottom on August 23, 1970 in Madras, Oregon. River's parents had been working as itinerant fruit pickers in California when they met. They joined the religious movement, Children of God, when River was two and moved to Venezuela as missionaries. After years of living in poverty and church practices they were uncomfortable with, the family left the movement. They eventually returned to the states and moved in with River's maternal grandparents in Florida. It was there they changed their last name from Bottom to Phoenix after the mythical bird.

In 1977, they moved to Los Angeles, and at their insistence, River began acting when he was ten years old. Although he never received any formal education, he could read and write, and between 1982 and 1993, he appeared in twenty-four television and film roles. He is probably best remembered for his role in *Stand by Me* released in 1986, and as Mike Waters in *My Own Private Idaho*, released in 1991.

River with Martha Plimpton in *The Mosquito Coast* (1986)

On the night of October 30, 1993, River, along with his younger sister, Rain, his brother, Joaquin, and his girlfriend, actress Samantha Mathis, went to visit the Viper Room, a West Hollywood club on Sunset Boulevard owned by Johnny Depp. It was reported that River went into the restroom and took drugs. The group left shortly after midnight. In the early hours of October 31, 1993, at the age of twenty-three, River collapsed on the sidewalk in front of the club, went into convulsions, and died.

An autopsy reported that his blood contained lethal doses of cocaine and morphine, as well as quantities of diazepam, ephedrine and marijuana.

Phoenix was cremated and his ashes were scattered at his family ranch in Micanopy, Florida.

Will Rogers (also known as Will Rogers, Jr.) was born in New York City on October 20, 1911. The son of humourist Will Rogers. Will Jr. grew up in Beverly Hills and attended school there. In 1935, he graduated Stanford University, and then published the *Beverly Hills Citizen* newspaper until 1953. Shortly after the beginning of World War Two, Rogers enlisted in the army. On January 3, 1943, he was elected Congressman, left the Army, served in Congress, and in 1944 he resigned from Congress and reenlisted in the army.

Rogers is probably best remembered for playing his father in the film *The Story of Will Rogers*, released in 1952. Between 1952 and 1982, he appeared in twelve television and film roles.

After retiring, Rogers lived on a ranch in Tubac, Arizona. In poor health, he committed suicide in 1993. He is buried next to his wife in the Tubac Cemetery.

Kurt Donald Cobain was born on February 20, 1967. He was an American musician and artist, best known as the lead singer, guitarist and primary songwriter of the grunge band Nirvana. Cobain formed Nirvana with Krist Novoselic in Aberdeen, Washington in 1985 and established it as part of the Seattle music scene, having its debut album *Bleach* released on the independent record label Sub Pop in 1989.

Married to Courtney Love, during the last years of his life, Cobain struggled with heroin addiction, illness and depression. On March 18, 1994, Love phoned the Seattle police, telling them that Cobain was suicidal and had locked himself in a room with a gun. Police arrived and confiscated several guns and a bottle of pills from Cobain. Kurt swore that he was not suicidal. He said he had locked himself in the room to hide from Love.

Love arranged an intervention regarding Cobain's drug use on March 25th. By the end of the day, Cobain had agreed to undergo a detox program. He arrived at the Exodus Recovery Center in Los Angeles, California on March 30th. He spent that first day talking to counselors about his drug abuse and personal problems and playing with his daughter. This was the last time Cobain saw his daughter.

The following night, Cobain walked outside, saying he was going to smoke a cigarette. He climbed over a six-foot-high fence, took a taxi to the Los Angeles Airport and flew back to Seattle. On April 8th, Cobain's body was discovered at his Lake Washington home by an electrician who had arrived to install a security system. Kurt had killed himself with a shotgun. A high concentration of heroin and diazepam was found in his body. His body had been lying there for three days. He was cremated and his ashes were scattered on McClain Creek in Olympia, Washington.

Stephen Keats was born in Brooklyn, New York on February 6, 1945. He graduated the New York School for the Performing Arts, and then served in the Air Force for two years. After discharge, he attended the Yale School of Drama.

After landing a part in *Oh! Calcutta!* on Broadway, Keats appeared in eighty-six television and film roles between 1973 and 1994.

For unknown reasons, Keats killed himself on May 8, 1994. His burial place is unknown.

Haing Ngor was born in Cambodia in 1940. He was a physician in his native country but after becoming a naturalized American citizen he became an actor. In 1985 he won the Academy Award for Best Supporting Actor for his performance in the film, *The Killing Fields*.

A scene from *The Killing Fields*

He also appeared in a number of movies and television shows, including *Heaven*

And Earth, and *Tupac, The Vanishing Son* miniseries.

On February 25, 1996, Ngor was murdered outside his home in Chinatown, Los Angeles. Three members of the "Oriental Lazy Boyz", a street gang who were reputed to have a history of armed robbery were charged with the murder. Prosecutors argued that the three killed Ngor because he refused to give them a locket that contained a photo of his deceased wife. Defence attorneys suggested the murder was a politically motivated, but offered no evidence to support this theory.

Critics of the theory that Ngor was killed in a robbery pointed out that $2,900 in cash was not taken. All three were found guilty on April 16, 1998

He is buried in Rose Hills Memorial Park in Whittier, California.

Roland Harrah III was born in Denver, Colorado on January 20, 1973. His family moved to Riverside, California in 1982. His first appearance at age eleven was in an episode of *Magnum, P. I.* Between 1984 and 1990, he appeared in six television and film roles, including *Braddock, Missing in Action III* (1988), and starring Chuck Norris.

For reasons unknown, he committed suicide on January 3, 1995. He was buried in Crestlawn Memorial Park in Riverside, California.

Hugh O'Connor was born in Rome, Italy on April 7, 1962. He was adopted by actor Carroll O'Connor and his wife when he was six days old.

At age sixteen, Hugh was found to be suffering from Hodgkin's Lymphoma. He overcame the cancer, but in the process became addicted to prescription drugs. This led him to cocaine and Heroin addiction. In spite of many months of treatment in rehab clinics, he was unable to break his addictions.

Hugh appeared in 146 episodes of the television production *In the Heat of the Night* between 1988 and 1995.

Extremely depressed by his inability to break away from drugs, he called his father and then shot himself on March 28, 1995. An autopsy determined that he had been using cocaine at the time. He was buried at Westwood Memorial Park in Los Angeles, California.

Keith Wayne was born in Washington, Pennsylvania on January 16, 1945. He only made one film appearance; *Night of the Living Dead* released in 1968.

He made his living as a singer for a number of years, and then became a chiropractor.

He killed himself on September 9, 1995. He was cremated and his ashes were given to his family.

The English Patient, released in 1996, won two of its nine Oscar awards for Best Film Editing and Best Sound. It was made with the first digitally edited soundtrack.

Don Simpson was born in Seattle, Washington, on October 29, 1943. He spent his childhood in Anchorage, Alaska, where he graduated West Anchorage High School and then took a degree at the University of Oregon.

Simpson was an executive at Paramount Pictures, but he lost his position as a result of addiction to cocaine and various prescription drugs. Friends say Simpson was spending more than $60,000 a month on drugs. He died on January 19, 1996, in his Los Angeles home. The coroner's report listed combined drug intoxication as the cause. It was later revealed that Don had been obtaining large quantities of drugs from fifteen different doctors and that police found 2,200 prescription pills at his home.

Ray Combs was born in Hamilton, Ohio on April 3, 1956. He moved to Los Angeles in 1983, where he entered show business by warming up audiences for various television shows. In 1986, he was invited by Johnny Carson to appear on *The Tonight Show.* The following year he was given a minor role in *Overboard.*

Between 1985 and 1995, he appeared on nine television shows. He is best known for replacing Richard Dawson as the host of *Family Feud.*

Following a domestic disturbance in 1996, Combs was placed in the psychiatric ward of Glendale Adventist Medical Center. He committed suicide on June 2, 1996, by hanging himself with bed sheets. He is buried in his hometown in the Greenwood Cemetery.

Glendale Adventist Hospital, 1509 E. Wilson Terrace, Glendale, California

Margaux Hemingway was born Margot Louise Hemingway in Portland Oregon on February 16, 1954. She was the granddaughter of Ernest Hemingway.

After working as a model, she first appeared in films in 1976, co-starring with her sister Mariel in *Lipstick*. In later years, she earned money by selling autographed nude photos of herself and appearing in a few "B" films.

Between 1976 and 1996, Margaux appeared in eighteen film and television roles, and during that period she married and divorced twice and became an alcoholic.

Margaux overdosed on Phenobarbital on July 1, 1996 and was cremated. Her ashes were interred in the Hemingway family plot, Ketchum Cemetery, Ketchum, Idaho.

Biggie Smalls (Christopher George Letore Wallace) was born on May 21, 1972 in Brooklyn, New York. His mother, Voletta Wallace, was a Jamaican preschool teacher, and his father, George Latore, was a welder. His father abandoned the family when Biggie two years old.

Biggie sold drugs to his schoolmates at the age of twelve. At age seventeen, Biggie dropped out of school and became involved in illegal activities on a full-time basis. In 1989, he was placed on five-year probation because of a weapons charge. The next year he served a nine-month sentence in prison in North Carolina for selling crack cocaine.

Biggie became involved in rapping while still in school. After serving his prison sentence, a New York promoter played a demo tape made by Biggie to the editor of The Source magazine. In 1992, The Source invited Biggie to make another demo tape. Uptown records heard the tape and signed Biggie to a production contract.

Biggie was six feet three inches tall, and weighed over three hundred pounds. He took the name Biggie Smalls from the film, *Let's Do It Again.*

He lost his recording contract when the owners learned that he was once again selling drugs. He changed his rapping name to The Notorious B.I.G. and used this name for the rest of his recording career. In 1994, Wallace made a recording that became a sales success when it reached number twenty-seven on the pop chart. That same year he recorded <u>Ready to Die</u> which became platinum.

Between 1993 and 2013, Wallace appeared in thirty-two television and film productions.

Wallace became engaged in a dispute with Tupac Shakur when Tupac told a Vibe reporter that Wallace knew that some hoodlums planned on robbing Tupac but didn't warn Tupac. Wallace denied this.

Tupac was shot and killed in Las Vegas in 1996. Wallace was accused of furnishing gang members the pistol. The following year, Wallace attended a party hosted by Vibe magazine and Qwest Records at the Petersen Automotive Museum in Los Angeles (6060 Wilshire Blvd.). After the party, as his group was driving away, Wallace was killed in a drive-by shooting.

Nancee Kelly was born Kelly Van Dyke in Danville, Illinois, on January 3, 1958. She was the daughter of Jerry Van Dyke, and the niece of Dick Van Dyke

Kelly grew up in the Hollywood/Los Angeles area and was a drug addict at an early age. She first appeared in two episodes of the television series, *My Mother the Car*, in 1966, and had roles in a total of two television shows and seven pornographic videos between 1966 and 1993.

She married actor Jack Nance, and committed suicide on July 15, 1991 by hanging herself. Her husband was also an alcoholic and drug addict and died in December, 1996 of injuries received in a street fight.

Nancee was cremated and her ashes scattered at sea.

Donald S. Cammell was born in the Camera Obscura on Castlehill, Scotland on January 17, 1934. He was a writer and producer with just one acting credit, *The 3 Drums*, released in 2007. He wrote four scripts and produced five films. When his upcoming Hollywood film, *Wildside,* was cancelled in 1996, he committed suicide.

Bridgette Andersen was born on July 11th, 1975 in Inglewood, California, and grew up in Malibu. Recognized to have exceptional intelligence, by the age of two, she was able to read and understand books by authors such as Ernest Hemingway.

Bridgette started her career early, working as a model, but she also appeared in television commercials and in television shows such as *King's Crossing*. In 1982, at the age of seven, she won a role in the film, *Washington Mistress*. That same year, she played the title role in the film, *Savannah Smiles* and was nominated for "Best Young Motion Picture Actress" by The Young Artists Awards.

After playing the part of the young Mae West in the television movie, *Mae West*, she starred in the TV series, *Gun Shy*, which resulted in a second nomination for a Young Artists Award. Besides those parts, her twenty-one screen credits between the years of 1982 and 1996 include the television movie, *A Summer To Remember*, in 1985, a starring role in *Fever Pitch*, playing opposite Ryan O'Neal, and roles in *Remington Steele*, *The Parent Trap 2*, and *Family Ties*.

Her last film was *Too Much*, in 1987. After that, she found little acting work until, in 1995, she made an appearance in the television series, *Unhappily Ever After*, her life significantly changing as she went from working as a busy actress to clerking in the Erewhon Health Food Store in Los Angeles.

Unfortunately, Bridgett became addicted to heroin while still a teenager. On May 18th, 1997 she accidently overdosed after mixing heroin with alcohol. She was twenty-one. Her body was cremated and the ashes scattered over Zuma Beach, Malibu.

Brian Keith was born in Bayonne, New Jersey on November 14, 1921. Because his parents had divorced, and his mother was working on the stage, Keith was raised by his grandmother. His step-mother was Peg Entwistle, a well-known actress. Entwhistle committed suicide in 1932 by leaping from the letter 'H' in the Hollywood sign.

Keith graduated East Rockaway High School in 1939. Two years later, shortly after the start of World War Two, he enlisted in the Marine Corps and served until the war's end in 1945 as a gunner in a Dauntless SBD dive bomber.

After the war ended Keith found work on stage in New York City. He went into television in 1952. Between 1947 and 1999, Keith appeared in 155 film and television roles. He was probably best known for appearing in sixty-seven episodes of *Hardcastle and McCormick* between 1983 and 1986.

Keith married three times and fathered six children.

Suffering from cancer, having financial problems, and just two months after his daughter Daisy committed suicide, he shot himself on June 24, 1997 and is buried in the Westwood Memorial Park in Los Angeles, California.

Daisy Keith was born in Hollywood on June 26, 1969. She was the daughter of Brian Keith. Daisy appeared in just one television show, *Heartland* in 1989, playing alongside her father. Daisy committed suicide on April 16, 1997 for no known reason. Daisy is buried next to her father in Westwood Memorial Park, Los Angeles, California.

Phil Hartman was born in Brantford, Ontario, Canada in 1948. His family moved to the United States ten years later, first settling in Connecticut, and later moving to California.

Hartman was an art student at Santa Monica City College, then an agent for a rock band. In 1972, he again studied art, this time at California State. Later, he started a graphic arts business specializing in album covers.

Working with Paul (Peewee Herman) Reubens, he helped create *The Pee-wee Herman Show*, originally a stage show and later an HBO production. While he was working with Reubens, he also did voice-overs for *The Smurfs*, *The 13 Ghosts of Scooby-Doo*, and *Dennis the Menace*.

Hartman is probably best known for his performances on *Saturday Night Live*. He starred in *News Radio* in 1995, and in the film, *Houseguest*, released in 1995.

Hartman was married and divorced twice before he married Brynn Omdahl in 1987. They had two children.

On May 27, 1998, he got into an argument with his wife over her addiction to alcohol, prescription drugs, and cocaine and threatened to leave her.

After Hartman went to bed, his wife shot him in the head. She later committed suicide.

Eduardo Sanchez and Daniel Myrick produced the independent film *The Blair Witch Project*, released in 1999 by little known distributor Artisan Films. This a documentary type horror movie that tells of a camping trip and ensuing investigation of a local legend. The movie has just three actors.

The roughly made black and white film soon became a cult favorite, and the most profitable film, grossing $140.5 million in the U. S., and $249 million worldwide. The film was budgeted at about $60,000.

George Lucas' *Star Wars Episode I: The Phantom Menace*, released in 1999, included characters that were entirely digitally rendered, such as Jar Jar Binks.

Dana Plato was born in Maywood, California on November 7, 1964. Her mother, unwed and sixteen-years-old, already had a one-year-old child at the time of Dana's birth, so she put Dana up for adoption.

Dana's adoptive parents had her working in television commercials when she was seven years old. She made her first film appearance in 1977 in *Return to Boggy Creek*. Between 1977 and 2002, Dana had roles in thirty television, film, and video game productions. She is probably best known for appearing in 132 episodes of *Diff'rent Strokes* between 1978 and 1986.

Dana, unmarried, became pregnant in 1984, and was dismissed from the series. She then worked in "B" films until her death.

Dana was said to have been a drug addict and perhaps for this reason she moved to Las Vegas in 1991 and attempted to rob a video store. She was arrested and received a sentence of five years' probation. A few months later she was arrested again. This time for forging a drug prescription. She served a thirty day sentence in jail.

On May 8, 1999, while visiting her boyfriend's mother in Moore, Oklahoma, Dana overdosed on Vanadom and Lortab. The coroner's report called her death a suicide. She was cremated and her ashes scattered at sea.

Dana's son, Tyler Lambert, killed himself with a self-inflicted gunshot to the head on May 6, 2010 in Tulsa. He was twenty-five. It was said he was also using alcohol and drugs.

Mary Kay Bergman was born in Los Angeles, California on June 5, 1961. Between 1991 and 2002, she worked in sixty-four radio, television, film, and video game productions. Between 1997 and 2002 her voice was used in forty-four episodes of *South Park*.

Unknown to most of her fans and friends, including her family, Bergman suffered from bipolar disorder. At age thirty-eight, on November 11, 1999, she committed suicide. She is buried at Forest Lawn Memorial Park in the Hollywood Hills.

Chapter Ten: the Twenty First Century

While filming *Taxi 2*, released in 2000, a car missed its mark and killed a camera man.

Lana Jean Clarkson was born on April 5th, 1962 in Long Beach, California. She grew up in Sonoma County, on the coast, just north of San Francisco. She had one brother and one sister, and went to Cloverdale High School. When she was sixteen, her father died, and her mother took the family to live in Los Angeles County where Lana found work as a model.

In 1982, Lana won a small part at Universal Studios in *Fast Times at Ridgemont High*. That same year, she was given an even smaller, unaccredited part in MGM's film *My Favorite Year*. In 1983, she worked in six television and film productions. Perhaps the best known of these were *Death Stalker*, and *Scarface*. All total, between 1983 and 2001, Lana performed in thirty-six television and film productions.

By the early 1990s, Lana's ability to land TV and film parts waned. She made a meager living operating a Web Blog where she sold signed copies of the films that she had appeared in. In 1997, Lana moved to Venice, where she started work on an independent production titled *Lana Unleashed*.

Several years later, she took a job at The House of Blues, on Sunset in West Hollywood. While working in the restaurant she met Phil Spector, a millionaire who made his fortune as a record producer. Spector had barely survived an auto accident in 1974. He suffered a head injury that required 300 stitches on his face and 400 on his skull, and had taken to wearing weird wigs.

Phil Specter

On February 3, 2000, Lana agreed to accompany Spector in a limousine ride that stopped at his mansion. Spector invited her in, telling the limousine driver they would only be a short while. Sometime later, the driver heard a gunshot. Spector came out brandishing a pistol and shouted, "I think I just shot her!" He was quoted as saying that Lana "kissed the gun", and that her death was, "an accidental suicide."

Spector put up one million dollars bail after being charged with Lana's murder, and his attorneys managed to delay the trial for four years. Spector's defense was based on a claim that Lana had shot herself. The first trial ended in a hung jury.

Spector was brought back to trial a year later and found guilty of murder. He received a sentence of nineteen years to life, and is serving his sentence at the California Health Care Facility (CHCF) in Stockton, California. He will be eighty-eight years old before he is eligible for parole.

1700 Grand View Drive, Alhambra, California, where Phil Spector murdered

Rick Jason was born in New York City on May 21, 1923. After Jason graduated college, his dad bought him a seat on the New York Stock Exchange. Jason sold the seat and enlisted in the Air Force, serving from 1943 until World War Two ended in 1945.

Jason then studied at the American Academy of Dramatic Arts.

He met Hume Cronyn while attending a play in New York City. This led to a role in *Now I Lay me Down to Sleep*, following which he was given a contract by Columbia Pictures and moved to Hollywood. Between 1953 and 1989, Jason appeared in sixty television and film roles. He is probably best remembered for working in 150 episodes of *Combat!* during the years 1962 through 1967.

Jason attended a reunion of cast members of *Combat!* in late 2000. For reasons unknown, he killed himself a week later on October 16, 2000. Rick was cremated and his ashes enshrined in a glass case at the Hollywood Forever Cemetery in Hollywood, California.

DVD sales in 2001 first exceeded VHS videotape sales.

2002: Movies-on-demand, a venture formed by Sony Pictures Entertainment, Universal Studios, Paramount Pictures, Metro-Goldwyn-Mayer and Warner Bros., started with the establishment of *MovieLink*. This was the first time a large supply of recent, popular movies became available legally on the Internet.

In 2002, an American stuntman was thrown into a support member of the Palackeho Bridge in Prague. The intended stunt was to show a man is being pulled behind a speed boat, hanging from a parasail. The stuntman was supposed to cut loose from the parasail and drop into the river. The stuntman, Harry L. O'Connor, playing Vin Diesel's double, could not release himself and he slammed into the bridge, dying instantly.

DVD rentals topped those of VHS videotape rental revenues in March, 2003.

Hollywood movie star Arnold Schwarzenegger was elected the 38th governor of California in 2003.

Charlie's Angels: Full Throttle, released in 2003, was the first Sony Pictures film, and it was the first feature movie to be published on *Blu-Ray Disc*.

In early 2006, the major Hollywood movie to be released in VHS videotape cassette format was *A History of* Violence, released in 2005.

Netflix became the first TV subscription service to offer legal ad-free, movies directly to a computer screen in 2007.

In 2007, the Writer's Guild of America went on strike. This was the result of a failure in negotiations with the Alliance of Motion Picture and Television Producers. The Writers Guild demanded increased pay for the movie and TV writers. When the 3-month strike ended in mid-February 2008, it was estimated that it had caused a loss of $2.5 billion dollars to the movie and TV businesses.

A fire at Universal Studios in 2008 destroyed a number of sets from old movies, including Courthouse Square, the clock tower from *Back to the Future*, and the King Kong exhibit on the studio tour.

The TV movie website *Hulu* was started in 2008.

In 2009, U.S. movie ticket sales exceeded income from the purchase of DVDs. DVDs began to outsell movies in 2002.

The first major buyout in the twenty-first century was *America Online's* purchase of Time Warner in 2009 for about $182 billion dollars. At the end of 2009, the merger ended when Time Warner announced that it would spin off AOL as a separate independent company.

In 2005, Viacom's Paramount Pictures acquired the 11-year-old DreamWorks studio, which had been founded in 1994 by Steven Spielberg, Jeffrey Katzenberg, and David Geffen. Paramount paid approximately $1.6 billion. DreamWorks demise marked the end of a Hollywood era. DreamWorks ended its 2 1/2 year partnership with Paramount in late 2008. A few months later, DreamWorks signed a long-term, 30 picture distribution deal with the Disney Company.

In late 2009, Walt Disney Co. bought Marvel Entertainment for $4 billion.

Carl Steven (Carlo Steven Krakoff) was born on November 4th, 1974 in Glendale, California. He was given his first television role on *Little House on the Prairie* (1981). Between then and 1996, he appeared in thirty-seven more TV and film parts, including *Star Trek III: The Search for Spock* as young Spock in 1984 and *Honey, I Shrunk the Kids* in 1989.

At age of eighteen, Carl decided to quit acting. He became addicted to prescriptions after having his tonsils out and began to steal.

In 2010, he was sentenced to thirteen years in prison for armed robbery. Carl died on July 31, 2011 of an overdose of heroin. He was serving his sentence in a prison in Tucson, Arizona at the time, and was only thirty-six years old.

Andrew Koenig was born in Los Angeles on August 17, 1968. His father is actor Walter Koenig known for his role as Pavel Chekov from the original Star Trek series. Andrew first appeared on the television production *Adam 12* at the age of five.

Koenig is probably best known for his work on *Growing Pains* from 1985 to 1989 where he played Mike Seaver's best friend, Richard "Boner" Stabone.

Between 1987 and 2008 he performed in eleven television roles. Koenig played the part of the Joker in *Batman: Dead End*, released in 2003.

In February, 2010, Koenig was reported to the police as missing. Nine days later he was found hanging from a tree in a Vancouver public park.

Andrew is buried in the Hollywood Forever Cemetery in Hollywood California.

Joey Kovar was born in 1989 in Chicago, Illinois. A known drug addict, Joey starred in television series *Real World: Hollywood*, where audiences watched him struggle to break free from drugs.

Kovar left the show in 2008 and entered a rehab center, returned, and then left again, fearing that the environment might cause him to relapse.

He admittedly was using cocaine and ecstasy when he joined the cast of another reality show, *Celebrity Rehab* in 2009.

Kovar told reporters, "You know, I guess in a way, I did feel a little bit betrayed — by some cast mates more than others. It was my understanding that things would change around the house in order to help keep me on the road to recovery but, unfortunately, the very first night back from rehab, every roommate but Will and Sarah went out and got messed up. To me, that was a little messed up."

Kovar died on August 17, 2012, in a friend's home in Chicago of a probable drug overdose.

Lisa Robin Kelly was born on March 5, 1970 in Southington, Connecticut. Her first acting job came at age twenty-one, in a 1992 episode of *Married with Children*. Following that, she appeared on many popular television shows, including *Murphy Brown, The X-Files, Sisters,* and *Silk Stalkings*. Her big break came at age twenty-eight, when she landed the role of Laurie Forman, the promiscuous elder sister of Eric Forman, on *That '70s Show*. She enjoyed some mild publicity during the first two years of the show, and appeared in the film, *Jawbreaker*.

During the filming of the third season of *That '70s Show*, Lisa became addicted to drugs, and was fired.

During the fifth season she appeared in the show again, and was offered appearances in thirteen episodes of the sixth season. She completed the first several episodes, and was then replaced by Christina Moore. Fox stated this was a mutual agreement. She has had only one acting credit since then, the 2005 film, *The Food Chain: A Hollywood Scarytale*.

Lisa entered a Los Angeles rehab facility in August, 2013. She died there on the 14th. In January, 2014, the Los Angeles Coroner reported that Lisa's death was due to multiple drug ingestion.

Robert Arthur (Robb) Knox was born on the twenty-first of August, 1989 in Bexley, England. At age eleven, he began acting on British television.

Robb was given the role of Belby in the film, *Harry Potter and the Half-Blood Prince*, which was released after his death, in 2009. He intended to play the same part in *Harry Potter and the Deadly Hallows*, but was stabbed to death on May twenty-forth, 2008, while attempting to help his brother who had gotten into a fight outside a bar in Sidcup, London. He was eighteen.

While shooting *Exit Wounds* (2001), stuntman **Chris Lamon** rolled out of a van, struck his head, and died six days later.

John Driftmier, director and camera man, was killed in a plane crash while filming *Dangerous Flights* in 2013.

Camera man **Roland Schlotzhauer** died when his helicopter crashed during filming of *The Final Season* in 2007.

Whitney Elizabeth Houston was born on August 9, 1963 in Newark, New Jersey. Her mother, Cissy Houston was a gospel singer and Dionne Warwick's cousin. Whitney was singing solo performances in the New Hope Baptist Church choir when she as eleven. She went to Mount Saint Dominic Academy, in Caldwell, New Jersey. As a teenager, she occasionally performed with her mother on stage and in nightclubs.

Her first recording job came at age fourteen singing backup in <u>Life's a Party</u>, a single produced by the Michael Zager Band, and the following year, she once again sang backup in <u>I'm Every Woman</u>, a Chaka Khan hit. Whitney became a model in 1982 and later sang lead vocalist in the Columbia Records album, <u>Paul Jabara and Friends</u>.

She attended the 1989 Soul Train Music Awards ceremony, met Bobby Brown there, and they married in 1992.

Whitney had acting roles in seven movie and television productions between 1984 and 2012 and performed as a singer fifty-two times on television and in movies.

She divorced Brown in 2007. He then sued her over custody of their daughter and demanded support payments for himself and the child, but got nothing.

Whitney admitted publicly in 2009 on the Oprah Winfrey show that Brown had got her started on drugs. She said that he mixed cocaine in with his marijuana.

Houston died on February 11, 2012, in her Beverly Hills hotel suite.

The coroner's report cited the cause of her death to be an overdose of Xanax and other prescription drugs mixed with alcohol.

The Beverly Hilton Hotel, Los Angeles, where Whitney Houston died in Room 434.

Jeremy Elliot Applegate was born Paul Andrew Boyce, on August 29, 1965 in San Jose, California. In 1989, he appeared in *Heathers*, and then in 1996, he had a minor role in Jim Carrey's *The Cable Guy*. He also did some television work.

On March 23, 2000, Applegate committed suicide by gunshot He was thirty-four.

Jeremy was cremated.

Christopher Pettiet was born on February 12, 1976 in Dallas, Texas. He appeared while still a child on *SeaQuest DSV*, *Star Trek: The Next Generation*, *Judging Amy*, and *Undressed*. He is probably best known for playing the young Jesse James in the television series, *The Young Riders*. Christopher's movie roles include *Point Break*, and *Don't Tell Mom the Babysitter's Dead*, both released in 1991.

All together he worked in twenty-six television and film productions between 1990 and 1999. His final appearance was in *Judging Amy* in 1999.

He died of an accidental drug overdose on April 12, 2000, at the age of twenty-four and was cremated. His ashes were scattered off of Topanga Canyon Road in Santa Monica, California.

Justin Charles Pierce was born in London, England, but raised in New York City. He took up skateboarding and soon began skipping school, getting into trouble when his parents divorced. After he quit school, he was arrested for drugs.

One day when Justin was skateboarding in Washington Square in New York City, a film director saw him and cast him in the film, *Kids* (1995.) The film was a success and Justin won an Independent Spirit Award for his performance.

After he moved to Los Angeles, he appeared in such films as *A Brother's Kiss* and *Looking for Leonard,* which was released after his death. He also did some television.

On July 10, 2000, Justin hung himself in his room in a Las Vegas hotel. He was twenty-five.

Richard W. Farnsworth was born in Los Angeles, California on September 1, 1920. Farnsworth grew up in Los Angeles during the 1929 depression. When he was sixteen, he began to work in films as an expert with horses. Between 1937 and 1999, he appeared in eighty-five television and film roles. He is probably best known for his portrayal of Bill Miner in the 1982 film, *The Grey Fox.*

Farnsworth was found to have prostate cancer in 1992. Six years later his doctors informed him that he had terminal bone cancer. He was in considerable pain while he worked in his final film, *The Straight Story*, released in 1999. For his work in *Straight Story*, he received an Academy Award Nomination for Best Actor.

Farnsworth committed suicide by shooting himself on October 6, 2000 and is buried in the Forest Lawn Memorial Park in the Hollywood Hills.

Jennifer Maria Syme was born on December 7, 1972 in Pico Rivera, California. At age eighteen she moved to Los Angeles, where she went to work for David Lynch. Lynch gave her a small part in *Lost Highway*, released in 1997, and she landed a role in *Ellie Parker* in 2000. Later, she worked for the Red Hot Chili Peppers.

Jennifer was invited to a party at Marilyn Manson's home on April 1st, 2001. A guest took her home shortly before dawn and she decided to return to the party. On the way she ran into parked cars on Cahuenga Boulevard in Los Angeles. Thrown from car, she was instantly killed. Syme was twenty-eight years old. Police found two rolled up dollar bills containing a white powder in her car. They also found several prescription drugs.

Syme is buried in Westwood Village Memorial Park Cemetery in Los Angeles.

David Lynch dedicated his film, *Mulholland Drive*, to her.

Glenn Quinn was born on May 28, 1970 in Dublin, Ireland. He, his mother, and his two sisters came to the United States in 1988. They settled in Long Beach, California where Glenn worked at various blue-collar jobs while attempting to find acting parts.

After doing commercials, he landed several small parts in various productions until he was hired to play, Mark, the older daughter's love interest, on the *Roseanne Show*. That gig lasted seven years. From 1999 to 2003, he portrayed Allen Doye in the television series, *Angel*.

Glenn fell from a horse while working on location in England. His back was seriously damaged, and this may have started him using drugs.

On December 3, 2002, Glenn overdosed on heroin at the age of thirty-two. He is buried in the Forest Lawn Memorial Park (Cypress) in Orange County, California.

Bonny Lee Bakley was born in Morristown, New Jersey in 1956. She was raised by her grandmother in Glen Gardner, N J. After dropping out of high school when she was sixteen, she went to New York City to try to become a model. When she was twenty-one, she married her first cousin, Paul Gawron.

In 1989, allegedly holding drugs for rocker Jerry Lee Lewis, she went to jail for possession. That same year she spent more time in jail for passing bad checks. Bonny then began earning living sending nude pictures of women to men. They were told she would come for a visit if they sent her money.

Bakley claimed to have had a child by Jerry Lee Lewis in 1993, but Lewis had DNA tests made, and they disproved this. Using the income from her nude photo business, Bakley was able to purchase several houses in Memphis, and another on the outskirts of Los Angeles.

In 1999, Bakley met Robert Blake at Chuck McCann's birthday party. She was dating Christian Brando at that time. Blake took Bakley to bed. He said she had assured him that she was taking birth control pills. Friends of Bakley said that in fact, she was taking fertility pills, and she soon became pregnant with her fourth child.

Bakley thought that Christian Brando was the father. When a DNA test determined that it was Blake, not Brando, who was the father of Bakley's youngest child, Blake agreed to marry her. This was her tenth marriage.

On May 4, 2001 Blake and Bakley ate dinner at Vitello's Restaurant on Tujunga Avenue in Studio City. After eating, Bakley was killed by a gunshot to the head. She was sitting in Blake's automobile at the time. Blake said he was not present but had gone back to the restaurant.

Blake was arrested April 18, 2002 for murder, soliciting murder, and conspiracy to commit the murder of his wife. On April 22, 2002, he pleaded not guilty to one count of murder and two counts of solicitation of murder. April 29, 2002, Bakley's four children filed a wrongful-death lawsuit against Blake and his former handyman/bodyguard, Earle Caldwell.

July 25, 2002, Blake's adult daughter, Delilah Blake, gained custody of Bakley's child, Rosie, while Blake put up one and one-half million dollars bail. He was then released from jail and placed under house arrest.

December 20, 2004, opening statements began in the criminal trial. The defence hoped to deflect suspicion from Blake by pointing the finger at Christian Brando, but that tactic failed due to a lack of evidence. Blake, his fans, and the media smeared the reputation of Bonny, his wife and the mother of his child.

Ronald "Duffy" Hambleton and Gary McLarty, both former stuntmen, testified that Blake had told them he was looking for someone to kill Bonny. On March 4, 2005, jurors began deliberations. March 16, 2005, Blake was acquitted of first-degree murder and one count of solicitation of murder. The trail was deadlocked on a second solicitation charge after jurors were split 11-1 in favor of acquittal. September 1, 2005 opening statements began in the civil trial. On October 25, 2005, Christian Brando invoked the Fifth Amendment when he took the witness stand. After closing arguments on November 3, 2005, jurors began deliberations.

On November 18, 2005, jurors found Blake "intentionally caused the death" of Bonny by a 10 to 2 vote, and he was ordered to pay Bonny's children thirty million dollars in damages. They voted against implicating Caldwell.

4349 Tujunga Avenue, Los Angeles. Where Bonny had her last meal.

She is buried in Forest Lawn Memorial Park (Hollywood Hills) in Los Angeles, California.

Lani O'Grady was born Lanita Rose Agrati in Walnut Creek, California on October 2, 1954. Her first acting appearance occurred in 1967 when she had a part in the television series *High Chaparral*.

She appeared in fourteen television and movie roles between 1967 and 1990 and may be best remembered for her appearances in the role of Mary Bradford in 112 episodes of *Eight Is Enough* between 1977 and 1981.

In 1992, Lani was diagnosed as having agoraphobia. She was also suffering from memory blackouts. Because of this, she took drugs for a brain chemical imbalance. No longer able to act, she became a talent agent.

O'Grady was found dead in her home on September 25, 2001. According to the autopsy report, her blood contained deadly amounts of Vicodin and Prozac. It was not determined if her death was an accident or suicide. Lani was cremated and her ashes were scattered in Hawaii.

Matthew Ansara was born in Los Angeles on August 29, 1965. His parents were Barbara Eden and Michael Ansara. Barbara was enjoying fame at the time as the mischievous genie in the television hit show, *I Dream of Jeannie*, while his father was probably best known for his work in the television series, *Broken Arrow* which ran from 1956 to 1960.

An only child, Matthew made his stage debut at nineteen months old when his mother held him and sang to him while appearing on *The Mike Douglas Show*. When he was fifteen, he appeared in his mother's series, *Harper Valley P.T.A.*

Barbara Eden with her son, Matthew

Matthew attended the University of California, Santa Barbara Valley College, and UCLA. He dropped out of all of these schools and is reported to have developed an addiction to heroin at this time.

Barbara Eden said, "I first knew Matthew was in trouble in 1984, when he was nineteen. He had chosen to live with his father after I remarried, but came back to live with me when my second husband and I divorced. He'd flunked out after one semester at the University of California at Santa Barbara and was supposed to be commuting to Valley College. I noticed that he slept a lot. Then, one day after he'd left for school, I saw that he'd forgotten his books. I raced out to the college and walked all over that campus looking for him. Finally I went to the registrar's office and found out he wasn't even registered. When I confronted him at home, he got angry, threw things and stomped out. That night he still hadn't come back, so I called his father. We searched for him everywhere, even under freeways. For months we had no idea where he was. Then a friend of Matthew's, who took him in, told us he'd spent most of that time living on the streets."

Matthew married Julie Karolyne Hoefer in 1993, but they divorced in 1995.

Then, when he was thirty-five, Matthew finally seemed climb out of the pit, and managed to break the drug habit. He turned his energy to amateur bodybuilding (he was six feet four inches tall), and that seemed to help. In 2001, he appeared in *To Protect and Serve* which opened to favorable reviews.

On June 26, 2001, Barbara Eden received a phone call informing her that her only child, Matthew Ansara, was dead. Six hours earlier, police had found Matthew slumped over in his truck at a gas station in Monrovia, Calif. The coroner's report blamed his death on an overdose of heroin. At the time of his death, he was playing the part of an inmate in the upcoming prison thriller *Con Games*.

Regarding Matthew's death, Barbara said, "He had shot up with a dose of unusually pure heroin, and it was too much for his heart. And I had another shock: Along with a syringe, the police found vials of anabolic steroids in his truck. To bulk up for bodybuilding competitions, he had been injecting himself with this dangerous drug. Even when he was getting in shape, he did it like an addict— obsessively. He was unable to do anything in moderation."

Matthew is buried in Forest Lawn Memorial Park (Hollywood Hill) in Los Angeles, California.

Lucas' second *Star Wars* pre-quel: *Attack of the Clones,* released in 2002, was the *first* major Hollywood motion picture to be filmed entirely with digital video (at 24 fps)

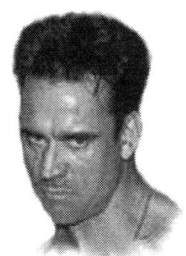

Trevor Goddard was born in Croydon, Surrey, England, on October 14, 1962. He grew up in Bromley, Kent. Trevor moved to New York City in 1986, where he found work in television. Between 1989 and 2003, he appeared in thirty-nine television, film and video game roles. He portrayed Lt. Cmdr. Mic Brumby in forty-two episodes of the television series, *JAG*, from 1998 to 2003.

On June 7, 2003, Goddard's body was discovered in his North Hollywood home. He was involved in divorce proceedings at the time and' perhaps for this reason, overdosed on a mixture of Vicodin, Temazepam, cocaine, and heroin.

Elliott Smith was born in Omaha, Nebraska on August 6, 1969. He grew up in Austin, Texas. Smith began his musical career by playing in Heatmiser, a local Austin rock band. His work as a soloist started in 1994 when his music was released by the recording labels Cavity Search and Kill Rock Stars. DreamWorks Records gave him a contract in 1994, and he recorded two albums for them.

Smith's music was used in the film, *Good Will Hunting*, released in 1998. As a result, he received an Oscar nomination for the Best Original Song.

He died in 2003 from stab wounds to his chest. His cause of death remains officially inconclusive. There were defense wounds on his arms, which led to consideration of murder, but his girlfriend testified that he had stabbed himself. The coroner called his death a suicide.

Elliot was cremated and his ashes scattered.

Jason Raize was born Jason Rothenberg on July 20, 1975 and grew up in the Catskills. After attending a summer Shakespeare workshop in his teens, he found his calling as a singer and actor and eventually moved to New York City where he attended the American Musical and Dramatic Academy.

After performing in regional theatre in such plays as *Phantom of the Opera* and *The Rocky Horror Show*, Jason won a role in the national touring company of *Jesus Christ Superstar* starring Ted Neely. That led to other parts and, in 1997, he decided to try out for the upcoming Broadway production of Julie Taymor's *The Lion King* and won the role of Simba. *He* also was the voice of Denahi in the Disney animated film, *Brother Bear.*

Jason as Simba

Besides the plays he performed in and his goodwill work for the U.N., Jason sang in concerts and made a couple of records. He also performed in a nationally syndicated program called *Keeping it Wild with Jason* where he visited exotic locations such as Africa and Australia to learn about animals in their natural habitat.

In 2003, Jason decided to return to Australia, as his stepmother, Sarah MacArthur said, he "needed to step back and catch his breath" and think about his career. He went to work on a horse ranch, and on February 3, 2004, a missing person's report was filed. On February 7, 2004, Jason was found hanged in a shed on the property. Jason death was determined to have happened on the day he disappeared and ruled a suicide. He was cremated and the location of his ashes is unknown. Jason was twenty-eight.

The Orpheus Theatre in Oneonta now issues two Jason Rothenberg Raize Scholarships each year to help teens who need financial aid attend the theater's summer music theater workshops.

While filming *Crossbones* in 2004, **Neal Fredericks,** camera man, was killed when his plane crashed.

Robert Pastorelli was born in New Brunswick, New Jersey on June 21, 1954. After a boxing career cut short by a near fatal car crash, Robert turned to the theater during the 1970s.

In 1982, he moved to Hollywood where he appeared in sixty-one film and television roles between 1982 and 2005. He may be best remembered for his portrayal of Eldin Bernecky in forty-four episodes of the television series, *Murphy Brown.*

Pastorelli was placed under investigation in the murder of his girlfriend, twenty-five year old Charemon Jonovich, at their Hollywood Hills home in March, 1999. He was not charged, but in 2004, when he found out that the police were reopening their investigation, Pastorelli evidently killed himself by overdosing on a mix of cocaine and morphine. A syringe, a spoon and a plastic bag with white powder were discovered near his body. He is buried in Saint Catherine's Cemetery in Sea Girt, New Jersey.

Spalding Rockwell Gray was born in Providence, Rhode Island on June 5, 1941. He taught poetry at the Esalen Institute near Big Sur, and then, in 1967, settled in New York City.

Between 1970 and 2003, Gray appeared in forty-two film and television roles. He appeared in nine episodes of the television series, *The Nanny* between 1997 and 1999.

Gray was involved in an automobile accident in June, 2001 while vacationing in Ireland, and was left with a partially crippled leg as well as a fractured skull that required the placement of a titanium plate. Gray became deeply depressed, and on March 7, 2004, he disappeared. His body was later discovered in the East River. Reports have it that Gray committed suicide by jumping from the Staten Island ferry He is buried in the Oakland Cemetery in Sag Harbor, New York.

John Drew Barrymore was born John Blyth Barrymore on June 4, 1932 in Los Angeles, California. His parents were John Barrymore of the famous Barrymore family and the actress Dolores Costello. After his parents separated when he was a baby, he rarely saw his famous father.

John began his acting career as John Barrymore Jr, but changed his name to John Drew Barrymore in 1958. He appeared in many low budget films, did some Italian movies, and worked in television, but his drinking and drug use in the 60s kept him from finding real success. Seemingly following in his father's footsteps, he struggled with addiction until he became a derelict, estranged from his family and friends.

Even though they were estranged, from 2003, until he passed on November 29, 2004 from cancer brought on by the addictive lifestyle he lived, his daughter, Drew Barrymore, paid his medical bills.

On hearing about her father's death, Drew Barrymore released a statement saying, "He was a cool cat. Please smile when you think of him."

John was cremated and his ashes scattered in the Joshua Tree National Monument.

Hunter Stockton Thompson was born on July 18, 1937 in Louisville, Kentucky. After his father died, his mother supported the family of four by working as a librarian.

Hunter joined the Air Force when he was eighteen. He left the Air Force in 1958 after being recommended for early discharge for having a rebellious attitude.

He worked for a while for a newspaper in Pennsylvania and then moved to New York City where he used the G. I. Bill to study writing at Columbia University.

He worked for Time Magazine for a short while as a copy boy but was fired for insubordination. His next job was with The Middletown Daily Record in Middletown, New York. His attitude and actions again got him fired.

Hunter spent a year in Brazil and upon returning to the U. S. in 1963, he married Sandra Conklin. They had a son and then divorced in 1980.

A job with the National Observer ended when the paper refused to print one of his stories. He moved on to San Francisco where he became part of the hippie culture and wrote for the Berkeley underground paper *The Spyder*.

The editor of *The Nation* gave Thompson a job in 1965 and published one of his articles about his experiences with the Hells Angels motorcycle club. That led to some book offers about the Angels. After Hunter refused to share his profits with the gang, they gave him a "stomping."

His book, *Hell's Angels: The Strange and Terrible Saga of the Outlaw Motorcycle Gangs*, was later published by Random House and Hunter received good reviews for his work.

Thompson wrote articles for various national magazines during the late 1960s, including *The Hashbury is the Capital of the Hippies* published in 1967 by Times Magazine. The article criticized the hippie culture as populated with newcomers that were in it just for the drugs.

Experiences during a trip to Las Vegas, which became the 1971 book *Fear and Loathing in Las Vegas,* was published by Rolling Stone. It became a best seller. The New York Times said it was "by far the best book yet written on the decade of dope".

In 1980, *Where the Buffalo Roam* was released.

Thompson had six novels published between 1980 and 2011. He appeared in several movies in 1996 and 1998.

He killed himself with a pistol on February 20, 2005. His funeral was paid for by Johnny Depp, allowing for Hunter's ashes and colorful fireworks to be fired from a cannon on a Colorado mountaintop in a spectacular display.

Charles Rocket was born Charles Adams Claverie in Bangor, Maine on August 24, 1949. He appeared in twelve episodes of *Saturday Night Live* in 1980 and 1981. Between 1984 and 2004, he had roles in seventy-eight film and television productions. On October 7, 2005, Rocket's body was found lying in a field in Connecticut. He had bled to death from a severed artery in his throat. The autopsy report called his death a suicide. He was cremated and his ashes scattered.

Tara Correa-McMullen was born Shalvah McMullen in Westminster, Vermont on May 24th, 1989. She moved to Venice, California in 1996, where she attended Venice High School. At age fourteen, Tara landed the part of Graciela Reyes, a gang member, in the television series, *Judging Amy*. Her mother worked for a casting company, and in 2005 got Tara a role in the film, *Rebound*.

On October 21st, 2005, Tara was shot and killed by a gang member while standing outside her apartment building in Inglewood, a suburb south of Los Angeles. She was sixteen.

Chris Penn was born on October 10, 1965 in Los Angeles, California. His brother Sean is also an actor, and his brother Michael is a musician.

Chris worked for the Loft Studios when he was twelve, making his first appearance in films in *Charlie and the Talking Buzzard* in 1979. Between 1979 and 2007, he performed in sixty-four movies, television productions, and video games. He may be best known for his roles in the original *Footloose,* starring Kevin Bacon, made in 1984 and *Reservoir Dogs,* written by Quentin Tarantino, released in 1992.

Chris with Matt Dillon, Nicolas Cage, and Vincent Spano in *Rumble Fish* (1983)

Penn was known to be a drug addict, but he died of heart disease in his Santa Monica condo on January 24, 2006. The autopsy report stated that the presence of Promethazine and Codine in his blood was a contributing factor. He is buried at Holy Cross Cemetery in Culver City, California.

Adrienne (Shelly) Levine, born on June 24, 1966 in Queens, New York, began her acting career at age ten in the Stagedoor Manor Performing Arts Training Center. Her first professional appearance was in *Annie* in Jericho, New York. She then majored in film production at Boston University

She appeared in *The Unbelievable Truth* in 1989 and in 1990 had a part in *Trust*. She also wrote, co-starred in, and directed the 2007 film *Waitress*, which won five awards.

Television appearances included *Law & Order*, and *Oz*. Her last film was *Factorium* in which she had a small acting role. She was also involved in the writing and directing of the film.

On November 1, 2006, she was discovered hanging from a shower rod in the bathroom of her apartment in Manhattan. At first the police thought she had committed suicide, but shoe prints that did not match hers were found in the bathtub, and according to her husband money had been taken from her purse. An Ecuadorian illegal immigrant who was part of a construction crew working at the building in which Shelly lived, was arrested and charged with her murder. He later confessed, saying that Shelley had caught him in her apartment rummaging through her purse.

Benjamin Hendrickson was born in Huntington, New York on August 26, 1950. He took drama classes at the Juilliard School, and later appeared on the stage. He had roles in seventeen film and television productions between 1976 and 2006. He may be best remembered for his appearances as Hal Munson in 158 episodes of the television series, *As the World Turns* between 1986 and 2006.

Henderson suffered from serious bouts of depression which were amplified by his mother's death in 2003. He was found on July 3, 2006 at his home in Huntington, New York, with a gunshot wound in the head. The autopsy report labeled his death a suicide. His burial place is unknown.

Jon Dough was born Chester Anuszak in Pennsylvania on November 12, 1962. He earned a degree in Biology at Albright College in Reading, Pennsylvania in 1985, and following his brother's example, became a model for gay magazines.

Between 1986 and 2007, Dough appeared in 872 pornographic videos. He is known for having had sex with 101 women over a period of three days in a video titled, *The World's Luckiest Man,* which was released in 1997. For reasons unknown, Dough hung himself on August 27, 2006.

Daniel Wayne Smith was born in Limestone County, Texas on January 22, 1986. He was the son of Anna Nicole Smith, and the stepson of multi-millionaire J. Howard Marshall II. Daniel's parents divorced in 1987, and his mother raised him.

Daniel appeared in two movies in 1995 and 1996. He is probably best known for appearing in twenty-six episodes of the television series, *The Anna Nicole Show*, seen in 2002-2003.

It was reported that Anna Nicole had been given a prescription for methadone by using a false name. She was in her eighth month of pregnancy at the time. Ford Shelley claimed that while Anna's Bahamas home was being inspected, Methadone was found in her bedroom refrigerator.

Daniel came to visit Anna Nicole after she delivered a daughter at Doctor's Hospital in Nassau, The Bahamas.

The President and CEO of the hospital said, "Daniel Smith --- spent the entire evening in the room and remained as a visitor with his mother and newly born sister. On Sunday, September 10, 2006, Daniel was observed to be asleep, but at 9:38 a.m. a nurse was called and doctors were summoned after Daniel was found to be unresponsive."

Daniel was pronounced dead at 10:05 a.m.

It was reported that Daniel stole methadone from his mother, and accidently overdosed.

Anna Nicole Smith (Vickie Lynn Hogan) was born on November 28, 1967 in Houston, Texas. She quit high school at age eighteen to be married.

Her second marriage was to oilman multi-millionaire J. Howard Marshall, sixty-two years older than her. For some reason many believed that she married him for his money.

Anna appeared in eight television and film roles between 1994 and 2007, and acted as creative consultant for the *Anna Nicole Show* which aired fourteen times in 2002.

Anna Nicole died of an accidental overdose of prescription drugs on February 8, 2007. She is buried in the Bahamas.

Richard Jeni was born in Bensonhurst, Brooklyn on April 14, 1957. He was an honor student at Hunter College where he graduated with a degree in Comparative Politics.

He appeared in eight television and film roles between 1988 and 2007, including thirteen episodes of *The Platypus Man* in 1995, but he suffered from severe clinical depression which caused psychotic paranoia.

Richard died of a gunshot wound to the head on March 10, 2007. He is buried in the Moravian Cemetery in New Dorp, New York.

Brad Renfro was born in Knoxville, Tennessee on July 25, 1982. At age ten, he was discovered by a casting director and given a leading role in *The Client*, starring Susan Sarandon. *The Client* was one of the big hits of 1994.

The following year he was named Hollywood Reporter's "Young Star." He won the lead in *Huck* that same year and appeared in *Sleeper* with Robert DeNiro and Kevin Bacon the next year.

At age fifteen, Renfro was arrested after two small bags of cocaine and one bag of marijuana were discovered in his possession. He agreed to random screening for drugs and was not charged. Renfro and a friend tried to steal a 45-foot yacht from Fort Lauderdale harbor on August 28, 2000. They were arrested and charged with grand theft and criminal mischief. The judge gave him probation. A little over a year later he was arrested for public intoxication and driving without a license.

Renfro was charged with attempted possession of heroin by the LAPD in December, 2005. He pleaded guilty and was again put on probation. He spent ten days in jail in 2006 for DUI and attempted heroin possession.

In June, 2007, he violated his probation and was warned that if he violated probation two more times, he would be sentenced to jail time.

Six months later, Renfro was found dead in his Los Angeles apartment. The coroner ruled that his death was caused by acute heroin/morphine intoxication.

Twenty-six-year-old **Nathan Clutter**, the star of *Paradise Hotel 2*, killed himself in October, 2007 by leaping from a cell-phone tower.

Ashleigh Aston Moore (Ashleigh Rogers) was born on September 30, 1981 in Sunnyvale, California. She began her acting career when she was four-years-old.

In 1992, at age 11, she was awarded the roles of Alpha and Donna, characters in *The Odyssey*, a Canadian children's television series. Ashleigh is probably best known for playing Chrissy in the movie *Now and Then*. Between 1993 and 1997 she earned thirteen credits in television and movie parts. In 1997, Ashleigh gave up acting.

Ashleigh died on December 10th, 2007, of an accidental overdose of heroin. She was twenty-six-years-old.

John Berg was born in Wichita Falls, Texas on April 5, 1949. He graduated from Wichita Falls High School in 1967, and then went to Tulane University.

After working in various positions in New York City, he started acting and was seen in roles in television soaps such as *General Hospital*, *The Bold and the Beautiful*, and *The Young & the Restless*. He then moved to Los Angeles and continued his career in television there. All in all, he appeared in seventeen television productions between 1998 and 2007.

On December 15, 2007, for reasons unknown, Berg took his charcoal grill into the bedroom of his home at the 6500 block of Nagle Avenue in Los Angeles. He then lit it, evidently went to sleep, and suffocated from the carbon monoxide fumes the grill produced.

While filming *Red Cliff* (2008/2009), a boat was set on fire and killed stuntman **Lu Yanqing.**

Heath Ledger was born on April 4, 1979 in Australia. He moved to Hollywood in 1998 to further develop his career. In 1999, he appeared in *10 Things I Hate About You.* The following year, he appeared in the Revolutionary War epic, *The Patriot*, with Mel Gibson. Heath also produced and directed music videos and aspired to be a film director.

He married the actress, Michelle Williams, in 2004, and their daughter Matilda Rose was born the next year.

That same year, the film Heath is most known for, *Brokeback Mountain,* was released. For his performance as the cowboy, Ennis Del Mar, Heath won the Academy Award for Best Actor.

Michelle and Heath divorced in 2007.

A few months before his death, Ledger finished filming the *Dark Knight* with Christian Bale. After his death, his performance as the Joker garnered Heath the Academy Award for Best Supporting Actor, becoming the first actor to receive the award posthumously.

Ledger was found dead on January 22, 2008 in his apartment, in the Manhattan neighborhood of SoHo. A coroner's report concluded that he died of an accidental overdose of prescription drugs that included painkillers, sleeping pills and anti-anxiety medication.

Heath was cremated in Australia and his ashes were interred in his family's plot at Karrakatta Cemetery next to his grandparents.

De'Angelo Wilson (De'Angelo Ke'Shine Hill Wilson), was born in Dayton, Ohio on March 29, 1979.

Wilson appeared in twelve television and film roles between 2003 and 2012. He is probably best known for his role in *Antwone Fisher*, released in 2002.

Wilson hung himself on November 26, 2008 in Los Angeles. The coroner's report called his death a suicide. According to his mother, he believed that his acting career was over, and he was deeply depressed. His friends paid to have his body sent back to Ohio.

John A. Costelloe was born on November 8th, 1961 in Brooklyn, New York. He worked as a Brooklyn Firefighter for eleven years, retiring in 1998.

John played a Firefighter named Jim Witowski in the series, *The Sopranos*, and had roles in eight other television and film productions between 1989 and 2008. For reasons as yet unknown, John shot himself in the head in his Sunset Park, Brooklyn home on December 16, 2008. He was forty-seven at the time of his death.

Louis Byron also known as Lou Perry, was born on August 15, 1941. He was employed as production manager of the Texas Pavilion at the World's Fair in San Antonio in 1968. Later he became a cinematographer, working for the Filmhouse in Austin. Lou performed in 1982's *Poltergeist*, and in *Last Night at the Alamo*, released in 1984. Two years later he was seen in *The Texas Chainsaw Massacre Part 2*.

On April 1, 2009, a 26-year-old man, just released from prison for aggravated robbery, murdered Lou with an axe.

Lucy Gordon was born on May 22, 1980 in Oxford, U. K. She went to Oxford High School, and in 1997 moved to New York City. After living there for several years, she moved to Paris, France. There, she was spotted by an agent from a modelling agency, and appeared as one of the faces on Cover Girl magazine, before moving starting an acting career. She made her film debut in the 2001 as Sarah in *Perfume*. In 2002, she landed a role in *Four Feathers*.

Gordon was found dead in her Paris flat on May 20, 2009. She left two notes, but there has been no explanation for her reason to commit suicide by hanging herself. However, a close friend had committed suicide shortly before she did, and neighbors reported that she and her live-in boyfriend had a serious argument that same night.

David (Jack) Carradine was born John Arthur Carradine in Hollywood on December 8, 1936. His parents divorced in 1944, when Jack was seven years old.

Jack graduated High School and then attended Oakland Junior College and San Francisco State College. He dropped out of college and then joined a group of 'beatniks' in San Francisco's North Beach and Venice.

He attempted to dodge the draft and failing was called into the army in 1960.

He made his first television appearance in 1963 on *Armstrong Circle Theatre*. His first film part was in *Taggart*, released in 1964.

Jack appeared in *The Royal Hunt of the Sun* on Broadway in 1965 and won a Theatre World Award for Best Debut Performance. When *The Royal Hunt of the Sun* closed, Carradine returned to Hollywood to star in the television series *Shane*.

He co-starred in *Boxcar Bertha* in 1972 with Barbara Hershey, who was living with him at the time. His next television role, which lasted three seasons, was in *Kung Fu* (1972–1975).

Oddly enough, even though he was a television star, he was arrested for attempted burglary and malicious mischief in 1974 after breaking into a neighbor's home, where he cut himself on broken glass, and bled on the furniture. He was nude at the time and spaced out on peyote. Charges were dropped, and Carradine was placed on probation.

Carradine received much praise for his lead role *Bound for Glory*, released in 1976.

Carradine joined his half-brothers Keith and Robert in *The Long Riders* in 1980. He appeared in *Safari 3000*, and was then again arrested; this time for possession of marijuana. He received a suspended sentence, claiming that the South African government had framed him for dancing in public with Tina Turner.

Carradine was arrested two more times in the 1980s on DUI charges.

Carradine's film and television career went into a tail-spin during the 1980s and 90s, but he once again became popular with his role in the two *Kill Bill* films, released in 2003 and 2004.

On June 4, 2009, while on location in Bangkok shooting *Stretch*, Carradine was found naked, hanging by a rope, in his hotel room. It was first thought that he had committed suicide, but reports later said that he had accidentally killed himself while engaged in autoerotic asphyxiation.

Two of his former wives stated that his sexual appetites included self-bondage.

He is interred in the Forest Lawn Memorial Park (Hollywood Hills) in Los Angeles.

Michael Joseph Jackson was born on August 29, 1958 in Gary, Indiana. His father worked in a steel mill and also performed in a local rhythm and blues band.

Michael had three sisters and five brothers. His brothers, Jackie, Tito, and Jermaine assembled a band in 1964. Two years later, Michael and his brother Jermaine began performing with the band as lead vocalists, and the name of the group was changed to The Jackson Five. Between 1966 and 1968, The Jackson Five toured throughout the nation's Midwest, and then signed with Motown.

Between 1972 and 2012, Michael was involved in 147 television and film productions. He acted in thirteen, and wrote the music used in all of the 147. His income from these various enterprises is said to have been 125 million dollars in 1989 alone.

Michael and Lisa Marie Presley married in 1994. Lisa, Elvis' daughter, made a public statement that she and Michael had sexual relations, but this was thought to be a public relations effort to offset rumors about Michael's interest in young boys. He and Lisa divorced two years later.

He then married Deborah Rowe, a nurse. Rowe was already pregnant with Jackson's son at the time. They had a daughter one year later, and then divorced in 1999.

Michael's third child was produced through artificial insemination.

In 2003, Michael was arrested and charged with child molestation, but he was found not guilty by a jury.

Michael died on June 25, 2009, of what is said to have been cardiac arrest brought on by unusual drugs administered by his physician. Michael suffered from insomnia and the drugs were intended to help him sleep. His death occurred two weeks before the opening of his come-back concerts, *This Is It*.

Michael was buried in the Forest Lawn Memorial Park in Glendale, California.

As of April, 2013, a lawsuit filed by the Jackson family against the promoters of Michael's last concert was underway. Michael's family argued that the promoter's hired the doctor that gave Michael the surgical aesthetic that killed him, and were therefore responsible for his death.

One of the defence lawyers had this to say about Michael: "We're talking about Michael Jackson," Putnam said. "This is a man who would show up in (court in) pajamas. This is a man who would stop traffic and get out and dance on top of his car. This is a man who would go to public events with a monkey named Bubbles. This is a man who said he slept in an oxygen chamber."

Michael Jackson's home at 100 N. Carolwood Drive
in the Holmby Hills section of Los Angeles

Michael Roof was born in Tampa, Florida on November 24, 1976. In the late 1990s, he travelled across the U. S. working in comedy clubs under the name "Chicken." Between 2000 and 2005, he appeared in six television and film roles, including a lead part in *Black Hawk Down*, which was released in 2001.

Roof's wife reported him missing on June 9, 2009. His body was found hanging from a tree in Snellville, Georgia.

Roof suffered from bipolar disorder, and he is said to have been depressed over severe financial problems. He is buried in Dunnellon Memorial Gardens in Dunnellon, Florida.

Ryan Alexander Jenkins was a reality show contestant on, *Megan Wants a Millionaire* and later starred in *I Love Money*.

He was married to model Jasmine Fiore, and it was said that they had domestic problems. His wife's body was found stuffed in a suitcase on August 15, 2009. The suitcase had been thrown in a dumpster. She had been strangled; her teeth and fingers were missing, and she had been cut into pieces.

Investigators later found Jenkins' suicide note. It had been written three days before he committed suicide, and was discovered on his computer's hard drive. The note expressed his deep love for his wife and praised her beauty. It then discussed the extreme jealousy that he experienced over her sexual involvements with other men. Police investigators believe that the note explains what Jenkins was thinking about while sitting alone in a rundown motel in British Columbia. He was being hunted internationally as a primary suspect in Jasmine Fiore's murder at the time.

An arrest warrant was issued for Jenkins on August 20, and three days later, his body was found hanging in his motel room.

Brittany Anne Murphy was born on November 10, 1977 in Atlanta, Georgia. After her parents divorced when Brittany was two, her mother took her to Edison, New Jersey. She went to Edison High School, and then to the Verneb Fowler School in Colonia, New Jersey. When Brittany was thirteen, her mother took her to Hollywood, where she got a role in the television show, *Blossom*.

Between 1991 and 2012, Brittany appeared in sixty-four television and film productions. This included voice work in 231 episodes of *King of the Hill* from 1997 to 2010.

Because of severe changes in her weight there were questions about the possibility that she was using drugs. Brittany denied this adamantly.

Brittany and Simion Monjack were married in 2007.

Emergency medical assistance was requested for the Monjack home on December 20, 2009. Responders found Brittany lying on the bathroom floor and took her to Cedars-Sinai Medical Center where she was pronounced DOA. The coroner reported that the many over-the-counter drugs found in her blood stream were likely the cause of death.

Another call for medical aid was made on May 23, 2010 to the same address, six months later. Responders found Simon Monjack dead. The coroner's report stated that he died of acute pneumonia and severe anemia.

Brittany is buried in the Forest Lawn Memorial Park in the Hollywood Hills.

After appearing on the reality show, *Kitchen Nightmares* in 2007 and receiving a scathing review from the show's host, **Joseph Cerniglia** killed himself in September of 2010. He died after jumping off the George Washington Bridge in New York City. Joe was thirty-nine.g

In November, 2010**,** after dining with his parents**, Julien Hug**, a onetime *Bachelorette* contestant, was found dead in the rugged desert terrain near Palm Desert, California. He died from a self-inflicted gunshot to the head. He was thirty-five years old.

The note he left for his parents:

I'm sorry to have to do this to you. I love you both tremendously. You two are the best parents. I've suffered from severe depression for years. I feel awful and don't know how to cope. If life's not enjoyable, why stick around?

Ronni Chasen was born Veronica Cohen on October 17, 1946 in Kingston, New York. Her first film related job was for her brother, director Larry Cohen. He put her in charge of publicity for his film, *Hell Up in Harlem* released in 1973.

Later, Chasen won recognition in Hollywood for her PR work with *On Golden Pond*, and *Wall Street 2: Money Never Sleeps*.

On November 16, 2010, Chasen was returning home after attending the premiere of *Burlesque* when she was shot five times and killed by an unknown assailant.

Ronni was buried in Hillside Memorial Park in Culver City, California.

Perry Moore was born in Richmond, Virginia on November 4th, 1971.

A 1974 graduate of the University of Virginia, Moore resided in New York City with his homosexual partner, Hunter Hill. Moore produced *I Am David* in 2003, and three of the *Chronicles of Narnia* films between 2005 and 2010. He also wrote the screenplay for *Lake City* in 2008.

Moore overdosed on drugs on February 17, 2011, at age thirty-nine.

Michael Christopher "Mike" Starr was born on April 4, 1966. Although he is best known as the original bassist for the grunge band Alice in Chains, Mike was featured in the third season of the television series, *Celebrity Rehab with Dr. Drew*, in 2010 where he was trying to kick his addiction to methadone. His next television appearance was on *Sober House*, documenting his struggle to stay clean, which he managed to do for six months and seven days.

On March 8, 2011, Mike's body was found, his death was the result of a prescription-drug overdose. Mike was forty-four.

Rod Lauren Strunk was born Roger Lawrence Strunk in Fresno, California on March 20, 1940. In 1943, his family moved to Tracy, California.

While Rod was still a teenager, RCA gave him a recording contract resulting in appearances on the Ed Sullivan show in 1959, and the Dick Clark show the following year.

Between 1962 and 1969, Rod had roles in fourteen film and television productions, but then his popularity fell.

He met Nida Blanca, a young actress, while working in the film, *Once Before I Die*, released in 1966, in the Philippines, and married her ten years later.

Blanca was murdered on November 6, 2001, and Rod was held by the Philippine authorities as a suspect. They claimed that Rod hired someone to stab Blanca to death when she asked for a divorce. There was inheritance money at stake.

Rod asked for permission to travel to the U. S. in order to visit his mother, stating that she was dying of cancer. He was allowed to do so, but once stateside, he fought extradition requests to bring him back and won.

Evidently, the pressures of the ongoing investigation were more than he could handle, and on July 11, 2011, he killed himself by jumping from the second floor of a motel.

Amy Jade Winehouse was born in the Southgate area of North London on September 14, 1983. She began writing music when she was fourteen, and in July, 2000, she was appointed lead female vocalist for the National Youth Jazz Orchestra. She became known for her original music, an unusual blend of rhythm and blues, reggae, soul, and jazz.

She made one appearance as an actress in 1997, in an episode of the television series, *The Fast Show*, and forty-three times as a performer or writer on television and in movies.

Amy became an alcoholic, and soon destroyed her career by showing up for concerts highly intoxicated. She cancelled all public appearances in 2007, blaming emotional strain.

2008 was a banner year in Amy's career when she became the first British female to win five Grammys, including Best New Artist, Record of the Year, and Song of the Year.

So in 2009, she tried again to perform at the Saint Lucia jazz festival, but ended leaving the stage in the middle of her performance after forgetting the lyrics.

Although Amy sang with Tony Bennett on *Duets II*, which was released in 2011, and again in *Body and Soul,* released that same year, when she showed up at one of her concerts too drunk to sing, the audience booed her off the stage.

On July 23, 2011, Amy Winehouse's bodyguard found her unconscious on her bed. He could not rouse her and called 911. The EMTs reported her dead when they arrived.

The coroner's report said that Amy died of alcohol poisoning.

On July 25, 2011, she was buried at Edgewarebury Lane Cemetery in north London.

Russell Armstrong, cast member of *The Real Housewives of Beverly Hills*, and ex-husband of Taylor Armstrong, was discovered by Taylor at his Los Angeles home on August 17, 2011. Armstrong had hanged himself. Armstrong owed in excess of one and one-half million dollars as a result of his excessive lifestyle.

James Kent "Jimmy" Leeward was born in Brackenridge, Pennsylvania on October 21, 1936. Leeward performed as an actor in three films between 1980 and 2006. He was an aircraft stunt pilot in four films between 1983 and 2009. He not only raced aircraft, but also owned Leeward Air Ranch.

Leeward crashed into the audience viewing the National Championship Air

Races at Reno Stead Airport, in Nevada on September 16, 2011. As a result, Leeward and eleven people were killed; sixty-nine were injured.

Nick Santino was born on January 24th, 1965 in Brooklyn, New York. He was placed in an orphanage at age five months and spent the next sixteen years bouncing from foster home to foster home. Santino, a very self-reliant individual, put himself through engineering school and earned an MBA in finance. He then completed a two year course of study at the American Academy of Dramatic Arts.

Nick worked in several off-Broadway productions before landing a part in *All My Children* in 1970. A year later he became a producer/director.

Facing pressure from his Upper East Side condo, Nick euthanized his Pit Bull dog, Rocco. He did this on his forty-seventh birthday. That decision caused such guilt and depression that on January 25th, 2012, Nick committed suicide at his Manhattan condominium complex by overdosing on prescription drugs. He left this note:

<u>Rocco trusted me and I failed him. He didn't deserve this.</u>

Nick was cremated.

While filming *The Expendables 2* (2012), during a staged explosion, a stuntman was killed and another was critically injured.

Donald Cornelius was born in Chicago on Sept 27, 1936. He was a Marine during the Korean War, and then became a police officer. He appeared in three movies between 1976 and 1988.

In 1970, Cornelius used $400 of his personal money to start *Soul Train* on a Chicago television station. He made himself host as well as executive producer and developed the show into a nationally syndicated institution. *Soul Train* was the first in the dance show genre to specialize in the musical tastes of American black teenagers. Because of its popularity, black music, dance, and fashion became recognized by mainstream America.

Aretha Franklin said Cornelius "united the young adult community single-handedly and globally. With the inception of *Soul Train*, a young, progressive brother set the pace and worldwide standard for young, aspiring African-American men and entrepreneurs in TV -- out of Chicago. He transcended barriers among young adults. They became one."

Cornelius moved *Soul Train* to Los Angeles in 1971, where he featured musical artists such as James Brown, Marvin Gaye, and the Jackson 5.

Teen Dance Party was featured on *Soul Train*, and it spotlighted the dancing abilities of the best young dancers in the LA area. One of *Soul Train's* most popular features was known as the 'line", where the dancers appeared in a line and took turns performing their best dance moves. Among the show's performers were Rosie Perez, MC Hammer, and Jeffrey Daniel, who taught Michael Jackson how to do the moonwalk.

On February 1, 2012, Cornelius committed suicide. He had been in poor health for some time, and might have been suffering from early onset of dementia or Alzheimer's disease.

Julie Patzwald was born on March 11th, 1980 in British Columbia, Canada. She appeared in fifty television and film productions between 1997 and 2010, and was best known for her performances in *John Tucker Must Die,* released in 2006 by Twentieth Century Fox, *Shattered,* released in 2007, and *Rampage,* released in 2009.

Suffering from severe, chronic pain, Julie took her own life on in April, 2012 in Vancouver, Canada.

Sylvester Stallone's son, **Sage Moonblood Stallone**, was found dead in his Hollywood apartment on July 13, 2012. Early reports say that he either committed suicide or accidently overdosed on drugs.

Gavin Smith was born on December 10, 1954 in the San Fernando Valley area of Los Angeles, California. Reaching the height of 6'6", he became a sought-after basketball star during his high school and college career.

After college, Gavin acted in a few films, including the 1994 film, *Cobb*, where he had a small role as a bartender, but then he decided he was better suited for a job in the business side of the film industry. Working for 20th Century Fox as a film distributer, Gavin was responsible to get the films to the theaters they were scheduled to appear in and was credited with helping films such as *Titanic*, and *Avatar* succeed. By 2012 he was Fox's regional branch manager for theaters in the Dallas and Oklahoma City areas.

Although Gavin was very successful in business, his personal life was beset with marital, financial, and substance abuse difficulties, and on the night of May 1, 2012, Gavin left a friend's house, where he had been staying, and simply vanished. The police were unable to find anything out about his disappearance until February 2013, when Gavin's Mercedes-Benz, was found in a Simi Valley, California storage facility. The man who rented the storage facility was the husband of one of Gavin's drug rehab friends.

On October 26, 2014, over two years after his disappearance, a group of hikers found a shallow grave containing a skull, some bones, and clothing in a rural area near Palmdale, California, which proved to be Gavin's remains.

The cause of death was not initially known, but at a press conference held the day Gavin's body was discovered, investigators shared their theory. Gavin was killed in his car shortly after he disappeared. They believe the cause of death would prove to be a homicide caused by blunt force trauma.

Johnny (Jonathon Kendrick Lewis**) Lewis** was born on October 29, 1983 in Los Angeles, California. As a Scientologist, Johnny appeared in the church's training films and he was also a sponsor in Narconon, their drug rehab group.

He left the group in his early twenties, but had been working in television since he was a teenager, with roles in *Boston Public* in 2000, *The Guardian* in 2001, and *American Dreams* in 2002, among others.

He made his first film in 2004 with a role in New Line Cinema's, *Raise Your Voice*. He then appeared in *Upperclassman* in 2005, and *Aliens vs Predator: Requiem* in 2007. In all, Johnny appeared in over thirty television and film productions, but he was perhaps best known for playing "Half-Sack" Epps, in the television series *Sons of Anarchy*

Johnny was involved in a motorcycle accident on October 30th, 2011 and suffered head injuries. He refused treatment, but later began to show signs of odd behavior. His medical discharge summary, dated January 11, 2012, states that he was suffering from basal skull fracture, and was likely hemorrhaging internally.

Although his injuries were well documented and he never tested positive for drugs, the doctors continued to say Johnny's problems were drug related.

His bizarre behavior led to three arrests 2011 and 2012. His probation officer even expressed concern that Johnny had mental health issues and was addicted to drugs, but the actor was still released from jail on September 24th, 2012.

Two days later, on September 26th, 2012, Johnny was found dead on the driveway of the home of his landlady at 3605 Lowry Road in the Los Feliz area of Los Angeles, California. Inside the house, they found his landlady's body.

Neighbors reported that they saw a man jump the fence from the murder house, attack two people next door, and then jump back over the fence. According to the report made by the Los Angeles Police Department, Johnny then either fell or jumped from the roof of the garage, or patio of the murder house. There was no indication that Lewis had been pushed or that he jumped from the roof in an act of suicide.

An autopsy report stated that Lewis did not have any drugs or alcohol in his system when he died, but had suffered partial strangulation and had fingernail marks on his neck when he died. His death was ruled accidental.

The police determined that Johnny broke into the house and murdered his landlady.

Brian Gerber was born in 1971. A Hollywood producer, he committed suicide on September 12, 2012 by driving his Toyota Prius off a 600 foot cliff on a highway near La Cañada Flintridge in the mountains north of Hollywood. Gerber produced 20 television shows and films between 2000 and 2012. He was probably best known for his work on Leonardo DiCaprio's documentary *The 11th Hour*.

Director **Tony Scott** was born June 21, 1944 in England. He was the younger brother of Director Ridley Scott. Tony committed suicide on August 19, 2012 by climbing an eighteen-foot high bridge fence and leaping into the Los Angeles Harbor.

Scott became a well-known director in the 1980s with such films as *Top Gun* and *Beverly Hills Cop II*. In later years, he directed *True Romance, Crimson Tide, Enemy of the State*, and *Unstoppable*. Scott co-produced the 2012 hit, *Prometheus,* and was said to be planning a sequel to *Top Gun*.

His motivation for suicide is as yet unknown. He is buried in Hollywood Forever Cemetery in Hollywood, California.

After a forty-year-old auctioneer named **Mark Balelo** appeared on the television show, *Storage Wars,* he was found dead in his car in February of 2013 from carbon monoxide poisoning. A few days before, Mark had been arrested for possession of methamphetamines.

Cory Monteith was born on May 11, 1982 in Calgary, Alberta, Canada. His father was in the military and his mother worked as an interior decorator. His parents divorced when he was seven years old. He lived with his mother and an older brother in Victoria, British Columbia. Possibly because he had no father he was an ill-behaved child, using drugs and often skipping school. Cory quit school at age sixteen, became a petty thief and continued using drugs. He went through a rehab center when he was nineteen, and again at age thirty-one, shortly before his death.

After deciding to become an actor Cory found work in television in small roles.

An audition tape won him the part of Finn Hudson, a character in the TV series, *Glee* and this led to movie roles in films such as, *Monte Carlo* (2010) and *Sisters and Brothers*(2011).

Cory met actress Lea Michele in 2009 and they became romantically involved, remaining together until his death.

Cory was staying at the Fairmont Pacific Rim in Vancouver in July, 2013. As he was expected to check out on the 13th and failed to do so, the hotel management sent someone to his room. This person discovered Cory's body. The coroner's report ruled out violence and stated that Cory had died from an accidental overdose of heroin and alcohol. He also had codeine and morphine in his system.

Gia Marie Allemand was born on December 20, 1983 in Queens, New York. She grew up on Long Island and Staten Island. Gia's parents divorced when she was ten. Gia graduated Lindenhurst High School in Long Island in 2001. Her mother had her modeling while she was still a baby and she worked for corporations such as Johnson and Johnson and Gerber. Gia began a full-time modeling career in 1992 at age nineteen. She is popularly known for her swimsuit ads in Maxim. She also worked for Dream It Make It, consultants for models.

In 2010, Gia landed a role in *The Bachelor: On the Wings of Love*, an ABC reality show, in 2010, and in the same year she appeared on *The Ellen DeGeneres Show.* Gia's next television appearance was on ABC's *20/20,* followed by another reality show, *Bachelor Pad.*

In 2013, Gia was working as a dance instructor and was romantically involved with Ryan Anderson who played basketball for The New Orleans Pelicans. On August 12, 2013, Ryan came home and discovered Gia hanging by the neck from a stair railing. She had attempted suicide using an electric cord. Ryan told investigators that he and Gia had argued at lunch time over her belief that he was seeing other women. After driving her to the drug store, he dropped her off at the apartment and told her he did not love her anymore as he drove off.

Investigators reported no signs of violence. A note was found. It read:

<u>"Mom gets everything."</u>

Gia was rushed to University Hospital by ambulance. Doctors there put her on life support, but said that her prognosis was grim. She died that same night. She was twenty-nine years old.

Lee Thompson Young was born on February 1, 1984 in Columbia, South Carolina. He was best known for his role as the title character on the Disney Channel television series *The Famous Jett Jackson*, and as Chris Comer in the movie, *Friday Night Lights*.

At age ten, Young played the part of Martin Luther King in the play, *A Night of Stars and Dreams* at a repertory Theater in Greenville, South Carolina. After doing Community Theater, he moved to New York in 1996.

In 1997, he auditioned for the part of Jett Jackson in *The Famous Jett Jackson*. In June 1998 the Disney Channel picked up the show, and it later went on to become a Disney movie released in 2001.

After the cancellation of *The Famous Jett Jackson*, Young had guest spots in CBS's *The Guardian*. He had a part in the movie, *Friday Night Lights* portraying Chris Comer and a part in the Jamie Foxx movie, *Redemption: The Stan Tookie Williams Story*. Young appeared in the feature film, *Akeelah and the Bee*, playing Akeelah's brother, Devon. He played National Guard rookie, Delmar, in *The Hills Have Eyes 2*.

On August 19, 2013, Young failed to appear for an episode of *Rizzoli & Isles*. Police found him dead in his apartment. The coroner confirmed cause of death to be a self-inflicted gunshot wound. After funeral services were held at Inglewood Park Cemetery, Lee was buried in Lakeview Park Cemetery in York, South Carolina. In Hollywood, Paramount Studios held a three hour memorial service on the studio lot.

Philip Seymour Hoffman was born on July 23, 1967 in Fairport, New York. His mother was a judge, and his father worked for Xerox. His parents divorced when he was nine years old, and he was raised by his mother. Because of his mother's love for the theater Hoffman was exposed to many productions, and age fourteen joined his school's drama club.

After graduation he attended New York University's Tisch School of Arts. He worked as an usher in order to pay his living expenses and graduated in 1989. His first acting role came in 1991 when he appeared in the television series, *Law and Order* episode, <u>The Violence of Summer</u>. Minor film parts followed through the 1990s. During those years he made a living waiting tables.

His first appearance in a movie came in 1991 when he appeared in *Triple Bogey on a Par Five Hole*, an independent production. His part as a police officer who is assaulted by Paul Newman in *Nobody's Fool* won him recognition. His performances in *Magnolia* and *The Talented Mr. Ripley* in 1999 resulted in him being named Best Supporting Actor by the National Board of Review.

In 2005, Hoffman won the lead in the film, *Capote* and this part won him an Oscar for Best Actor. Hoffman received three Tony nominations and three nominations for Best Supporting Actor during his career. He also earned recognition for his work on the stage and as a director.

In 2007, he starred in *Before the Devil Knows You Are Dead* and *Charlie Wilson's War*. New York magazine stated his work as Gust Avrakotos in the latter "carried the film". His performance won him an Academy Award for Best Supporting Actor.

Hoffman's last performance on stage was in the role of Willie Loman in *Death of a Salesman* in 2012. The play received mixed reviews. His last completed film role came in 2013 when he appeared in *The Hunger Games: Catching Fire*. He was working in the production of *The Hunger Games: Mockingjay – Part 2* at the time of his death. His character was digitally recreated in order to complete the film.

Hoffman appeared in more than fifty films over a period of twenty years.

Hoffman was in a relationship with Mimi O'Donnell during his last fourteen years. They had one son and two daughters. They separated just a few months before his death.

Hoffman admitted to using drugs as a young man, and went through a rehabilitation program when he was twenty-two. He claimed to have been drug free until 2012 when he started using heroin and prescription drugs. In 2013, he spent ten days in a rehab center.

A friend of Hoffman's found him dead in his West Village apartment on February 2nd, 2014.

The New York City Medical Examiner has determined that his death was due to an accidental drug overdose. Philip was cremated.

Sarah Jones, assistant camera man, died while filming *Midnight Rider* in 2014.

On February 20th, 2014, twenty-seven-year-old camera assistant, **Sarah Jones,** was killed while filming a dream scene for a biopic about Southern rock star, Gregg Allman, entitled *Midnight Rider.* The cast and crew were working on an old railroad trestle bridge in Georgia, when a freight train suddenly appeared.

Scrambling for safety, the crew members couldn't get a bed they were using in the scene all the way off the tracks. The train hit the bed sending shards of metal into the air. One of those shards struck Sarah and threw her into the moving train. She was killed instantly.

L'Wren Scott (Laura Bambrough), was born on April 28th, 1964, and raised by adoptive parents in Roy, Utah. At age twelve, she had already grown to six feet in height, finally reaching six feet three inches.

After graduating high school, Scott moved to Paris, France, where she found work as a model. In 1992, Scott returned to the U. S. and settled in Los Angeles, California, where she established herself as a stylist. She designed the ads for *White Diamonds*, Elizabeth Taylor's perfume business.

In 2001, Scott met Rick Jagger of *The Rolling Stones*, and they became romantically involved.

Madonna chose Scott to design the clothing she wore for photographs used in a 2009 issue of W Magazine. Two years late she did the same thing for Julia Roberts. Scott also served as costume designer to films such as *Diabolque,* released in 1996, and *Ocean's Thirteen* released in 2007.

On March 17th, 2014, Scott hanged herself in her Manhattan, New York apartment. She left no note, and there is no explanation for this act. The Chief Medical Examiner ruled her cause of death to be suicide. Scott was interred at the Hollywood Forever Cemetery in Los Angeles.

Born Peaches Honeyblossom Geldof-Cohen on March 13, 1989, **Peaches Geldorf** was the second daughter of musician and Live Aid founder **Bob Geldof**. Her mother was Paula Yates, who died of a heroin overdose when Peaches was eleven.

After Peaches finished school, she worked as a journalist and then moved into modeling where she became the face of the Miss Ultimo collection. After she lost that contract due to nude pictures and suspected drug use, she appeared in a six-part television series, *OMG! with Peaches Geldof.*

On 7 April 2014, she was found dead at the age of twenty-five, at her home in England. The police found drug paraphernalia at the house, and the cause of death was recorded as opiate intoxication, but there was no evidence she had committed suicide. Peaches had been using methadone for a couple of years, but had started using heroin again a few months before her death

John Winkler was a thirty-year-old production assistant working for the Comedy Central show *Tosh.0*. He rented an apartment in West Hollywood on Palm Avenue after moving from Puyallup, Washington (40 miles south of Seattle) in November, 2013. He was a graduate of the Seattle Film Institute. Winkler's ambition was to become a television producer.

On April seventh, 2014, Winkler went to a friend's apartment where he discovered a man holding the friend and another man hostage by using a knife.

When Winkler attempted to escape by running through the front door of the apartment deputy sheriffs shot and killed him.

Robin McLaurin Williams was born on July 24, 1941, in Chicago, Illinois. His parents were Laurie McLaurin, a former model from Mississippi, and her husband, Robert Fitzgerald Williams, an executive at with Ford Motor Company. As both parents worked, Robin was often left in the care of the family's maids. A lonely child, he was very shy. When he was sixteen, the family moved to California. There, he enrolled in a public high school, joined the drama department, and began to conquer over his shyness. After high school, he eventually enrolled in a Marin community college where he studied acting. Three years later, he won a full scholarship to Julliard in New York City.

In 1976, Robin left Julliard and joined his family in Marin County, California, where he earned his living working the comedy clubs in San Francisco. Later he moved to Los Angeles, where he developed his signature frenetic improvisational comedy style. He later admitted that during this time he started using cocaine to help relieve stress.

Robin appeared in several television shows, but is probably best known for playing the part of the alien Mork from Ork in the popular series, *Mork and Mindy* in 1978.

Pam Dawber and Robin in *Mork and Mindy*

His success as Mork led to the starring role in the 1980 film, *Popeye*.

Robin in *Popeye*

In 1982, he starred in *The World According to Garp*. His next film was *Good Morning, Vietnam!* for which he won a Golden Globe for Best Actor. All in all, from 1977-2015, Robin appeared in 106 television and film roles, winning five Golden Globes, a Screen Actors Guild award, and an Academy Award for the 1997 film, *Good Will Hunting*.

Struggling with drug and alcohol abuse, when his son was born, Robin entered rehab. He remained clean until 2003 when his problems with alcohol returned and led to more rehab time. Through the following years, he amassed an amazing amount of film and television work, doing one-man tours, comedy performances and charity work. As a result, his physical health suffered, and in 2009, he developed heart problems and had to have surgery.

On August 11, 2014, struggling with severe depression and having been diagnosed with Parkinson's disease, Robin Williams hung himself. He was cremated and his ashes were scattered in San Francisco Bay.

Elizabeth Peña was born on September 23, 1959 in Elizabeth, New Jersey to Mario Peña, a Cuban actor, writer, and director who co-founded the Latin American Theatre Ensemble, and Estella Margarita Peña, a producer. Her family then moved to Cuba and lived there until she was eight, when they returned to the United States and settled in New York City.

Elizabeth attended the prestigious High School of Performing Arts in New York City with Esai Morales and Ving Rhames. She graduated in 1977, and her first film was in *El Super* (1979). She worked steadily, appearing in films such as *La Bamba* with her former classmate, Esai Morales, *Lone Star*, and *Rush Hour* with Jackie Chan. Her television work included the series, *I Married Dora*, *Numb3rs*, and the hit comedy, *Modern Family*.

On October 14, 2014, Elizabeth passed away in Los Angeles from acute gastrointestinal bleeding caused by cirrhosis of the liver due to alcohol. She was fifty-five.

Stephanie Elyse Moseley was born Vancouver, Canada in 1984. Her passion for dance began at the early age of two. She had such talent, she performed the role of Claire in the Nutcracker Ballet when she was five. After growing in her craft and performing around the world, Stephanie moved to Los Angeles in 2004. With her agent's help, her career took off, touring with celebrities like Beyoncé, Jennifer Lopez, Mariah Carey, Britney Spears, and Usher. Her film credits include: the televisions series, *Hellcats, Once Upon a Time, Psych,* and movies like *Snow White,*

Twilight, Breaking Dawn and *Sparkle*. On December 8ᵗʰ, 2014, Stephanie was killed in her Los Angeles apartment, along with her rapper husband, Earl Hayes, who she married in 2008. They had been arguing about infidelity when Earl shot her and then turned the gun on himself in an apparent murder/suicide. Stephanie was thirty.

Sawyer Sweeten and his twin, Sullivan, were born on May 12, 1995 in Brownwood, Texas. When they were six months old, their parents, Timothy Sweeten and Elizabeth Millsap moved their family to California. The twins were sixteen months old when they were cast in the sit-com *Everybody Loves Raymond* along with their older sister, Madylin, playing the children of Ray Romano and Patricia Heaton. The series ran for nine years.

The cast of Everybody Loves Raymond

On April 23, 2015, Sawyer, for reasons unknown, sat on a family member's front porch in Austin, Texas and shot himself in the head. He was nineteen years old.

Amanda Peterson was born on July 8, 1971 in Greeley, Colorado. At the age of nine, she persuaded her parents to allow her to audition for the movie, *Annie*, competing with 8,000 other girls in a casting "cattle call," and winning a role as one of the orphans. Amanda went on to act in commercials and television until in 1985, when she appeared in the movie, *Explorers*, with River Phoenix. Her biggest hit was playing the role of Cindy Mancini and co-starring with Patrick Dempsey, in the hit movie, *Can't Buy Me Love*. In 1988, Amanda won the Young Artist Award in the category of Best Young Actress Starring in a Television Drama Series for her role in the Emmy Award-winning television series, *A Year In The Life*. Amanda's body of work crossed genre lines to include westerns, romance, science fiction, thrillers, dramas, and comedies.

Sadly, even with all her talent and success, Amanda struggled with substance abuse, having been arrested four times over the past two decades in her hometown of Greeley, Colorado, most recently on a May 2012 DUI and drug paraphernalia charge.

On July 5, 2015, Amanda Peterson's body was found in her Greeley, Colorado apartment. She had been dead for two days. Although her family speculated she had passed from sleep apnea, the Weld County coroner's office in Colorado confirmed that she had died of acute morphine toxicity from an accidental overdose, after self-medicating to deal with the pain from a hysterectomy. Amanda was forty-three years old.

Prince was born Prince Rogers Nelson on June 7, 1958 in Minneapolis, MN. His mother, Mattie Della Shaw, was a professional singer, and his father, John Lewis Nelson, was a pianist and songwriter (It is said that Prince wrote his first song, a piece titled, "Funk Machine", at age seven.

Prince's parents separated when he was ten, and he began an unstable period where he lived with his father sometimes, and sometimes with his mother and stepfather. He finally became a member of a neighbors home, attended Minneapolis' Bryant Junior High School, and later, Central High School.

In 1975, at age 17, Prince joined a band known as '*94 East*'. The band was formed by Pepe Willie, who was married to Prince's cousin, Shauntel. Prince contributed guitar tracks, and co-wrote the song, '*Just Another Sucker*'. One year later, he was given a recording contract by Warner Bros., which led to the releasing of his album, '*For You*'. His last album, '*Hit n Run Phase Two*', came out in 2015. He is credited with 179 TV and album soundtracks, nine TV and video acting parts, and eight video directions.

Prince was married twice. His wives were: Manuela Testolini (2001–2006), and Mayte Garcia (1996–2000). He fathered one son, Gregory Nelson.

Prince died at his home in Chanhassen, Minnesota, on April 21st, 2016, after taking an overdose of the drug Fentanyl (approximately 80 to 100 times more potent than morphine and roughly 40 to 50 times more potent than pharmaceutical grade (100% pure) heroin). He was 57 years old. It is reported that he was suffering from AIDS.

Prince's home and studio at Chanhassen, Minnesota

The Children of the Stars:

A complaint most often made by Hollywood's children is that they never had the comfort and guidance of parents. Their real parents were always on the verge of a divorce or were already divorced. Even if the mother was not an actress, she was devoted to caring for the actor father and she did not have enough energy left to raise children properly. If she was not devoted to the husband and his needs, she was soon divorced. Actors don't have time for children if they want to make it big.

Gregory Peck's son, Jon, committed suicide, leaving Gregory in severe depression for two years. Peck explained, "When you're working you have to get up at five in the morning. When you come home at the end of the day you're too tired to talk to your children. You can't give them the time they need, and all you really have to give them is time. If not, you lose them."

In 1983, **Gary Crosby** published his autobiography, *Going My Own Way*, revealing his own alcoholism and how messed up his childhood was as a result of his mother's (Dixie Lee Crosby) alcoholism and his father's (Bing Crosby) emotional and physical abuse. Gary said Bing referred to Gary as Bucket Butt and beat his sons until they bled. His brothers, Lindsay and Dennis, confirmed Gary's story, and both later committed suicide by gunshot, Lindsay in 1989, and Dennis in 1991.

Drew Barrymore recalls, "Until I was five years old my father and I were very close. Then my parents separated, and I had a nervous breakdown. I was nine at the time. By the time I was eleven, I was a drunk, and by the time I was fourteen, using drugs."

Tatum O'Neal's brother, **Griffin**, has stated that the O'Neal children were "traded like dogs" between Ryan and his various divorced wives.

Marlon Brando's daughter, **Cheyenne**, hung herself after saying, "I have come to despise my father for the way he ignored me when I was a child".

Michael Blosil, son of **Marie Osmond**, leaped to his death from the roof of his apartment building after fighting drug addiction and depression for most of his life. He had already attempted suicide after his parents divorced.

Mackenzie Phillips told Oprah Winfrey that her father raped her when she was eighteen, and for ten years they carried on a sexual relationship. She also told stories of how her father, **John Phillips**, taught her how to roll a marijuana cigarette when she was ten, and injected her with cocaine when she was seventeen. Mick Jagger had intercourse with Mackenzie when she was eighteen. Her father, John, watched. Mackenzie reportedly said Jagger told her, "I've been waiting for this since you were ten."

Redmond O'Neal, son of **Ryan O'Neal** and **Farrah Fawcett,** served prison time on drug charges.

Michael Douglas' son **Cameron** was sentenced to nine years in prison for selling heroin in New York City. His original sentence was doubled when he was discovered attempting to smuggle drugs into the prison. He spent six months in solitary confinement for misbehaving and was only released from solitary after Michael Douglas pleaded for mercy for his son at the 2013 Emmy Awards.

Sylvester Stallone's son, **Sage Moonblood Stallone**, was found dead in his Hollywood apartment on July 13, 2012. Early reports say that he either committed suicide or accidently overdosed on drugs.

Art Linkletter's daughter **Diane**, leapt to her death in 1969, allegedly under the influence of LSD.

Mary Tyler Moore's son shot and killed himself.

Paul Newman's son, **Scott**, died in 1978 of a valium and alcohol overdose.

Carroll O'Conner's son, **Hugh**, committed suicide after fighting drug addictions for sixteen years.

James Arness took four years to recover after his daughter **Jenny Lee** committed suicide by drug overdose in 1975. Four years later his wife, **Virginia**, also overdosed on drugs.

Marlon Brando's son, **Christian**, murdered a man. He later became involved with Bonney Lee Baker, the future wife of Robert Blake. Many believe that Blake either murdered Bonney or had the job done.

River Phoenix' parents were hippies who used drugs and named their children River Jude, Joaquin Rafael, Libertad Mariposa, Summer Joy, and Rain Joan of Arc. River overdosed on drugs.

Ryan O'Neal's daughter, **Tatum**, lost her grasp on the rungs of the Hollywood ladder to success because she could not break her addiction to heroin. Tatum stated that her mother, Joanna Moore, was far more interested in getting high than caring for her children.

References

Final Curtain, Everett Jarvis and Lois Johe, Citadel Press, 1998

Sal Mineo: His life, Murder, and Mystery, Carroll & Gaff, 2000

Montgomery Clift: A Bio-bibliography, Mary C. Kalfatovic, Greenwood, 1994

Eighty Silent Film Stars, George Katcherm, McFarland, 1991

Laid Bare: A Memoir of Wrecked Lives and the Hollywood Death Trip, John Gilmore,

Amok Books, 1997

Manson: The Unholy Trail of Charlie and the Family, John Gilmore, Amok Books, 2000

Carole Lombard: A Bio-bibliography, Robert D. Matzen, Greenwood, 1988

The Hollywood Murder Casebook, Michael Munn, St. Martin's Press, 1987

The Film Lover's Companion, David Quinlan, Citadel Press, 1997

Movie Stars of the 30s, David Ragan, Prentice Hall, 1985

Former Child Stars, Joal Ryan, ECW, 2000

Screwball: The Life of Carole Lombard, Larry Swindel, William Morrow, 1975

Wired: The Short Life & Fast Times of John Belushi, Bob Woodward, Pocket Books, 1985

Mayer and Thalberg: The Make Believe Saints, Samuel Marx, Random House

The Life and Legend of Tom Mix, Paul E. Mix, A. S. Barnes, 1972

The Night the Laughter Stopped: Joan Rivers Talks About the Hope and Despair of Husband Edgar's   Brush With Death, People, December 10, 1984.

Judy: A Legendary Film Career, John Fricke, Running Press, 2011

Veronica, Veronica Lake, Bantam, 1972

When The Stars Went To War, Roy Hoopes, Random House, 1994

George Sanders: An Exhausted Life, Richard Vanderbeets, Madison Books, 1993

W. C. Fields by Himself: His Intended Autobiography by W. C. Fields and Ronald J. Fields

Prentice Hall, 1973

Janis Joplin: Rise Up Singing, Ann Angel, Amulet Books, 2010

Never Met a Man I Did not Like, Will Rogers, Joseph H. Carter, Jim Rogers, William Morrow, 1991

When The Legend Became Fact - The True Life of John Wayne, Richard Douglas Jensen, Raymond Street Publishers, 2012

Sal Mineo: A Biography, Michael Gregg Michaud, 3 Rivers Press, 2011

The Killing of the Unicorn: Dorothy Stratten, 1960-1980, Peter Bogdanovich, Bantam, 1985

Plain Beautiful: The Life of Peggy Ann Garner, Sandra Grabman, BearManor Media, 2005

The Life and Films of Buck Jones: The Silent Era, Buck Rainey, World of Yesterday, 1988

The Unruly Life of Woody Allen, Marion Meade, E-Reads 2010

Walter Slezak, Ronald Cohn and Jesse Russell, VSD, 2012

Auto Focus: The Murder of Bob Crane, Robert Graysmith, Berkley 2002

David Carradine: The Eye of My Tornado, Marina Anderson, Transit Publishing, Inc. 2010

Heroes, Lovers, and Others: The Story of Latinos in Hollywood, Clara Rodriguez, Oxford University Press 2008

D.W. Griffith: An American Life, Richard Schickel, Limelight Editions 2004

67910109R10178

Made in the USA
Charleston, SC
28 February 2017